Business Policy and Strategy

OTHER AUERBACH PUBLICATIONS

Agent-Based Manufacturing and Control Systems: New Agile Manufacturing Solutions for Achieving Peak Performance
Massimo Paolucci and Roberto Sacile
ISBN: 1-5744-4336-4

Curing the Patch Management Headache
Felicia M. Nicastro
ISBN: 0-8493-2854-3

Cyber Crime Investigator's Field Guide, Second Edition
Bruce Middleton
ISBN: 0-8493-2768-7

Disassembly Modeling for Assembly, Maintenance, Reuse and Recycling
A. J. D. Lambert and Surendra M. Gupta
ISBN: 1-5744-4334-8

The Ethical Hack: A Framework for Business Value Penetration Testing
James S. Tiller
ISBN: 0-8493-1609-X

Fundamentals of DSL Technology
Philip Golden, Herve Dedieu,
and Krista Jacobsen
ISBN: 0-8493-1913-7

The HIPAA Program Reference Handbook
Ross Leo
ISBN: 0-8493-2211-1

Implementing the IT Balanced Scorecard: Aligning IT with Corporate Strategy
Jessica Keyes
ISBN: 0-8493-2621-4

Information Security Fundamentals
Thomas R. Peltier, Justin Peltier,
and John A. Blackley
ISBN: 0-8493-1957-9

Information Security Management Handbook, Fifth Edition, Volume 2
Harold F. Tipton and Micki Krause
ISBN: 0-8493-3210-9

Introduction to Management of Reverse Logistics and Closed Loop Supply Chain Processes
Donald F. Blumberg
ISBN: 1-5744-4360-7

Maximizing ROI on Software Development
Vijay Sikka
ISBN: 0-8493-2312-6

Mobile Computing Handbook
Imad Mahgoub and Mohammad Ilyas
ISBN: 0-8493-1971-4

MPLS for Metropolitan Area Networks
Nam-Kee Tan
ISBN: 0-8493-2212-X

Multimedia Security Handbook
Borko Furht and Darko Kirovski
ISBN: 0-8493-2773-3

Network Design: Management and Technical Perspectives, Second Edition
Teresa C. Piliouras
ISBN: 0-8493-1608-1

Network Security Technologies, Second Edition
Kwok T. Fung
ISBN: 0-8493-3027-0

Outsourcing Software Development Offshore: Making It Work
Tandy Gold
ISBN: 0-8493-1943-9

Quality Management Systems: A Handbook for Product Development Organizations
Vivek Nanda
ISBN: 1-5744-4352-6

A Practical Guide to Security Assessments
Sudhanshu Kairab
ISBN: 0-8493-1706-1

The Real-Time Enterprise
Dimitris N. Chorafas
ISBN: 0-8493-2777-6

Software Testing and Continuous Quality Improvement, Second Edition
William E. Lewis
ISBN: 0-8493-2524-2

Supply Chain Architecture: A Blueprint for Networking the Flow of Material, Information, and Cash
William T. Walker
ISBN: 1-5744-4357-7

The Windows Serial Port Programming Handbook
Ying Bai
ISBN: 0-8493-2213-8

AUERBACH PUBLICATIONS

www.auerbach-publications.com
To Order Call: 1-800-272-7737 • Fax: 1-800-374-3401
E-mail: orders@crcpress.com

Business Policy and Strategy

The Art of Competition

Seventh Edition

Cheryl Van Deusen

Steven Williamson

Harold C. Babson

Auerbach Publications
Taylor & Francis Group
Boca Raton   New York

Auerbach Publications is an imprint of the
Taylor & Francis Group, an informa business

Auerbach Publications
Taylor & Francis Group
6000 Broken Sound Parkway NW, Suite 300
Boca Raton, FL 33487-2742

International Standard Book Number-10: 0-8493-8324-2 (Hardcover)
International Standard Book Number-13: 978-0-8493-8324-3 (Hardcover)

Library of Congress Cataloging-in-Publication Data

Van Deusen, Cheryl A.
    Business policy and strategy : an action guide / Cheryl Van Deusen, Steven Williamson, Harold C. Babson.
        p. cm.
    Rev. ed. of: Business policy and strategy / Robert G. Murdick [et al.]. 6th ed. Boca Raton, Fla. : St. Lucie Press, c2001.
    Includes bibliographical references and index.
    ISBN 0-8493-8324-2 (alk. paper)
    1. Industrial management. I. Williamson Steven A. II. Babson, Harold C. III. Title. IV. Title: Business policy and strategy. 2001.

HD31.B8543 2007
658.4'012--dc22   2007060375

Visit the Taylor & Francis Web site at
http://www.taylorandfrancis.com

and the Auerbach Web site at
http://www.auerbach-publications.com

CONTENTS

PREFACE

This seventh edition could well be considered a memorial edition dedicated to a distinguished academic colleague, Robert G. Murdick, who suffered an untimely death during the preparation of the sixth edition, *Business Policy and Strategy, An Action Guide*. For this edition only, all royalties will be donated to his widow in appreciation of his contributions to the field.

The importance of business policy and strategy has surged to the forefront of the business world. Globalization of business, deregulations, mergers, acquisitions, strategic alliances, and international joint ventures, coupled with a new emphasis on creating shareholder value, have created great uncertainties in the global environment.

Traditionally, university students complete a series of courses on the functional areas of business without considering broad policies and the interrelationships among the various functions and the external environment. When the student takes a policy/strategy course, the big picture and primary concerns of business are often lacking. It is the purpose of this text to supplement the typical case book and computer simulations used in teaching business strategy and provide a basic review of the key functional areas while integrating them into the larger strategic picture.

The authors wish to express their gratitude for the welcome contributions to Chapter 1 from Carolyn B. Mueller along with chapter authors Paul A. Fadil, Young Tae Choi, Cheryl Frohlich, Antony Paulraj, and William Sodeman. We also wish to express our gratitude for outstanding support from Leanna Payne, Michelle Green, and Carolyn Gavin. Further it is very important that Gary Fane, University of North Florida professor of accounting, be acknowledged, as Gary and Steven team-taught the graduate policy class for a number of years, and Steven's ideas presented in this text were very much influenced by Gary. Lastly, without the guidance and counsel of William (Tommie) Tomlinson, this edition would not be a reality.

Cheryl A. Van Deusen
Steven A. Williamson
Harold C. Babson

CONTRIBUTORS

Young-Tae Choi, Ph.D.
Department of Marketing and Logistics
Coggin College of Business
University of North Florida
Jacksonville, Florida

Paul A. Fadil, Ph.D.
Department of Management
Coggin College of Business
University of North Florida
Jacksonville, Florida

Cheryl Frohlich, Ph.D.
Department of Accounting and Finance
Coggin College of Business
University of North Florida
Jacksonville, Florida

Antony Paulraj, Ph.D.
Department of Management
Coggin College of Business
University of North Florida
Jacksonville, Florida

William A. Sodeman, Ph.D.
College of Professional Studies
Hawaii Pacific University
Honolulu, Hawaii

ABOUT THE AUTHORS

Cheryl A. Van Deusen, Ph.D., is an associate professor of strategic and international business in the Coggin College of Business at the University of North Florida. She earned her Ph.D. from the University of South Carolina in strategy and IB, an M.B.A. from Appalachian State University with an emphasis in Human Resources, and her B.S. from Virginia Tech. Dr. Van Deusen joined the Coggin College of Business in 1998. She is the past chair of the Academy of International Business–Southeast USA Chapter, the co-faculty advisor for the University of North Florida Society for Human Resource Management, and the president of Beta Gamma Sigma, the business honor society.

Dr. Van Deusen usually teaches business strategy and international management but also teaches human resource management classes such as employee benefits planning, compensation, and international human resources. Primary research streams include cross-cultural management issues, national and organizational culture, and organizational learning, concentrating on mergers and acquisitions. Understanding the relationship between exploitation of current processes and procedures as compared to exploration for new methods of performing organizational activities and the subsequent impact on firm performance is a long-term research stream of interest.

Prior to earning a Ph.D., she worked in the hospitality industry for almost ten years. Starting out as a front desk manager, she rose through the ranks to become a resort general manager for an oceanfront and golf resort development company. Then she was a corporate quality manager for a publicly traded company operating resorts in 11 states and the U.S. Virgin Islands. With over 4000 employees, she was responsible for implementing a corporatewide quality and training program and established and implemented corporatewide standards. Her position also involved coaching the general managers on how to increase their productivity and create effective performance evaluations. Change management was a primary focus of the company.

Most of Dr. Van Deusen's consulting activities have been with senior level managers implementing organizational change. To date, she has consulted both domestically and internationally in seven countries, primarily in the South Pacific region. A group of academicians established a non-profit foundation where they work with the CEOs and COOs of major organizations trying to improve their overall effectiveness to encompass organizational change efforts in governmental and private organizations. Firms facing downsizing, privatization, and outsourcing and small business start-ups in both union and non-unionized environments are typical examples.

To complement her scholarly activities, Dr. Van Deusen raises Arabian horses and competes in 100-mile endurance races and shows.

Steven A. Williamson, Ph.D., is an associate professor of management in the Coggin College of Business at the University of North Florida. In addition to teaching, he directs two university institutes: the Institute for Management Development and Organizational Quality and the Paper and Plastics Education and Research Institute. He also is the principal of Management Development, Incorporated, a management-consulting firm.

He earned a B.S. in business administration from Memphis State University, an M.S. from the University of Arkansas, and a Ph.D. from Memphis State University. Prior to joining the faculty at the University of North Florida in 1984, he taught at Memphis State University and Georgia Southern College. Currently, Dr. Williamson's primary teaching assignment is in the M.B.A. program, where he teaches the required "Strategic Management and Business Policy" seminar and graduate electives in research and consulting. His international experience includes teaching strategic management in Paris and international business in London.

Dr. Williamson has directed numerous organizational and management development activities. He has served as a consultant, researcher, and facilitator for local, state, and federal agencies and private sector organizations. His private sector experience includes organizations in the banking, manufacturing, insurance, transportation, chemical, communications, supply chain, and health care industries. He also is certified as a neurolinguistic programming practitioner and coach.

The majority of Dr. Williamson's recent efforts have been focused on strategy development and implementation, quality systems implementation, and international entrepreneurship. He is a recognized expert in organizational management and is often asked to assume the role of guest speaker by civic and professional organizations.

He is a licensed private pilot and, in his spare time, he enjoys flying his Piper Cherokee on cross-country trips.

Harold "Hal" C. Babson has served as instructor and administrator for 42 years at institutions that include Villanova University, West Chester University, George Washington University, Northeastern University, the University of Delaware, and Robert Morris College.

Mr. Babson also held a management position for five years with Boeing Services Corporation at the Department of Energy Coal Research Center in Pittsburgh, Pennsylvania.

For the past 21 years, Mr. Babson has served as chairman of the Business Management Department at Columbus State Community College in Columbus, Ohio, the second largest community college in Ohio.

Throughout his career in education, Mr. Babson has served as consultant in various capacities for organizations that include the Commonwealth of Massachusetts, the Pennsylvania Department of Vocational Education, The Insurance Institutes, and Blue Cross/Blue Shield of Maryland, as well as numerous small businesses, chambers of commerce, and government agencies in Ohio.

Mr. Babson is currently serving on two boards, the Council on Ethical Leadership and the Electronic Classroom of Tomorrow, on numerous advisory committees, and is a member of several professional organizations in Columbus, Ohio including ASTD, Rotary, and The Society for the Advancement of Management. In addition, he serves as an accreditation site team member for the Association of Collegiate Business Schools and Programs.

Mr. Babson has won several teaching awards and was recently inducted into Iota Lambda Sigma, the national honor society for adult/vocational education teachers and administrators.

1

THE IMPORTANCE OF BUSINESS STRATEGY AND THE EXTERNAL BUSINESS ENVIRONMENT

THE HYDRA

The term "Hydra" is from Greek mythology (see Figure 1.1). The Hydra was a giant swamp monster with seven dragonlike heads, each on a long, spiny, dragonlike neck. Each of the monster's heads turned, moved, and attacked with the speed of a cobra. To complicate matters, the Hydra's breath was toxic enough to bring death. Thus, if a would-be dragon slayer was brave enough to survive the sheer fright created by the Hydra's physical appearance, and fortunate enough to evade the beast's ferocious heads snapping and attacking, he was still at mortal risk from the Hydra's noxious breath. Also, the Hydra had been granted the power of regeneration by the Gods. If a champion successfully cut off one of the Hydra's heads in a fight, two would instantly grow back in its place and some legends credit that the Hydra had as many as 100 heads; in addition, its central head could not be harmed by the weapons of man. It was a fierce, formidable killing beast. All who confronted the Hydra were certain to perish.

Hercules, mortal son of Zeus, was required to slay the Hydra as his second labor of penance. Hercules, accompanied by his charioteer Iolus, journeyed to the Hydra's lair using a swift chariot. Hercules drew the Hydra out of its hole by shooting flaming arrows into the pit and soon found himself involved in a long and difficult battle to conquer the deadly

Figure 1.1

beast. It was only by securing the assistance of Iolus that he was finally able to prevail. As Hercules cut the monster's heads off one by one, Iolus would cauterize the wound with a flaming torch to prevent further regeneration of the lethal heads.

Finally, the Hydra was left with one last fierce head, but Hercules found this head to be impenetrable to his mortal weapons, whereupon Hercules took up his very large and heavy club and crushed the Hydra's last head. Then, after tearing the head from the Hydra's body with his bare hands, he buried it deep in the earth, placing a large boulder over it that no mortal could ever move.

Having finally conquered the Hydra, Hercules dipped his arrows in its poisonous blood to use against future enemies, to create wounds that would never heal.

Strategic planning is the modern-day organizational equivalent of the Hydra. The process of strategic planning seems most at home in the morass of seemingly endless committee meetings, where the air of creativity and thought is stifled by the toxic breath of traditional culture and inertia. As one approaches the process of strategic analysis and planning, its many "ferocious heads" warn of possible looming danger. Just as firms begin to believe that they have everything covered, another head rears up. These heads are uncovered information and knowledge, which confirm that you need to know even more. They also include the heads of self-interest and political attitude, which have little to do with productive behavior. However, until a firm conquers strategic planning, it is, at best, doomed to wander without direction, and at worst, will cease to exist.

Having conquered strategic planning, the results and knowledge obtained become the arrows tipped with the Hydra's poisonous blood, using which a firm is able to inflict wounds that will not heal upon its competition.

STRATEGIC PLANNING DEFINED

Strategic planning is the development of a competitive strategy or the planning that sets the long-term direction of the organization. Its purpose is to guide the organization to accomplish its mission and to organize the allocation of resources. Strategic planning seeks to maintain a viable fit between the organization and its ever-changing environment. The objective of strategic planning is to continuously shape and adjust the organization's business and outputs to ensure that they produce the desired return on invested capital.

THE IMPORTANCE OF STRATEGIC PLANNING

All things being equal, the organization that plans the best will perform the best. The importance of strategic planning and the concepts associated with it surfaced in the 1970s. Strategic planning is an ongoing process. The strategic plan may look ahead five, ten, or even twenty years but it should be revisited annually. It is necessary to review the strategic plan, the assumptions on which it is based, and include new internal and external information to maintain the validity of the plan. Plans of this nature are known as *rolling plans*. The relevance of strategic planning and its benefits include:

- Strategy is an ongoing process. An organization must continue to adapt each year as the environment changes, while analyzing the validity of its past predictions.
- It seeks to maintain a viable fit between the organization and its ever-changing environment.
- It assists organizations to adapt to the ever-changing environment, thus increasing the stability relational fit between the organization and its environment.
- It assists firms to identify resource allocation and reallocation needs.
- It is long term, with planning horizons among U.S. firms usually ranging from five to fifteen years; in Japan long term can mean as much as a hundred years.
- A good strategy is one that capitalizes on organizational strengths and minimizes internal weaknesses, as it utilizes organizational resources to avoid or minimize environmental threats and exploit environmental opportunities.

How often does the predicted future come to pass? Never! So why bother with planning? Is it a waste of time? No, because it determines the firm's direction and helps it to plan for contingencies; the greater the planning, the better an organization performs. The further the firm projects into the future, the better off it will be.

Fiction versus Fact

Myths and misconceptions often reign in the realm of strategic planning. These misconceptions may cause confusion about the purpose and goals of planning and result in a lack of buy-in from employees. To better grasp what strategic planning is, it is important to examine what it is not.

- *Fiction — Strategic planning is a linear, smooth process.*
- Fact — "Strategic planning is not a linear process that flows seamlessly from step to step, as many books would suggest. Rather, it proceeds in fits and starts, revisiting earlier steps in some situations and skipping ahead in others" (King, 1998, p.35). Strategic planning should be considered as having a feedback loop at every stage, whereby new information requires previous assumptions to be reviewed for relevancy.
- *Fiction — Strategic planning should only be developed by upper management and selectively shared.*
- Fact — "Little of the actual development of the plan can be delegated, but it must be a product of extensive listening and the gathering of input from all levels of the company .... The final plan must be shared with all levels, in varying detail depending on their responsibilities"[1] if it is to be implemented.
- *Fiction — Strategic plans are the same as operational effectiveness.*
- Fact — "Improvements in operational effectiveness make companies move closer together as they compete using similar management techniques, which are easily imitated. Strategic changes, by contrast, seek to differentiate from rivals to improve sustainability and profitability."[2]
- *Fiction — Nonprofit organizations do not need strategic plans.*
- Fact — "At the sector level, it is clear that nonprofit organizations are vulnerable to the same environmental changes that are having an impact on public and for-profit organizations. At the organizational level, a strategic planning process can be a valuable exercise only if it includes methods for demonstrating improved performance."[3]
- *Fiction — Every organization needs a strategic plan.*
- Fact — "Strategic planning is not for every business. You probably don't need it if you are satisfied that your business is stable and

yielding a satisfactory living for you and your family. It's a lifestyle question."[4]

Resistance to Strategic Planning

Why do some CEOs resist strategic planning? There are many reasons including increased performance visibility and accountability. In addition, the prevailing wisdom ingrained in many organizations is to regard the future as a mere extension of the past, and thus, the executives of such firms do not see a need to prepare for the future and its changes. "The managers at Xerox didn't notice (a decrease in earnings) because they were blinded by their past successes. They expected the future to be a continuation of the past ... the results of this attitude were tragic."[5] Bluntly stated, some companies just do not want to devote the time, energy, and money to the strategic planning process because it is arduous, and the results of the effort are not readily apparent. "Ask any company to name its most loathsome management process, and the answer is likely to be strategic, tactical, and financial planning."[6] Additionally, it has often been said by CEOs that strategic planning reduces ones ability to take advantage of environmental opportunities that may present themselves and thus limits the organization's flexibility. Strategic planning helps to keep organizations focused on their mission objectives. Because organizations have finite resources, deviating from the plan to pursue opportunities unrelated to the mission may actually reduce a firm's ability to compete in its primary business.

Why do some CEOs have corporate jets? Because they want them. Sometimes, organizations are run by CEOs for their own benefit and not the benefit of the shareholders or stakeholders. In these situations, strategic planning can represent a transparent, accountable process where numerous issues regarding potential mismanagement can be addressed. Although strategic planning can provide a forum for the reallocation of funds or the restructuring of organizational assets, much has been written about several CEOs mismanaging corporations for their own selfish gain. This phenomenon is known as *agency theory.*

APPROACHES TO STRATEGIC ANALYSIS AND PLANNING

Top companies use guidelines to streamline the strategic planning process and produce an invaluable tool for better decision making. Despite the model chosen, there are common attributes to all strategic plans. "While the best firms update the tactical plan annually, they make developing a strategic plan an event-driven activity, contingent upon major shifts in the business operating environment and not just because the calendar says it's June."[7]

The most effective strategic plans are readable, clear, well written, and well communicated. "If written clearly, it will be understandable by a 10th grader; otherwise, it's probably too jargon-filled or stilted."[8]

There are three basic approaches to strategic management. They are:

1. The hierarchical approach requires all activities to be grounded by the vision, the guiding principles, and the mission. With regard to formal planning models, the hierarchical approach is the oldest and its roots can be traced back to ancient history. As old as it may be, the hierarchical approach, when effectively applied, still adds value by creating the overarching organizational purpose for existence and promoting oneness of purpose among its members.

2. The eclectic approach is based on past and present activities — where firms wish to acknowledge what is working or has worked as a formal strategy. "It is the stuff that floated down the river" or "stuck to the wall" and is thus worth continuing and, therefore, its use is continued. It is a justification of past actions and not planning *per se*. However, any firm that has survived utilizing this approach for a prolonged length of time has most likely developed a system that used the successful activities and transformed them into a kind of loose, ill-defined strategy that has provided some direction.

3. The internal/external analysis approach requires that the organization be evaluated based upon its adaptability to the external environment. This approach has most often been identified as a SWOT analysis — SWOT being an acronym for strengths, weaknesses, opportunities, threats. The SWOT analysis has been taught in business schools for at least the last 50 years and almost every corporate strategic plan includes a SWOT analysis. Further, most executives, managers, and business students are familiar with the SWOT concept. Thus, the concept is pervasive within the context of business and yet, it has most often been operationalized in such a vague fashion as to become less than meaningless, and the poor operationalization may mislead the organization from using its real abilities. A thorough knowledge of a firm's capabilities and limitations is necessary before any event occurring in the environment can be acknowledged as being either an opportunity or threat. An environmental event, by definition, is organization neutral; it only becomes an opportunity or threat to a given organization when it is perceived and evaluated by the organization, based upon the organization's ability to respond through awareness of its strengths and weaknesses.

The Hydra model recognizes the importance of all three foundations of strategic analysis and planning: the hierarchical approach, the eclectic approach, and the internal and external analysis approach. All three play an important role in understanding a firm's strategy and developing the firm's future. Exclusion of any one of the three would never get the final head torn from the Hydra's body.

MANAGERIAL STRATEGIC DECISION MAKING

Every day, thousands of new businesses are conceived by entrepreneurs, and thousands of new ventures and expansion projects are conceived by existing firms. The question always arises as to why some entrepreneurs and firms succeed whereas many others fail. Why are some firms initially successful and then fail as they mature is another frequent question; and finally, why do some firms seem to grow old, decline, and die, when others rejuvenate and reinvent themselves and seem to live on into perpetuity? The specific answers to these questions are many and varied but, in one way or another, can be laid directly at the feet of the entrepreneur or the management that makes the decisions and controls the resources. The outcome would be heavily weighted toward success if these decision makers were both familiar with the concepts of strategic management and applied that knowledge in the execution of their decisions. However, it can be concluded from the number of failures that there are many decision makers lacking the required knowledge and skills.

WHY BUSINESSES FAIL

Although managers cannot control all the events that affect their businesses, most businesses fail because managers fail. The history of American business shows that many businesses, large and small, have a relatively short successful life span. Obviously, few (if any) executives want their businesses to fail. They want to perpetuate the lives of the firms that they manage and increase the profits. Why then is the track record poor? There is only one answer — managers either do not know how to determine the specific actions necessary to maintain the ongoing health of their organizations or they lack the required execution skills.

Why shouldn't managers know what to do? Haven't they had prior experiences in a variety of business situations? Haven't they read books and taken courses on the concepts, practices, procedures, and thinking in every area of business? The answer is an obvious "maybe."

The skill that managers need most is the ability to analyze and diagnose complex decision problems. From this analysis, managers also must be able to formulate understandable action terms. This means that managers must first be able to identify a situation that requires action, then identify several good alternative courses of action, identify the constraints on each alternative, and finally evaluate the alternatives relative to each other. Managers must have the courage to not only decide on the best action, but also subsequently take that action. Equally important to making the right decision and taking action is the ability to correctly analyze the results of the action taken and correctly attribute the results to the correct cause.

Both practicing business executives and students in business policy courses have a variety of backgrounds, skills, and natural abilities. It is well known that most students are ill-prepared for their capstone course of business problem solving. It is less well known that many business executives are unprepared for their present jobs or unprepared to advance into general management.

ENVIRONMENT OF THE BUSINESS SYSTEM

Any firm may be just one decision away from prosperity or oblivion. It has often been said that it isn't how many good decisions a CEO makes that determines the success of a firm; instead, it is how few bad ones and, in fact, avoiding that one particular bad strategic decision that may cripple an organization. Still others have indicated that, in business, the mediocrity of a CEO is rewarded for these very same reasons, and most succeed with the *"don't rock the boat" syndrome*. It is just as important to understand what makes a given business successful as it is to acquire the ability to analyze, diagnose, and cure a troubled firm.

LEGITIMACY: THE ROLE AND RESPONSIBILITIES OF BUSINESS IN SOCIETY

Calvin Coolidge, president of the United States, 1923–1929, while in office, stated that "the business of business was business." Businesses are created not for societal benefits, but to make money. The fact that they provide benefits to the society in which they exist is a peripheral and ancillary result of their financial success and not their primary reason for existence. However, all too often, business managers have a restricted perspective of their business. They see their business firm as an institution empowered with innate rights and specific obligations only unto itself. An educated manager realizes that businesses, as they exist in our society, do so only because society believes that it is best served by such institutions. This rightness of an institution is called its *legitimacy*.

Businesses gain legitimacy by satisfying their stakeholders to a sufficient degree, and by acting in a morally responsible manner toward them. The following are considered common stakeholder groups:

1. Shareholders
2. Customers
3. Employees
4. The general public and communities
5. Special-interest groups
6. Suppliers
7. Governments
8. Competitors
9. Lenders
10. Unions

The process of evaluating a firm on its ability to meet its key stakeholders' goals is generally referred to as the balanced scorecard approach. The balanced scorecard employs various metrics to determine a firm's performance with regard to each stakeholder group considered critical to the firm's success. This approach also has been somewhat institutionalized in the Malcolm Baldrige National Quality Award, which requires that the quality award applicant address specifically how information is gained from its key stakeholders, and how its performance and improvement efforts are measured.

A company does not have to completely satisfy all stakeholders to achieve legitimacy and stay in business. It is impossible to maximize all goals of all stakeholders simultaneously. Satisfying one or two powerful stakeholder groups may be enough to provide legitimacy. However, if a powerful stakeholder group is not sufficiently satisfied, it may also be enough to force the company out of business. Therefore, managers must establish policies for each stakeholder group and clarify the degree of social responsibility that it will accept.

SUMMARY

This chapter began with the ancient Greek myth of Hercules' slaying of the Hydra and concluded with the firm establishing its legitimate right to exist. Hopefully, the strategic manager will take heart from Hercules when undertaking his or her own quest to develop a strategic analysis and plan. By any account, developing a strategic analysis and plan is a prodigious feat and the modern-day equivalent of slaying the Hydra. The CEO and his or her executive team must never lose sight of the need of strengthening the firm's current position while insuring that the firm isn't sacrificing its future. This book will introduce many new ideas and attempt to integrate the functional areas of business with strategic planning to develop topic relevancy.

REFERENCES

1. Mariotti, J., Failing to Plan Is Planning to Fail, *Industry Week*, 247(13), 1998, p. 66.
2. Brooks, A., Organizational Strategy, *Supply Management*, 3(12), 1998, p. 49.
3. King, K.N., How Are Nonprofits Using Strategic Planning [and Is It Worth Their While]?, *Nonprofit World*, 16(5), 1998, p. 34.
4. Anonymous, Small Business: If Your Firm Is Ready for Change, Consider Strategic Planning, *The Los Angeles Times*, August 19, 1998, p. 7.
5. Gibson, R., Rethink the Future, *Executive Excellence*, 15(12), 1998, p. 13.
6. Hackett, G., Prime Your Planning Process, *Financial Executive*, 14(5), 1998, p. 4546.
7. Ibid. 46.
8. Mariotti, op cit. 67.

2

CRITICAL BEGINNINGS

VISION STATEMENT

"One of the keys to a good strategic plan is that everyone [can understand] the company's vision, that is to say where it wants to be in the future."[1] A vision statement should be focused on the future, usually looking out no more than three to five years. "A vision statement should project to a point in time far enough from the present so that the future for the organization is unpredictable."[2] Visualizing the focus of the organization three to five years in the future can be extremely difficult. The vision statement should be revised, as needed, to keep it fresh and useful. It should incorporate the company's main goals, as well as illustrate how the company plans to achieve these goals. According to a recent survey, "54 percent of all companies and government organizations [have] developed vision statements over the last few years ... however, about 75 percent of these vision statements [were] poorly written and fail[ed] to provide a clear vision of where the organization wants to be in the future."[3] For this reason, it is important to focus on the process of the development to ensure that the vision will be an effective tool for the organization.

CHARACTERISTICS OF A GOOD VISION

An effective vision should describe the desired state that the company wants to develop into in the next three to five years. It should be concrete, visual, and descriptive of an ideal condition that provides direction for the company and all of the internal stakeholders of the organization. The vision should be brief and focused, easily understood, and remembered by the employees. The vision should be verifiable; measures used should be indicative that the goals of the vision are being met. The vision should be inspirational and paint a picture of the future of the company. It should be challenging so that executives and employees can set and achieve ambitious goals. The vision should be appealing to all employees and shareholders. Finally, the vision for the company should be the vision of the CEO and, if applicable, the vision of the board of directors. Ultimately, it is the job of the senior management, including the board of directors, to ensure that the company is a success. They must see the vision, believe in it, and be able to communicate it, if this result is to be achieved.[4]

A vision is created in the hopes that it will provide direction for the company and, therefore, its employees. Communication of the vision to all employees is essential. Employees that are on the front line of the organization offer the closest link to its customers. These workers also deal with the day-to-day company operations. For this reason, it is important that the vision be clear and easily understandable. If the vision is full of catch phrases and trendy words, then it will not be tangible and therefore not understood. An inspirational vision will assist the firm's personnel in developing a positive attitude with regard to the organization's direction. Having a vision that is clearly stated, inspirational, and motivating is critical to achieving employee "buy-in."

The vision statement impacts many aspects of the company's operation. "Decision making and investments are difficult without a clear vision against which to evaluate each new opportunity or problem that inevitably comes up."[5] Consultants and other members of the company that can be used as resources will produce better results if they have a clear vision statement to work with. Once the goals of the vision have been achieved or have become obsolete, the vision must be revamped, revised, and rewritten so that it can remain a tool that will continue to be inspirational and challenging in the future.

To summarize, vision statements should:

- State where the company wants to be in the future, long term, usually three to five years into the future.
- Be concrete, visual, and descriptive of an ideal condition that provides direction and guidelines.
- Be brief — usually two to three sentences.
- Be inspirational, challenging, and motivational.
- Ensure that the vision is the CEO's and, if applicable, the board of directors' perception of what the firm will look like in the future.

The CEO, in his role as the figurehead, must live the vision and lead by example. A vision must be more than a mere "slogan." The CEO must communicate the vision to all. Lee Iacocca (of Chrysler Corporation fame) and Herb Kelleher (CEO of Southwest Airlines) are examples of CEOs who successfully communicated their visions to their employees and stockholders.

VISION STATEMENT DEVELOPMENT

Companies have many options available to them when attempting to create a vision statement. One method may be to hire a consultant and send the top management to a resort for a few days until they come up with the vision the company will pursue. The consultant's responsibility is to keep all egos in check and keep everyone moving in the right direction to complete the task as effectively as possible. The end product will likely be filled with trendy words and phrases that attempt to communicate the plan for the company. However, after the task is completed, those who participated in the creation of the vision would be hard-pressed to articulate the meaning behind the words or the true outlook (vision) of the company.[6] Another alternative is to look at the vision statements that other companies have used. Pick out parts that are appropriate, change some of the words and phrases, make sure that they fit the company focus, and put them into use. The CEO may purchase a book of visions and pull together phrases and sentences that other consultants or other executives have used in their vision. This is also known as using cookie-cutter phrases that could fit after the name of any company. A more effective method of developing a vision statement is to pretend it is five years down the road and that you are being interviewed by the *Wall Street Journal*. The reporter has asked you to describe your organization's major accomplishments over the last five years. What do you want to tell the reporter?

GUIDING PRINCIPLES AND COMPANY VALUES

Purpose and Goals

A company's values should become the ethical guide that determines how business will be conducted. For this reason, the values trump and determine the firm's mission, in that the values must be congruent and supportive of the firm's mission if it is to be accomplished. Values are the principles that determine how an organization operates and earns profit. Values must be lived by all levels to be effective. These principles determine the strategies that will be developed and the methods of strategy implementation employed to achieve success. If a person is in disagreement with the values of the organization, he or she will leave the organization or conform only within their limits of tolerance. In essence, "Values, or deeply held principles and beliefs, can be powerful motivators that, when shared, form a foundation for corporate culture."[7]

Organizations are said to have a "syntality" or a joint personality influenced by everyone in the organization, but some people contribute more to it (executive versus the hourly employee). The syntality thus determines the organization's norms and values. The founders of the organization have the greatest influence on its values.

Identification of Guiding Principles and Company Values

The guiding principles may be listed as follows:

- Value statements should be short and clear.
- Company values closely reflect the personal values of upper management. Can a leader impose his or her values on an organization if the culture already exists? It is easier for a CEO to influence the organization if it is a newer company than one that has been in existence for a long time.
- When conflict exists between stated values and a firm's actions, believe the action. "But when a company's stated values clash with its actions, employees grow cynical and angry and often quit or check out mentally."[8]
- Values must be operationalized (i.e., integrity may be a value, but how is integrity demonstrated in the corporate environment?).
- A problem many organizations encounter is that they do not consider the customers' needs as standards. Customer needs should be a value because those who put customers first, succeed.
- Values that are operationalized determine to a large extent how well the organization will do.
- It is best if organizational values are not directly linked to religious values. This is because an organization's value statement often becomes a public document and differences in religious beliefs have often become the source of conflict.

Identification of Values

Three of the more common methods used to develop organizational value statements are:

1. The *open listing approach* uses nominal groups and brainstorming to help identify values usually with the aid of a facilitator over several meeting periods.
2. The *stakeholder listing approach* is similar to the open listing approach; however, values are characterized by those who have special interest in the success of the organization including owners, customers, employees, the community, suppliers, and creditors.
3. The *business-function listing approach* requires that values be sorted and determined by individual business functions. Hence,

the finance department will have different values from human resources. Though customized in their respective function in the organization, all should support the corporate values.

The process needs to [begin at the top and] cascade down to the individual departments, to the employees themselves.[9]

Recommendations for writing a good statement include:

1. Involve everyone.
2. Allow customization.
3. Expect and accept resistance.
4. Keep it short.
5. Avoid religious references.
6. Challenge it.
7. Observe the values.[10]

Examples of Typical Values

The following values (or similar values) are often stated by corporate America and serve as examples:

- We require adherence to a strict ethical code, which ensures that we operate above reproach.
- We acquire businesses that only support our strategic plan.
- We will make training opportunities available to all employees.
- We will meet our customer expectations.
- Our company's vision, values, and mission will drive our business decisions.

MISSION STATEMENT

Whereas a vision statement focuses on the future, the mission statement should focus on the present. It is typically about two to four sentences long and describes what the organization does and the reason for the organization's existence.[11] There is no single, cookie-cutter mission statement format appropriate for all organizations, nor do mission statements have to be lengthy. Differences will occur, but perhaps the key point is that an effective mission statement specifies guidance for strategic plans. It is often the most visible part of a strategic plan.

An effective mission statement will clearly portray the organization's reason for existence. The mission statement must be reflective of the organization's values and provide a sense of the means by which it will accomplish its vision. It will include all of the key elements necessary to discern the organization's direction and should provide a basis for employee decisions. The mission statement should be very specific that it applies only to the concerned organization.

History of Mission Statements

A growing number of organizations, including both corporations and community groups, have been utilizing mission statements since the 1980s. These mission statements give "direction, purpose, and perspective" to those both inside and outside of the organization including management, staff, clients, and prospects.[12]

Mission Statement Development

A company mission statement is much more difficult to develop than one would expect. Developing a mission statement involves taking the time to reflect on what the company has accomplished and what it wants to accomplish.[13] "One of the main reasons for writing a mission statement is to develop a road map showing management where the company should be and giving general directions for how to get there."[14] The questions to answer in developing a mission statement include:

Who are the appropriate stakeholders involved?
Where does the company want to place its focus?
What development process is used?
What measurement techniques should be utilized to ultimately determine its effectiveness?

The process of developing the mission statement is as important as the mission statement itself in that it determines its effectiveness and its ultimate success.[15] The mission development process should be seen as a collaborative process that includes all stakeholders and not as a top-down, autocratic exercise. Although it is critically important for the views of the executive management to be embodied in the final document, the document itself must be owned by all. The mission statement should reflect the existing direction of the organization, as well as lay the foundation for the future. Stakeholders should commit to paper what they already know about the organization.[16] A successful mission process should allow for creativity. "Thus, it would appear to be far better for an organization's mission development team to follow an original process rather than simply take one from a textbook and impose it on the organization."[17]

Most mission statements are basically the same in content. It is the stakeholders' interpretation of the mission and their ability to communicate it to others that makes it effective.[18] The mission statement is a tool that can get everyone in the company moving in the same direction. Therefore, when communicating the mission statement, the company must focus on all stakeholders. "The two areas in which administrators should consider placing greater emphasis in disseminating their mission are customers and shareholders; these are the stakeholders who do not seem to get the attention they require."[19] Mission statements are typically communicated through posters, employee manuals, the annual report, and plaques. Other communication methods include newsletters, company seminars, workshops, training sessions, and word-of-mouth. The least utilized, yet most effective, method is word-of-mouth. This is a low-cost method that is often overlooked. Once the mission statement gains widespread acceptance and support, the process should be considered complete.

Stakeholders' Involvement in the Development of a Mission

In developing a mission statement it is important to solicit input from all stakeholders. An excellent mission statement is the product of many different stakeholders' perspectives. Input should be sought from those stakeholders with the greatest investment in the direction and success of the organization. Those stakeholders include the shareholders, represented by the board of directors, the firm's management and nonmanagement personnel, and even its customers and suppliers. The process of developing the firm's mission belongs to the CEO and executive management, without whose commitment the mission statement becomes meaningless. Research indicates that the more stakeholders that are involved in mission development, the greater the likelihood that they will assume ownership, thus increasing commitment and satisfaction.[20]

Often, the actual development of the mission statement is facilitated by either an internal or external consultant appointed by the CEO or the executive management team. The facilitator then leads the mission development team, task force, or committee composed of the selected stakeholders. Organizational stakeholders selected to participate in the mission development team should represent the diversity of the organization and include both management and nonmanagement members of the organization. The facilitator should encourage input from all members of the mission development team to ensure that all perspectives are voiced, while at the same time, keeping the group on task. It is important that this mission development team does not become bogged down in the wording of a document, but instead focuses on the critical components that need to be articulated within the mission. After having gathered the input of the mission development team, the facilitator can draft a document, which can then be put forward for review.

Beyond the internal review of the draft mission statement, the firm may also benefit from an external review by key or select customers and suppliers. The external review may provide the firm with additional insight that it would otherwise not have, and at the very least, demonstrate the firm's commitment to its external stakeholders. Approval of the mission statement by external stakeholders is very important, as the mission will inevitably become a public document and subsequently a public relations tool. All key stakeholders should be solicited for feedback on the draft, and all feedback should be taken into consideration when composing the final statement.[21]

Focus of the Mission Statement

The mission statement should keep an organization focused on the objectives it wants to accomplish in relation to its key customers, products, and services. It should be utilized by the firm when evaluating prospective business opportunities to ensure that would-be resource expenditures are in keeping with the company's mission.[22] The mission should answer specific questions, such as the following:

- Who are the customers of the organization?
- Where does the organization compete geographically?
- What are the major products or services?
- What is the organization's basic technology?
- What is the organization's attitude toward growth and profitability?
- What are the organization's strengths and competitive advantage?
- What public image is desired?
- What are the fundamental beliefs and values?
- Does the mission statement address the wishes of key stakeholders?
- Does the statement motivate people?

Answering these questions will help make the mission statement a viable tool to enable the company to achieve its objectives. Further, mission statements should be reflective of the organization's business environment as well as its internal processes. The organization should analyze the external environmental factors that influence its competitive stance, positioning itself to leverage whatever core competency it possesses. This will enable the firm to serve its customers better. "The organization is most likely to achieve its mission objectives [if it focuses] on those areas where [it] can develop and maintain a competitive advantage."[23]

Mission Statement Measurement

An effective mission statement clearly states why an organization exists. Many mission statements are eloquently stated, but they fail to include measurable objectives. Using the analogy that the mission statement is the road map for the company, the measurable objectives are the mile markers. For a company to know where it is going, it needs these landmarks. Without specific measurement standards, a firm will not know if it has achieved its mission. Every company should ask itself, when writing a mission statement, how it intends to measure the stated objectives. A stated objective may be eloquent and even address the emotions of a stakeholder group, but if it cannot be measured, it should not be included, as inclusion will only confuse the issues and detract from the more measurable objectives that provide real direction.[24]

Mission statements should include a measurement objective based on some financial aspect such as profitability or the bottom line. It is important for companies to end the mission statement on a financial note because of "the recency effect:" the last thing a person sees, hears, or reads tends to remain more clear in the mind.

Mission statements must be comprehensible; they must be simple, clear, and concise. Company jargon should also be avoided. All stakeholders should be able to comprehend the mission statement message. This comprehension is crucial to the firm's achieving its corporate goals. Mission performance metrics are relevant only if the management receives timely feedback that allows adjustments of operations.

Mission measurements also need to be reliable. Measurements are considered reliable when the data provides consistent results. There should be no room for bias or the ability to make the numbers fit desired results.[25]

Mission Statement Benefits Should Exceed Costs

All organizations should weigh the benefits and the cost of the mission measurement. The organization must be careful not to get carried away. It is critical that the benefits exceed the cost. The measurements should be simple and straightforward, but care should be taken not to sacrifice their quality. "A corporate map of missions will do what the ordinary road map is intended to do, provide direction, as well as organize many of the activities associated with the journey."[26]

Each company's mission statement should be different because each organization is different. Mission statements are designed to provide the organization with strategic direction. Good mission statements are developed by involving the appropriate stakeholders and they reflect the values of the firm. Once a suitable mission is developed, it must be reviewed periodically to ensure that it remains reflective of the firm's guiding principles and direction.

SUMMARY

Many firms either have no clearly stated vision, guiding principles, or mission (VGPM), or have a VGPM that is nonreflective of its reality. If you are assisting such a firm in the development of its strategic plan, you should select these components as the starting point. However, if a firm's vision, guiding principles, and mission do not exist or do not reflect reality, it is often necessary to determine them from a firm's actions when completing a competitive analysis.

Strategic planning is built around the objective of continuously shaping and adjusting the organization's business and outputs to ensure that they produce the desired return on invested capital.

The first steps in the plan consist of vision, values, and mission development. Guidelines have been provided to assist the strategist and the organization's stakeholders in developing each part. Once the process has been initiated, and a solid vision, values, and mission have been developed, the strategist will have a firm foundation on which to build the rest of the strategic plan.

REFERENCES

1. Brown, M.G., Improving your organization's vision, *The Journal for Quality and Participation,* 21(5), 18, 1998.
2. Zuckerman, A.M. and Russell, C.C., Jr., Creating a vision for the twenty-first century healthcare organization/practitioner application, *Journal of Healthcare Management,* 45(5), 294, 2000.
3. Brown, op cit. 18.
4. Ibid.
5. Ibid. 20
6. Ibid.
7. Shellenbarger, S., Companies declare lofty employee values, then forget to act, *Wall Street Journal,* B1, 1999.
8. Ibid. B1.
9. Farnham, A., State Your Values, Hold the Hot Air, *Fortune,* 127(8), 1993, p. 117.
10. Ibid.
11. Brown, op cit.
12. Anonymous, This Month's Focus: The Mission Statement, *Manager's Magazine,* 70(2), 1995, p. 30.
13. Ibid.
14. Bailey, J.A., Measuring your mission, *Management Accounting,* 78(6), 44, 1996.
15. Bart, C.K., Making Mission Statements Count, *CA Magazine,* 132(2), 1999, p. 37.
16. Nelton, S., Put Your Purpose in Writing, *Nation's Business,* 82(2), 1994, p. 61.
17. Bart, op cit. 38.

18. Darazsdi, J.J., Mission statements are essential, *Personnel Journal*, 72(2), 24, 1993.
19. Bart, op cit. 38.
20. Ibid.
21. Ibid.
22. Brown, op cit.
23. Bailey, op cit.
24. Ibid.
25. Ibid.
26. Ibid. 46.

3

UNDERSTANDING
EXISTING STRATEGY

Before one can identify the adjustments that need to be made to an organization's strategy, one must first determine if a strategy truly exists and, if so, be able to identify the strategy that is in place. Even though many organizations have a document in place labeled "strategy," there is no guarantee that the strategy this document represents has actually been implemented, and even less of a guarantee that the strategy documented is actually operational. The same can be said about an organization's vision, values, or mission statements. If a particular strategy is said to exist, and it is supported with a written plan, but one sees something else actually operationalized, one should believe only what is seen.

IDENTIFYING STRATEGIES

The strategist should focus on key areas when attempting to determine the strategy of a given firm. First, the strategist needs to look at the business the firm is in and then the industry in which it competes because, to some extent, the business and industry within which a firm operates determines the corporate strategy required for survival. Second, it is very helpful to know how the firm prices and markets its products or services, to whom it markets, and the profile of the customer. Third, where and how does the firm spend its money? (Many organizations have no clue where they are spending money, and there is no linkage among projects.) And finally, what performance measures are held sacred?

Many times, firms may believe that they have a strategy in place, when, in fact, they have only many programs, policies, and processes in place but have failed to implement any unified strategy. What they may have, in reality, could amount to nothing more than an eclectic assortment of organizational artifacts.

It should go without saying that an effective business strategy will be unified, directed, and have supporting goals that contribute to the firm attaining its overarching goals. The more profitable the firm, the more likely it has an appropriate unified strategy in place. And likewise, the more unprofitable a firm, the more likely that either the firm does not have a unified strategy in place, or it has enacted one that is wrong for its competitive position.

PORTER'S GENERIC BUSINESS STRATEGIES

Michael Porter has identified three generic business strategies. His first two strategies, low-cost leadership and product differentiation, are based on the product's appeal to the customer and the firm's ability to achieve above-industry-norm profits. The third strategy is known as a focused strategy and is based on the target market, that is, narrow focus (niche) or broad focus.

Low-Cost Leadership Strategy

Firms that compete in a commodity market seek production efficiencies and low overall cost structure. Utilizing a cost leadership strategy allows the firm to sell at or around market price and make above-industry-norm returns because of lower costs. Firms that adopt this strategy often utilize "operational leverage" to replace people with equipment, thus replacing a variable labor cost with a more fixed automation cost. Firms that automate and utilize a high operating leverage will perform better financially in a strong economy and worse in a weak economy.

Product Differentiation Strategy

A product differentiation strategy allows a firm to sell at a price higher than the market price for similar products because the product has been differentiated in some way from its would-be competitors, and thus it creates a perceived higher value and corresponding return. The simplest and easiest form of product differentiation to enact is based on differentiation by product features: more knobs, buttons, functions, and colors, but also is the easiest for competitors to copy. More difficult to develop, but also to copy, is product differentiation based on customer-perceived company and product intangible differences: quality, reliability, cutting edge, and reputation of firm. This type of differentiation may take a long time to develop, but may be well worth it.

Focused Strategy

A focused strategy is simply the application of one of the above strategies to a niche market. Within the overall scope of the market, a firm may seek to concentrate on a particular market segment within which they have found it possible to favorably compete. When a firm does this, they essentially have chosen to withdraw from the broader market and thus have imposed a limit on their market potential. The danger in doing this is that the niche they have chosen might be easily threatened by others entering the same niche.

STRATEGIC THRUST

A strategic thrust is an expenditure of funds that establishes the strategic direction of the firm; it is the new money spent today that determines where the firm will be in the future. It can be used to reinforce the current strategy or to set a new direction for the future; in either event, there must be a clear and uncompromised connection to the enterprise's mission. The funds available to support strategic thrusts are usually limited to a small percentage of a firm's overall net revenue. The actual available percentage varies from firm to firm, depending on each individual firm's own circumstances; however, in most cases, the available support for strategic thrusts is less than 6 percent. These uncommitted funds have sometimes been referred to as organizational slack. The remainder of the funds generated from operations goes to maintain the organization, that is, general operating expenses and investments. If a firm fails to view the expenditure of these uncommitted or slack funds strategically, it is likely that they will be utilized inappropriately.

Inappropriate Uses of Strategic Thrust Funds

Many times, CEOs or others with spending authority may utilize strategic thrust funds to take advantage of short-term opportunities that are not mission related. Whereas the short-term opportunities might seem to be viable opportunities at the time the funds are committed, the diversion of financial resources to activities that are unsupportive of the firm's mission are likely to negatively affect the firm's performance. First, the investments needed to reinforce current strategy and develop the future aren't being made, thus reducing the firm's long-term viability in favor of short-term gains. Second, the pursuit of short-term unrelated ventures will distract executive management and others from the primary mission of the organization and its core business. However, the pursuit of short-term opportunities at the cost of long-term viability, though ill-advised and indicative of a weak management, is nevertheless an honest mistake even if it is the result of poor judgment.

The misuse of uncommitted or slack funds unfortunately doesn't stop with honest mistakes. Indeed, there is also a dark side to this misuse, and there have been many instances in recent years where CEOs have ignored their fiduciary responsibilities to their stockholders, and their firms' long-term viability, in favor of personal gain. Some of these incidents have gained widespread public attention, for example, Enron, Adelphia, and WorldCom, whereas many lesser incidents have basically gone unnoticed. These unnoticed and questionable misuses of corporate funds include the familiar practices of providing excessive perks, benefits, salaries, and bonuses to CEOs and executives. Although, the practice of excessive generosity with oneself is self-serving and demonstrates agency issues, it is in most cases, quite legal, and largely accepted as normal practice. Often, the overall health of the organizations that pay the price for this excessive generosity to those few at the top is poor and declining. There would be many organizations that would be far healthier today if slack funds had been utilized in a strategic manner to ensure the future prosperity of the firm instead of being diverted to other uses.

VALUE CREATION

The concept of *value creation* is an expansion of value chain analysis. Value creation is the process by which the firm transforms its resources from raw inputs into a product or service that the customer is willing to purchase. The firm must in some way add value to resource inputs to garner from its customers a price that not only covers the cost of all of its resource inputs but also generates a surplus that allows it to sustain itself and prosper. This resembles the "open systems" model of organizations.

The Sequentially Interdependent System

The open systems concept (Figure 3.1) is a classic value chain. Value addition begins with the inbound logistics process, progresses through each step of the transformation process, and ends with the outbound

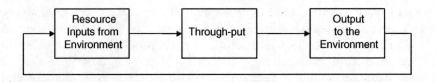

Figure 3.1 Open system.

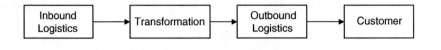

Figure 3.2 Traditional value chain.

logistics process. A manufacturing organization provides a simple example of this system. The technology at work is "long-linked." Only those activities that are identified as being part of the value chain add value for the customer.

The value chain concept (Figure 3.2) cannot stand by itself because it is a linear system, sequential in design (like manufacturing), and not all systems are sequential in nature, although all systems are likely to have some sequential process. There are other ways to create value for the customers. Organizations need to understand how they create value for their customers so that they can become or remain competitive and continue to exist.

The Pooled Interdependent System

The pooled interdependent system makes use of intensive technology. Multiple resources are used in service of the client. Customer satisfaction is derived from the sum total of the customer's experience. In essence, all of the organization's employees that come into contact with the customer, and many that don't actually have contact but provide services, which the customer uses, impact the customer satisfaction with the total organization. For example, the value of a college education as perceived by the consuming student is based on the student's satisfaction with the total institution and is influenced not only by the classroom faculty, but also all of the other university services and personnel with which the student comes into contact. In fact, it is the sum total of all of the independent reciprocal relationships between the student and the university that make it pooled interdependence. Other examples of pooled interdependent organizations are:

- Nursing homes — one-on-one care
- Hospitals
- Cruise ships — employees are there to strictly serve the customer, and the client becomes part of the organization, because one must follow the rules and regulations of the organization

In planning strategy, the organization must also consider that the customer is trapped (Figure 3.3). More often than not, the customer is locked into the organization for some length of time and cannot change providers

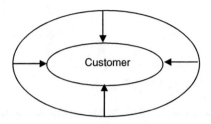

Figure 3.3 Value pool with one customer group.

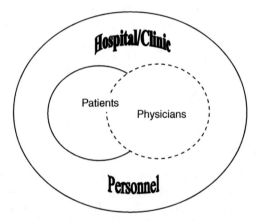

Figure 3.4 Value pool with multiple, but symbiotic, customer groups.

without paying switching costs. The greater the switching cost, the more likely the customer will stay with your organization. In this type of value creation process, customers are often called by industry-specific titles; in education, the customer is a student, and in health care, they are known as patients, by hospitality organizations as guests, correctional institutions as prisoners, and in many other environments as clients. All units of an organization need to be serving the customer well.

This type of organization sometimes seems to have a secondary customer that consists of a "core constituency." In the case of the hospital, it is the physicians that treat patients and conduct research. In the university environment it is the faculty that teach students and conduct research. The depiction shows the relationship between the two categories of customers and the organization (Figure 3.4).

The Reciprocal Interdependent System

The reciprocal interdependent system utilizes mediating technology to add value through convenience by facilitating the transaction. Examples

Figure 3.5 Value transaction model.

include banking, railroads, finance, and retail organizations. In effect, the organization that devotes itself to facilitating transactions actually has multiple customer groups. In retail and distributor organizations, those who deposit or supply the organization are as much of a customer as those who seek the products or services from the organization. This traditional middleman organization relies on suppliers purchasing its distribution services, and paying for those services by pricing the products below the consumer price, as much as it relies on consumers to purchase its consolidation and convenience services above the manufacturer's direct price. Too often, those firms engaged in this type of business only recognize the consumer or purchaser of the goods as the customer, totally missing the fact that they are in business to facilitate transactions. Distribution, consolidation, and facilitation are the only products that this kind of organization actually sells.

All energy should be focused on facilitating the transaction (Figure 3.5). If an organization understands this, it can manage its resources better to create value (examples include the transportation and communication industries).

Value Creation Lessons

Understanding the value creation process allows firms to deploy their limited resources where they will create the most value for the customer and, in turn, generate maximum profits for the firm. This knowledge provides the direction needed to strategically align the organization and insure the future. Thus summarizing:

■ Regardless of the value creation system in place, care should be taken when investing resources in non-value-creating activities because, regardless of the internal benefits received from these activities, they are not part of the product or service being purchased by the customer who will not knowingly pay for these activities.
■ In a sequential organization, serving the next person in the line is the goal; technology is long-linked. Teamwork is necessary only

because it relates to improving the sequential processing, and all effort should be related to protecting and improving the sequential linkages.

■ In a pooled organization, train employees individually; technology is intensive.

■ In a mediating organization, facilitate the transfer.

■ You only add value for what is contracted and only with those with whom you have contracted (customers, regardless of their label). An organization can destroy value with non-value-added activities.

CORE TECHNOLOGY[1]

Core technology refers to how an organization accomplishes its value creation activities. It deals with the transformation of inputs to outputs — not computers, electronics, or networks. Usually, large organizations are likely to employ all three types of technologies in different areas, but primarily add value to the customer via one model. Core technology is the process by which an organization adds value in providing a product or service to the consumer. Core technology can be classified as long-linked, intensive, or mediating. Long-linked technology, as a value chain, involves transforming inputs into products. Long-linked technology exhibits sequential interdependence in which the output of a given unit becomes the input of another's work process. Intensive technology focuses on using knowledge, housed within the firm, to solve customer problems by employing pooled interdependence, in which each task in the process is separate from the others. Intensive technology is referred to as a value shop, because the idea of a shop captures the concept that the firm is directed toward solving unique client problems, much like a machine shop or a job shop that produces unique customer products. A firm that employs intensive technology is thus selling the knowledge of its employees. The third type of core technology, mediating technology, is based on the idea of a value network. These networks link customers or clients who wish to be interdependent. The mediating technology of the firm facilitates exchange relationships among customers distributed in space and time.

CORE BUSINESS

The core business is exactly what its name implies — identifying the type of business in which an organization wants to be involved. Successfully identifying an organization's core business is vital to the success of that organization. There are three situations in which an organization can identify its core business. The first is in the planning stages of a new organization with the development of a business plan. The second is through the development of an existing organization's strategy; for an established organization that did not begin with an in-depth business plan that identified its core business, consequently developing the organization's strategy can identify the core business. Finally, the identification of the core business also occurs when an organization has identified its core business in the past, but feels the need to study and possibly reinvent its current business.

CORE COMPETENCY

In general terms, a business' core competency is an internal organizational process that allows it to successfully compete. It may or may not be a distinctive competency dependent on the capabilities of its competitors. In any given industry, the core competencies of the competing firms will differ. Not all core competencies are created equal; the power of any particular core competency is relative to those of the competing firms. A firm's core competency may reside either within or without a firm's value creation process but will always influence the firm's ability to survive.

There probably are very few strategic management terms that have been more confused or misused than core competency. Core competency is often confused with core business. In a manufacturing organization, if the general manager was asked to identify the core competency, likely as not, some part of the manufacturing process would be identified, even if the firm's actual processes lagged behind the competition. It just seems to be normal for those in organizations to identify the most obvious firm characteristic as its core competency. This misidentification may result in poor strategic decisions being made. A firm's core competency, regardless of where it lies, allows it to successfully compete.

Further, a core competency provides a firm with a competitive advantage. Thus, a firm does not have a core competency that it doesn't employ. At most, it can be said of such a condition that the firm has a potential core competency that could lead to a competitive advantage if recognized and deployed. There is real danger to any firm that may be successfully competing in its industry but has either failed to identify its core competency or identified it incorrectly. The danger stems from the firm's inability to protect what it does not recognize or utilize to the fullest. Firms in this position are apt to fall out of favor with their customers without ever knowing why, or make strategic decisions that enhance their misperceived competency while diminishing the effectiveness of the unknown competency. This situation is no more than attribution theory applied to the firm's performance.

INTERNAL RESOURCE AUDIT

Conducting an internal resource audit is critical to being able to analyze external opportunities and threats that come from neutral external events. The difference between the two is in how the company handles the events. If the company can adjust and adapt to the event, then it is an opportunity; if not, it is a threat. Because opportunities and threats are dependent on a firm's ability to react, and the ability to react is dependent upon its strengths and weaknesses, it is logical to evaluate internal capabilities prior to looking for environmental opportunities and threats.

Today, as in the past, many organizations utilize the SWOT (strengths, weaknesses, opportunities, and threats) approach as a strategic analysis tool. Although it is an excellent tool when properly used, most organizations fail in the identification of their strengths and weaknesses. Oftentimes firms identify their top management team as their number one strength (because of depth of experience) when, in fact, management may be their primary deficiency. In addition, people, that is, employees, have been mentioned as a firm's most valuable resource so often that the phrase is nothing more than a tired cliché. The problem with a SWOT analysis, as it is usually developed, is that it is too subjective and reflects the bias, attribution errors, and misconceptions of those involved. Thus, because of its lack of framework, it creates a tendency that leans toward accepting an organization's beliefs about itself and then reinforcing those beliefs with the analysis.

RESOURCE BASED VIEW (RBV) OF ORGANIZATIONS[2]

The RBV is a relatively recent approach to strategy development and requires the strategist to view organizations as a collection of resources. This approach requires that resources be identified and evaluated. Four broad categories of resources are possessed by organizations; they are:

1. Physical — property, plant, and equipment (anything tangible)
2. Human — people
3. Financial — money that is available to the organization
4. Organizational — all of the intangible resources (culture, various systems, morale, patents, intellect)

Strategists utilizing the RBV must correctly identify firm resources in as much detail as possible, and then evaluate the resource, based on its contribution to the organization relative to the similar resources possessed by competition. Correct identification of resources and a correct evaluation of those resources are critical to the RBV. As an example, firms have the tendency of exaggerating the importance of human resources and wrongly attributing organizational success to them. Strategists have the tendency of looking at a well-trained workforce and quickly evaluating the employees as a valuable (among other qualities) human asset when, actually, the employees themselves are only average in comparison to employees of other firms within the industry. That the employees may be better trained than those of other firms within the industry is likely a fact attributable to the organization's training system, not the employees.

Resources are evaluated based upon their value, rarity, immitability, and the extent to which the organization exploits the resource. In essence, a resource by making it to this list has been identified as valuable; after all, if it isn't valuable, recognition as a resource is unlikely. The more unique the resource is to the industry, the more value potential exists. The following matrix (see Table 3.1) examines the various outcomes an organization can expect from possessing a resource, based on the criteria listed above. Organizational exploitation of the possessed resources is critical to its success.

As shown previously, dependent upon the evaluation of the resource's value and rarity, and the degree to which the organization exploits the resource, the organizational outcomes vary dramatically. It has been demonstrated that the greater the value and rarity, the stronger will be the firm's competitive advantage from exploiting the resource. However, if a firm underutilizes a resource (by its failure to exploit the resource), it will find itself at a competitive disadvantage that is inversely related to the value and

Table 3.1   Resource Based View

Resource	Valuable	Rare	Non-immitable	Exploited	Outcome
R1	Yes			Yes	Competitive parity
R1	Yes			No	Competitive disadvantage — level 1
R1	Yes	Yes		Yes	Temporary competitive advantage
R1	Yes	Yes		No	Competitive disadvantage — level 2
R1	Yes	Yes	Yes	Yes	Sustainable competitive advantage
R1	Yes	Yes	Yes	No	Competitive disadvantage — level 3

rarity of the resource. The simple logic is that the more value attributed to a given resource, the more important it is for the firm to exploit that resource.

Many novice strategists also confuse the analysis by failing to apply the analysis to the competitive market within which the organization operates. As an example, consider a university that is attempting to analyze itself utilizing this technique. Its Ph.D. holding faculty members are one of its human assets, and in the general population they are very rare; however, in an educational environment they are common. Thus, the most that the Ph.D. faculty can provide to the institution is competitive parity, and that too is only if the institution exploits them within the system by utilizing the faculty for research and teaching. Using these same Ph.D.s in administrative tasks for which they are both over- and underqualified may put the institution at a competitive disadvantage. However, if the same institution has a system in place that ensures Ph.D. faculty members remain productive in teaching and research, that system might provide the institution with a competitive advantage.

Generally speaking, it will be the organizational systems and processes that lead to a competitive opportunity, and the organization's ability to exploit those systems fully, or at least more efficiently than its competitors, that will lead to a competitive advantage. Thus, by applying an RBV analysis to a firm's resources, the strategist can better utilize the SWOT analysis because strengths result from resources being exploited. Weaknesses will then either result from a lack of resources or the firm's inability to exploit the resource.

OUTSOURCING

Those aspects of the organization that are not considered core competencies may be good candidates for outsourcing. Outsourcing can be defined as a strategic decision to obtain goods or services from an outside agency versus making or providing the goods or services within the organization. Outsourcing is usually met with opposition in many organizations because it is often associated with the loss of jobs. It is essential that companies define and understand the primary objectives that they want to achieve through the use of outsourcing. Some objectives of outsourcing may be to improve management focus, gain access to better skills than currently available within the organization, enhance skills, or control costs. A cost-benefit analysis may also be beneficial in determining whether or not to outsource a noncore process. If a function can be performed in-house at a high quality and relatively low cost, then it is probably not a good candidate for outsourcing. Evaluating performance by the group should include an examination of service levels, customer satisfaction, costs, and attainment of agreed-upon goals (Figure 3.6).

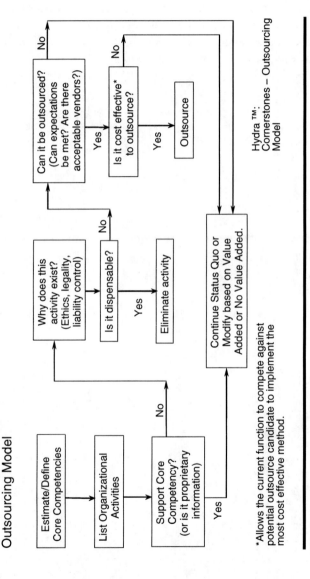

Figure 3.6   Outsourcing model.

Exercise

Based on your own observations, what strategy do you believe your own organization is currently pursuing? Is it an eclectic or planned strategy? What strategy would you propose for adoption?

Identify your organization's primary value-adding process and explain the ramifications of your decision.

Identify your organization's core business activities. What activities is the firm engaged in, beyond its core?

REFERENCES

1. Thompson, J., *Organizations in Action,* McGraw-Hill, New York, 1967.
2. Barney, J., Firm resources and sustained competitive advantage, *Journal of Management,* 17(1), 99, 1991.

4

IDENTIFICATION OF KEY PERFORMANCE MEASURES

Organizations conducting a strategic analysis or developing a strategic plan must incorporate performance metrics as a method of analyzing overall organizational performance. Traditional finance-based measures place an unbalanced importance on short-term results. Therefore, both financial and nonfinancial measures should be considered to achieve the long-term vision of the organization. Individuals within the organization need to be evaluated in areas and behaviors that they are responsible for and for what they control. All metrics must be meaningful, align with the organization's primary goal of customer satisfaction, and drive the organizational activities in the same direction. To attain this ultimate goal, it is imperative that all organizations know and understand their customers. Performance metrics, utilized to evaluate an individual manager's performance, must be developed to ensure that attainment of the desired performance at the individual manager level will lead to the organization itself meeting its own performance objectives.

The four primary control structures are as follows:

- Cost — production function, manager is only responsible for inputs
- Expense — no production function, manager only controls inputs consumed in achieving goals (research and development, accounting)
- Profit — pricing function, manager controls marketing mix, pricing decisions, advertising, and commission structure
- Investment — capital function, manager controls capital and working capital decisions (inventory, receivables, payables)

Oftentimes, senior management misaligns performance measures with structures. Effective performance measures are dependent on an accurate definition of structure and proper alignment that reinforces the appropriate behavior and goals. Performance measures must be in line with the particular function the manager presides over.

Both financial and nonfinancial metrics are needed for an organization to achieve an acceptable level of performance. Specifically, performance can be divided into four distinct categories: financial, customer, employee, and internal processes.[1] Whereas financial statements still provide a good indication of how well a company has performed, organizations need to know more about their customers, their critical business processes, and their employees.[2]

The following recommended performance measures are based both on historical financial data (lagging indicators) and current operational data (leading indicators).[3] Operational performance measures linked to a company's objectives, goals, and mission are superior to traditional financial measures.[4] To effectively manage the financial performance of the operation, management needs both lagging and leading performance measures.[5]

In establishing performance measures, organizations must benchmark by comparing their indicators within the industry, as well as within the company. Best practices need to be established by learning from industry competitors, as well as from internal company leaders. Additionally, products with differing characteristics can be benchmarked against each other. Businesses with similar business functions but differing products can be useful tools in the utilization of benchmarking. Benchmarking provides organizations with a useful measuring device for performance metrics. As important as it is to benchmark within the industry and firm, it is equally important to take a broader perspective and benchmark against completely different industries and their firms. External benchmarking involves the search for practices, systems, and processes that can be imported and applied to assist firms to focus on customers instead of direct competition, and thus break with the industry status quo with revolutionary gain.

It is crucial for organizations to track and make decisions on those skills, systems, and values that will determine the future success of the firm.[6] It is believed that a more balanced approach, with each metric having a customer-centric design, will allow the company to link performance to its corporate mission and strategy.[7] This balanced approach focuses on corporations as organizational units such as strategic business units, not on business processes.[8]

BENCHMARKING AND DETERMINING CURRENT PERFORMANCE

To engage in strategic planning or for that matter planning of any kind, organizations must be able to accurately determine their current level of performance. Many mature organizations have well-defined and long-standing performance metrics. Likewise, many organizations regardless of their maturity level, have poorly developed or ill-defined performance metrics. All organizations embarking on strategic planning need to reassess their key performance indicators to insure that strong showings on the indicators are truly indicative of strong organizational performance. For many organizations, it is necessary to redefine the key performance measures. Changing the measures changes the game. People and organizations naturally resist change — they don't like to give up the old. Therefore:

- A firm benchmarks by comparing itself to others either within the same industry or in totally different industries. Products can be very different but can still be benchmarked against each other. The first step in benchmarking is the identification of the key performance measures.
- The primary benchmark for a for-profit organization is net income.
- All key measures must have alignment, that is, align and move toward a common goal and control. The goal directs the behavior; the control compares performance to the goal after completion. Performance benchmarks should be identified in such a way that if they are reached, then so is the goal.
- The goal of a shareholder owned, professionally managed organization should be to maximize shareholder wealth. The goal of the family-owned-and-operated business is to allow its owners to live well. To meet either of these goals, firms must gain and retain customers; thus customer satisfaction becomes the primary goal.
- It is difficult to identify measures that act as solid controls and goals.
- Net profit has been used for many years. Net income is not necessarily a good measure because it is too easily manipulated (expenses can be cut to boost net income). Because net income is inadequate, how can any measure based in part on net income be good? Any one financial measure can be misused and bring about failure, but if we take one measure and manage the organization skillfully, other measures are not needed.

Often, income-related performance indicators are misused because of the performance/reward system. Employees will do only what is asked of them, and this may end up hurting the organization. The performance measure used should lead to or indicate organizational performance; however, this does not always happen. Things are usually measured because they are easy to measure, but that doesn't mean that just because we can measure it, we should. On the flip side, just because something is not easy to measure doesn't mean that we should ignore it.

Example: U.S. Steel

The performance measure that was used for quite some time was the number of tons of steel produced, however, this did not mean tons of steel sold. There were two types of steel being produced: boutique and mass. The boutique steel was in demand, but was produced in small quantities and the mass steel was not in as high a demand, but it was produced in large quantities. The performance indicator that used the number of tons produced encouraged production of mass steel, though it was not in demand. U.S. Steel ceased to exist partly as a result of using poor metrics.

Organizations should use meaningful measures by working from the customer backward, because customer satisfaction is the primary goal. If an organization does not understand customer satisfaction, it is lost. Care for the customer will ensure that the organization makes profits. All measures should be "customer concentric." To repeat, all performance measures should be tied to the customer. Stakeholder measures are important only when they impact or influence the customer.

To do this, all organizations must know and understand their customers. Most companies do not know or understand their customers. A customer is someone who utilizes a service that your organization offers. Moreover, all organizational goals and objectives should be aligned and go in the same direction. The alignment should be such that returns can be maximized. In Figure 4.1, the large arrow is the organization as a whole, and the smaller arrows represent departments within the organization. The goals and alignments of each of the departments should correspond with those of the entire organization. Unaligned goals, such as those indicated by the yellow arrow, must be either adjusted and brought into line or eliminated. Thus:

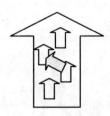

Figure 4.1   Misaligned goal.

- For an organization to find out what the customer wants and why they are a customer, they must be talked to and observed.
- The performance of sales personnel is most often measured by tracking the individual employee's sales-related activities (calls, lunch, and contacts); however, without a results component, effectiveness really isn't measured.
- When organizations establish minimum performance objectives, they are also, in essence, establishing the maximum performance that can be expected because, once the limit has been reached, most employees will tend to stop, as there is often no incentive to go beyond the minimum.
- To effectively measure current performance, organizations must look for the drivers. Financial performance is driven by customer and operational performance.
- All organizations must identify and then utilize the performance measures that are appropriate to the management of their firms.
- Measuring is a non-value-added activity; so something must be done with what is measured.

FINANCIAL PERFORMANCE MEASURES

Financial performance measures are used to track and monitor organizational performance. However, it is stressed that financial performance is a by-product of satisfying the customer and has little, if anything, to do with beating your competition. Financial numbers fail to provide a complete picture of an organization's performance and future. Customers do not buy products and services because of a company's financial performance because these figures reflect historical information and not where the company is going in the future.[9] Financial performance measures should only be one element of a well-balanced program of metrics, which, at its core, should focus on satisfying the customer.[10]

Net income, often used as a benchmark, is not necessarily the best performance metric measure because it can, as mentioned earlier, be easily manipulated by cutting expenses. Employees often perform based on the relationship between compensation and bonuses. This may result in higher short-term performance but can result in hurting the long-term viability of the company.

Economic Value Added, Return on Invested Capital, and Free Cash Flow

Understanding an organization's historical performance provides a fundamental perspective for developing and evaluating goals and strategies

Table 4.1 Evaluation of Past Financial Performance

Driver	Calculation	Relation to Value Creation
ROIC	NOPLAT/invested capital	An organization creates value for its shareholders only when it earns an ROIC over and above its cost of capital
FCF	NOPLAT net investment	ROIC and the proportion of its profits that the company invests for growth drive FCF, which in turn drives value
Economic profit	Invested capital × (ROIC WACC)	Combines size and spread (ROIC and WACC) into a dollar estimate of value added

going forward. In a traditional sense, an analysis of a company's past performance would entail an examination of the material changes in the financial statements, and the relating ratios and measures of such. However, it is important to note that the conventional methods of analysis do not take into consideration the value created by the firm. Therefore, a better approach to analyzing historical performance is to focus on the return on invested capital (ROIC), which is considered to be the primary driver of an organization's value. However, the firm's weighted average cost of capital (WACC) must be considered because if the ROIC doesn't cover the WACC, the firm is destroying value. ROIC and the two remaining core-value drivers, free cash flow (FCF) and economic profit, are regarded as very powerful analytical tools for evaluating the true operating performance of a company. Both the ROIC and FCF metrics include the use of net operating profit less adjusted taxes (NOPLAT). The calculations for all three drivers and their respective relation to value creation are shown in Table 4.1.

Notably, when using these drivers to analyze the historical performance of a company, ROIC should be calculated with and without goodwill, as both calculations present different measuring capabilities for an organization. For example, ROIC excluding goodwill is useful for comparing operating performance across companies and analyzing trends over time, whereas ROIC including goodwill is useful in measuring how well a company has used its investors' funds. The latter is primarily applicable to firms that have grown through acquisitions, as ROIC including goodwill is a principal indicator of whether or not the company has earned its cost of capital, taking into consideration the premiums it paid for the acquisitions.

To delve a bit further into ROIC, an example of a ROIC tree is presented in Table 4.2, showing the key elements of the rate and providing more insight into the actual drivers of ROIC. The component measures of ROIC are both industry and company specific, and as such, the ratios can be viewed as reflections of an organization's strategy, relative to its competitors.

Table 4.2 Return on Invested Capital (ROIC) Tree

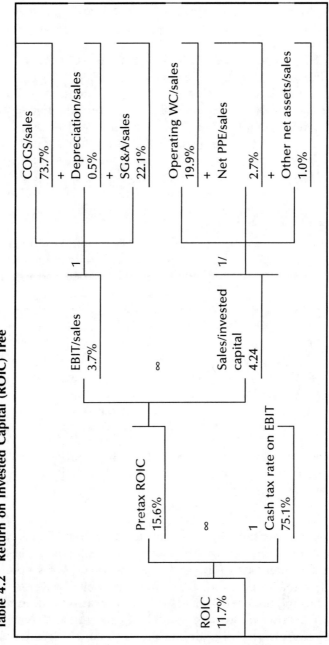

Consequently, a firm can set internal goals and controls regarding the measures that will ultimately enhance ROIC and lead to the creation of value. The following illustration utilizes cost of goods sold (COGS); earnings before interest and taxes (EBIT); sales, general, and administrative expenses (SG&A); working capital (WC); and plant, property, and equipment (PPE) in the calculations.

The FCF calculation depicts a firm's actual cash available for operations. As a performance measure, it is superior to net profit in predicting the firm's short-term financial welfare. FCF can be significantly different from net profits. FCF is the actual cash on hand, after adjustments have been made for noncash, but tax-deductible, expenses such as depreciation and amortization. As long as FCF is greater than the firm's total cash requirements for both creditors and shareholders, the firm will remain solvent. A large investment in operating capital or goodwill can result in a negative FCF balance, which would deplete the funds available for distribution. In such an event, a company would have to find additional resources, typically debt, to keep itself going.

Economic profit measures the dollars of economic value created by a company in a single year. The measure is dramatically different than accounting profit because economic profit or the economic value added (EVA) includes a charge for the cost of capital employed, and amortizes certain expenses whereas accounting profit does not. Firms seeking to maximize shareholder wealth often employ EVA as a measure of performance. Firms that increase EVA are utilizing capital efficiently and productively. EVA as a performance measure assists executive management to focus on the long-term welfare of the firm. Notably, EVA can be determined for divisions as well as for the company as a whole, so it provides a useful basis for determining managerial compensation at all levels. The fundamentals of the EVA concept require:

- Only investing in projects that return a profit greater than the industry average profit and the cost of capital employed
- Using assets more intensely
- Divestment of all nonproductive assets

EVA may be misleading in some circumstances. If a corporation is old and has owned appreciating assets for a very long time as in the case of a railroad, the value of its appreciating assets will be shown on its balance sheet at a historic value and, thus, invested capital will also reflect this historic value and not the true market value. For firms like this, the invested capital may be very misleading and when used in the EVA equation, the firm could easily show an optimistically positive ROIC when the historic book value of the asset is used, but actually have a grossly negative return if the current market value of the asset is estimated and used in the equation. As another example of the misleading nature of assets that fall into this category, consider the firms that are selling off bits and pieces of property and rights at a dramatically higher market price than the historical price at which they are valued on the books and thus creating an illusion by padding their operating bottom line with this false profit. It is unlikely that firms in this position will actually perform the calculation above as few could justify their continued existence based on the return they make from the actual value of the assets they control.

However, firms holding appreciating assets would argue that to reflect the true market price in their invested capital would be unfair and not accurately reflect their position. This case can be made, but if ROIC, EVA, and ROA are going to be used as true reflections of a firm's performance, the question is: shouldn't these firms measure their current performance to the current value of the assets that they employ to earn their current return? This approach, however unorthodox, is in keeping with Accounting's traditional matching philosophy.

The Profit Zone

Slywotzky and Morrison (1997) define the profit zone as the arena of a company's economic activity where high profit is achieved. This arena of high profit, once identified, helps an organization to sustain profitability and ultimately appreciate in value.[11] Organizations must identify the profit zones in which they operate both at the corporate and divisional levels. The key to entering the profit zone is customer-centric design, which requires that the organization focus first on the customer, and then work backward from there.[12]

Stock Price

The economic performance measures mentioned previously are vital to the success of an organization, but traditional measures of financial performance should not be overlooked. EVA and related metrics represent a new paradigm for firms, and incorporating stock price as part of the overall equation may help to make those in the organization more comfortable, as stock price is an easily understandable and visible measure. Value creation, profitability, and customer satisfaction are all included in the stock price of the company.

The value of stock price as a stand-alone measure of firm or executive performance is of questionable value, and care should be taken not to overemphasize its importance as a measure. The "stock market isn't necessarily rational" is a kind way of saying that the behavior of the market is driven by many forces, ranging from the optimism and pessimism of individual traders and analysts — and thus, the many different interpretations that are made from the same information — to the more insidious motivations of the players involved.

In addition, the market goes up and down as in the "bull and bear" cycle and often carries all the traded firms right along with it. In times of market prosperity, many firms and their executives ride the bull as the firm's value increases when the overall market expands, taking credit where no credit is due, because the increased value of the stock isn't the result of actual improvement in firm performance. However, when the market hits the skids and is being chased downward by the bear, the executives of firms are quick to point out that the downward movement of their firm's stock is the result of a temporary market trend, and not a result of poor performance on their part. The interesting aspect of the bull and bear phenomena is that it seems to be universally applied by firms and understood by most as a "family secret" — something that everyone knows and everyone knows that everyone knows, but everyone knows that no one is supposed to know. Divulging the family secret is similar in nature to "coming out of the closet," generally accepted as being in poor taste and at the least, will cast a shadow of disloyalty on the offending person.

Sales to Breakeven

This can be an important metric, as it may answer such questions as to how far sales can drop before a firm begins to lose money. When incorporated with other performance measures, it may help to define the operational strategy of an organization. In its simplest form, this measure utilizes sales in dollars to breakeven in dollars where the overall average company contribution margin is used. The more complex the organization and its product mix, the more likely that sales to breakeven will be simply a gross estimate, varying significantly from period to period, and depending on the product mix that is produced and sold. Like many other measures, it should not be used alone, but when used as one of several carefully selected performance indicators, it can add significantly to management's ability to understand the firm's performance.

CUSTOMER PERFORMANCE MEASURES (CPM)

In the following paragraphs are detailed some CPM that would help in achieving the set customer care goals.

Feedback and Complaints

Management must have metrics in place that accurately track both the feedback and complaints that follow a completed customer transaction or interaction, to understand and respond effectively to the needs of the customer. Two methods of collecting customer transactional satisfaction information are through the use of self-reporting cards and a self-reporting mechanism accessible to the customer through use of a code on the company's Web site. Firms must ensure that customers are getting what they purchased on time and are charged correctly.

Often, surrogate and distal measures are used to capture customer satisfaction because they can provide information that is based more on hard data than the perception-based customer satisfaction questionnaires. Tracking customer callbacks, returns, and warranty repairs through the use of check sheets or checklists is another method of determining customer satisfaction. After collecting the information, it must be transformed into analyzable data. Often the information is transformed with a Pareto chart that identifies problem severity and frequency and thus allows the management to focus on eliminating the most costly problem causes. Firms are unlikely to achieve long-term financial success if customers are not satisfied; and without the appropriate metrics in place, satisfaction cannot be measured.

Customer Tracking

It should be obvious that a firm needs to know who its customers are and understand their purchase behaviors and, yet, many firms seem just to be happy to have customers and do nothing to track them. Without tracking and understanding the customer, the management cannot know if they are effectively retaining customers and gaining repeat business, or effectively securing new business and growing their customer base. The second often-overlooked issue is the reason for customers purchasing from a given firm.

> *Customer repeat business:* Management needs to track the number of instances where customers have transacted repeat business or, on the contrary, ceased purchasing products/services altogether. Management should identify and analyze trends and the cause for either their repeat business, or lack thereof. The rationale is to understand whether the management and/or the sales force can provide some form of support/service at any given stage of the consumption life cycle, which would prevent the clients' departure or generate repeat business. Tracking this information can also provide firms with an indirect report on what actions their competitors are taking that they are not.
>
> *Percentage of new customer sales:* Tracking the number of sales made to new customers is important for several reasons. First, over a

period of time, this metric will develop an either increasing or decreasing trend that will indicate with a high level of detail whether an organization's business is growing or shrinking. The real inherent value and the second reason for tracking this metric is that, from an operational standpoint, by tracking these percentages along with the percentages of the rest of its customer base, the management should be able to predict the relative maturity of its client base and, from this information, forecast future demand. Thus, an understanding of its client-base maturity will allow a firm to logistically plan for its customer demands at a level of efficiency and effectiveness that otherwise would be impossible. Finally, if the percentage of new customer sales and number of new customers is low, it can be inferred that customers are not satisfied with the service level and are thus not recommending the firm to others or, even worse, recommending that the firm be avoided by others.

Customer Profitability

The customer base must be analyzed not just for feedback purposes, but also for determining the overall profitability of the relationship. Those clients that do not meet management-specified criteria for profitability and do not present any viable future profit opportunity, must be eliminated, as these relationships represent non-value-added components. This process is essential for a market-driven organization, and it dispels the myth that sales should be made at any cost to increase market share. Market share is only important when viewed as a result of a successful customer concentric strategy; as a driver of sales behavior it is destructive.

Customer Satisfaction Ratings

According to Kueng (2000), managers cannot know the quality of their organization's service level unless customers are asked. He further states that organizations rarely analyze customer information on a systematic basis. One way of gathering customer data is through the use of the SERVQUAL instrument. This instrument is a two-section set of questions, one addressing customer expectations, and the other addressing customer perceptions of the service they consume.[13] Another approach is to define quality criteria, and have customers rate both the degree of satisfaction and the importance of each criterion.[14] It is recommended that all organizations implement some form of this instrument, and data be gathered and analyzed from both the existing client base and those clients that no longer do business with the company.

Additionally, customer satisfaction needs to be measured in the form of service level or fill rate. Service level is measured in terms of actual demand met by the organization. To monitor customer satisfaction with the product shipped, returns need to be accurately tracked. Reason coding of returns will provide a measurement tool for product satisfaction as well as the ability to track problem areas. Return reason codes would need to track the following:

- Late delivery
- Not satisfied with product
- Ordered wrong product
- Salesperson error
- Delivery error
- Shipping damage
- Warehouse damage

Utilization of such return codes provides immediate feedback as to customer satisfaction with both product and service. This will provide organizations with information that can be utilized in improving service as well as the ability to track operational-service-related issues.

Service Level

This measurement is the probability of a stock-out not occurring. Although service level is also included as part of customer satisfaction, this metric is also important at measuring how an organization's internal processes are functioning. Service level is an important measurement in determining if the organization is able to meet the demands of the customer. Benchmarking within the company is imperative to determine how well each company is meeting demand. Benchmarking within the industry will generate feedback as to how to improve service. An increase in service level will improve customer service, add value, and ultimately increase profitability.

Number of On-Time Deliveries

This is a crucial metric as it ties in directly with customer service. It is an easy measure to track, and one that the management should analyze carefully. This is one of many proactive performance measures outlined in this paper, as it is intended to measure operational events. Proper design of this metric will lead organizations to provide the appropriate service level to clients in ways that will foster future loyalty and growth.[15]

Cycle Time

Cycle time is the time it takes a customer order to be fulfilled successfully. A reduction in cycle time will improve customer service, adding value, and ultimately increasing profitability.

Number of Reorders

This measurement can be defined as the number of customer orders that were not correctly completed the first time, and needed to be redone. This is an important measure, as it places emphasis on the internal processes of the organization, though having a direct link with customer service and satisfaction.

EMPLOYEE PERFORMANCE MEASURES

Employee performance measures should be applied to all organizations. Employee-related performance measures that actually measure performance in two distinct areas should be developed. The first set measures the firm's ability to utilize its human resources, and the second measures how well the firm meets the needs of its employees. Kueng (2000) emphasized the importance of the firm maintaining an acceptable quality of work life (QWL) for its employees. This should be done, not merely out of an altruistic desire to improve the life of employees, but because the efforts of human resources are required for organizational success. Many companies distribute a yearly employee survey that allows the employee to provide anonymous feedback for the firm. Some firms will go even as far as to link the management team's bonus program to the results of the survey.

Employee Attitudinal Questionnaires

Employee attitudinal questionnaires (i.e., job satisfaction, morale, quality of work life, etc.) may have a downside for organizations. First, the natural instinct of employees is to not believe the organization when they are told their answers and comments will remain confidential and there will be no personal repercussions from their responses; unfortunately, this often has not been the case. Thus, the answers tend to reflect the employees' perception of what may serve as the appropriate responses, and not their true feelings, thus invalidating the premise upon which the attitudinal survey is based. Second, attitudinal questionnaires ask the respondent to dredge up all the unpleasantness of the past and bring them to mind at one time. This may, in fact, have the unintended consequence of lowering an employee's opinion of the employer and thus lowering individual satisfaction and company morale. Third, employees rightly expect that if the employer takes the time and effort to ask the questions, then they should care enough to eliminate the troublesome issues that are identified through the process. However, as often as not, individual employees see no positive results from the exercise, which tends to reinforce the opinion that the firm doesn't care.

Employee Turnover Rate

To survive, an organization must have a stable core work force. It is important to understand and define the core within every organization. Core work force refers to employees in an organization that possess key skill and knowledge sets. These individuals are difficult and expensive to replace. Organizations characterized by a high degree of core turnover destroy value, as customer relationships are jeopardized and new hire and training costs negatively affect organizational profitability. This metric must be tracked and analyzed in a detailed manner, as management must uncover the reasons contributing to a high turnover rate. Noncore turnover is the turnover of employees easily replaced because they possess no specific skill set or knowledge important to the organization. Turnover among these employees is often counted on by management to hold down overall payroll costs. These are noncareer positions and are found in many service industries, a prime example being employees of the fast food industry.

There are two types of turnover, negative and positive. Negative turnover consists of employees that pursue opportunities outside of the firm. Positive turnover is a measure of employees that are promoted within the firm or make a lateral move to a different job position.

Frequency of Training

The rapidly evolving environment surrounding firms today require both the firm and its employees to adapt to new methods, processes, and technologies. To accomplish this, firms must invest heavily in the training and development of their personnel. If they fail to invest in continuous learning and employee development, obsolescence of employee skills is inevitable. Obsolete employees, like obsolete equipment, can't keep the company competitive. However, return on training investment (ROTI) is difficult to measure. The more advanced the training, the more difficult it becomes to measure ROTI.

Although the effectiveness and ROTI of training employees on a new mechanical process might be easy to do, the difficulty increases significantly as the skills to be developed become more cognitive as in management development. The success of cognitive skill development, at best, can only be estimated and, even then, not immediately. Thus, in times of economic pressure, firms often cut funding for employee development. The concept of EVA recognizes the difficulty in measuring ROTI and suggests that firms capitalize and amortize training and development costs for the purpose of calculating EVA, reducing the firm's temptation to cut expenditures in this critical area.

Whereas training and development programs are necessary and important to sharpen employees' skills and keep the organization competitive, they should be used in moderation. Direct training and development costs are expensive as are the losses due to decreased employee productivity costs. In addition, too much training may make employees feel as though they are full-time students.

Training metrics need to be maintained at the organizational and individual levels. These records also need to include the resources dedicated to training and some type of ROTI metric that estimates the benefit of the investment in training and employee development.

Advancement Opportunities

In organizations where advancement opportunities are sparse, employees may experience a psyche prison, feeling trapped and making those with transferable skills look for new positions outside the firm. Ensuring that employees increase their opportunities contributes to organizational effectiveness and enhances the overall quality of the workforce by promoting professional growth. In today's litigious societal environment, it also is very important for all firms to ensure that their advancement policies are consistently applied and that metrics are maintained that demonstrate the organization's commitment to equal opportunity and fairness.

Quality of the Work Environment

A work environment that does not permit optimal performance will frustrate those employees who seek to perform to the best of their abilities. Frustrated employees will lose their motivation to excel as they don't control the results of their efforts. The sources of this frustration are many and varied, and may include insufficient resources, outdated technology, low employee morale, and numerous others. Specific metrics used to assess the quality of the work environment, including many distal and indirect measures, may vary radically from firm to firm. They often are composite measures that include both employee and operational metrics. The important thing regarding this metric is that the management is made aware of the importance of the quality of the work environment for assessment and subsequent improvement.

INTERNAL PROCESS PERFORMANCE MEASURES

Internal process performance metrics address the efficiency and effectiveness of the various systems within an organization critical to its survival. These are many and varied and can be likened to the systems within a living organism. More explicitly, those elements depicted in the open systems model (OSM) (i.e., input, throughput, and output) all have multiple systems embedded within each stage or phase of the model. Therefore, the phases of the OSM can be used as the organizing strategy for developing the internal process metrics.

Input Metrics

Input metrics should include measures that monitor and evaluate all those systems that must perform prior to the throughput phase. Supplier, procurement, internal support, and front-end staging are all interrelated systems that must be performance tracked.

Supplier Metrics

Supplier performance is a key predictor of firm performance and therefore requires the firm to actively monitor and manage its supplier relations. The management of supplier relationships via performance measures makes it easier for organizations to price products for market dominance.[16] Nonvalue activities can be reduced or eliminated through a concentration of business with high-performance suppliers.[17] Tracking supplier performance is based upon on-time delivery, order accuracy with regard to standards and quantity, damaged goods, freight and handling charges, billing accuracy, supplier responsiveness and service level, order processing time or cycle time, and price consistency.

Procurement Metrics

The procurement area must be evaluated both on its efficiency and effectiveness in procuring the required inputs in a timely fashion. It also is necessary that the procurement office be held accountable for conducting business in an ethical fashion. Boundary-spanning activities such as procurement are often subject to illegal, unethical, or image damaging inducements for using a particular supplier or source of suppliers.

Avery (2000) contends that nearly 48 percent of every dollar that enters an organization leaves through procurement. Careful attention to the management of supplier contracts can add value to the organization. This point illustrates that it may be beneficial for firms to form and train a team that operates under a well-defined procurement strategy that is aligned with the corporate goals and mission. The goal of the purchasing/procurement team should be to take a long-term view of the agreements they negotiate.[18]

Avery (2000) further contends that the team should be trained to have a five-year view of the relationship with the supplier. As with any performance measurement, everyone in the organization must be aware of the contract management plan.[19] Research has indicated that an automated system works well for many organizations. Organizations should seek to maximize leverage with suppliers.[20] This can be accomplished with a systematic approach. Metrics should include well-defined parameters, should not be complicated, and should focus on improving company results. Most importantly, they should be well-communicated with suppliers.[21] Specific metrics for evaluating the procurement function include vendor performance to contract on all contract components. It is equally as important for the procurement function to be evaluated on its ability to insure the quality and timeliness of the input as it is to negotiate for low price inputs.

Front-End Staging Metrics

Except for those rare organizations that truly have a complete just-in-time supply system in place, front-end staging inventory practices need to be tracked with efficiency and effectiveness performance measures. The metrics that need to be put into place to access performance in this area will depend on the activities involved. They will normally include monitoring of all receiving activities as well as some type of quality check of the materials being received. Also included would be the actual staging and distribution processes. Many of the metrics utilized at this stage might be shared with the procurement stage.

Throughput Metrics

Throughput metrics are put into place to measure the efficiency and effectiveness of the transformation processes. These may include many statistical process control (SPC) measures, machine and employee productivity and performance measures, labor and material waste metrics, cycle time, and many others. The actual measures applied, to a large extent, depend entirely on the value creation method employed. However, the primary measures, already mentioned, although applied differently, seem to be of universal importance.

Output Metrics

The final stage of the OSM is output. Performance measures that are used in this stage, again, depend on the actual value creation method utilized by the firm. In manufacturing, the primary measures deal with the disposition of finished goods and the outbound logistics that puts these goods in the hands of the consumer. Measures would include both the efficiency and effectiveness of the process. Specific processes to monitor might include the movement of finished goods to the warehouse and all warehousing processes, as well as movement from the warehouse to the customers' locations.

SUPPORT FUNCTION METRICS

All areas of the firm not directly related to the value creation process also need to have performance metrics in place that measure the efficiency and effectiveness of their individual mission-related activities. This includes all of the indirect staff functions, customer service, administration, accounting, human resources, engineering, research and development, corporate relations, and many more. The effective and efficient performance of these units are every bit as important to the welfare of the firm as are those directly involved in the production process, regardless of the value creation process in use.

ASSET UTILIZATION

One of the keys to maintaining a positive EVA is through asset management. Assets need to be exploited to full potential, and nonperforming assets need to be eliminated. The following three metrics can assist management to identify and manage such assets:

- Fixed asset turnover ratio — sales divided by net fixed assets
- Total asset turnover ratio — sales divided by total fixed assets
- AR/DSO — accounts receivables divided by average daily sales

Utilization of fixed asset turnover and total asset turnover will allow managers to identify assets that may be underperforming or unprofitable. High AR/DSO is typically associated with higher bad debt expense. Proper tracking and maintenance of the AR/DSO will lead to lower overall expenses, through reduction in expenses related to collection as well as bad debt expense. The net effect of these metrics is to focus management upon factors that will have a significant and positive impact upon EVA.

INVENTORY TURNOVER

Inventory turnover (Inventory DSO) is measured by dividing total sales by the amount of inventory on hand. Higher inventory turnover reduces holding costs, yielding lower working capital. Better management of the supply chain will allow managers to increase inventory turnover. A high level of supplier performance is needed to successively manage the strategic supply chain. This is imperative in establishing a competitive market advantage.[22] This involves establishing strong relationships with an organization's suppliers. Because higher inventory turnover is typically related to lower inventory on hand, the imperative facing the management is to balance lower inventory levels while maintaining a high service level.

SUMMARY

Another issue that firms often confront is selecting too many measures, which results in ineffective use of everyone's time. Fewer vital metrics will provide more impact.[23] To communicate strategic directions through-out the organization, old measures should be reviewed and disregarded if they are not linked to key success factors.[24] Confusing terms should either be avoided or clearly defined in a dictionary of common measure-ment terms for everybody to fully understand.[25]

Many firms motivate employees by basing compensation on the results of the balanced scorecard.[26] For example, Merrill Lynch's balanced score-card for customer service representatives contains five levels for the final results. Each representative's yearly raise is based on the outcome of the year-end scorecard. Consistency and communication are vital to the suc-cess of the balanced approach. This approach should be used as an everyday management tool and not just as "a flavor of the week." As business objectives and goals change and evolve, so should the metrics for performance.[27] Performance management is important because it pro-vides feedback for performance improvement both at the individual and firm level.[28]

In summary, the development of meaningful performance metrics should not take place in a vacuum. To be truly meaningful, financial performance metrics should be selected and developed because they support the strategy and, therefore, the mission of the corporation. Addi-tionally, the measures we propose, as well as the measures management eventually selects, should not be static, but rather should adapt to the changing needs of the business. That is, the value that each of these financial performance measures provides should be revisited periodically as an extension of the strategic planning process. The contention is that the link between serving the customer (i.e. corporate values, mission, and strategy) and performance measures can be preserved only if adjustments that are made to the strategy are reflected in the performance measures.

REFERENCES

1. DeFeo, J., Measuring what matters, *Industrial Management*, 42(3), 31, 2000.
2. Ibid.
3. Rivers, D., Proactive performance measures, *Hospital Material Management Quarterly*, 20(4), 60, 1999.
4. Ibid.
5. Ibid.
6. Stivers, B. and Joyce, T., Building a balanced performance measurement system, *S.A.M. Advanced Management Journal*, 65(2), 22, 2000.
7. Frigo, M. and Krumwiede, K., The Balanced Scorecard, *Strategic Finance*, 81(7), 2000, p. 50.
8. Kueng, P., Process performance measurement system: a tool to support process-based organizations, *Total Quality Management*, 11(1), 67, 2000.
9. Rivers, op cit.
10. Goulian, C. and Mersereau, A., Performance measurement, *Ivey Business Journal*, 65(1), 53, 2000.
11. Slywotzky, A. and Morrison, D., *The Profit Zone: How Strategic Business Design Will Lead You to Tomorrow's Profits*, Random House, New York, 1997.
12. Ibid.
13. Kueng, P., Process performance measurement system: a tool to support process-based organizations, *Total Quality Management*, 11(1), 67, 2000.
14. Ibid.
15. Rivers, op cit.
16. Anonymous, Q&A: Performance Measurement: Why It's Important to measure Suppliers Well, *Purchasing*, 128(7), 2000, p. 36.
17. Ibid.
18. Avery, S., Measuring Performance Takes on New Importance, *Purchasing*, 129(3), 2000, p. 123.
19. Ibid.
20. Ibid.
21. Anonymous, op cit.
22. Ibid.
23. Frigo, op cit.
24. DeFeo, J., Measuring what matters, *Industrial Management*, 42(3), 31, 2000.
25. Ibid.
26. Frigo, op cit.
27. Ibid.
28. Stivers, op cit.

5

MONITORING AND FORECASTING THE ENVIRONMENT

Managers and leaders of organizations are facing ever-increasing levels of change from outside their organizations, driving the need to create corresponding modifications inside the organization. Unlike the organizations that operated in the more or less stable environments of the past, the organizations of today operate in a dynamic environment, which seems to be evolving at an ever-increasing rate. Even staid and well-established firms involved in the production or distribution of well-known, name-brand products that have influenced the culture to the point that day-to-day life has been affected, have found that they must adapt to survive. Gibson believes that the lesson of the past three decades is that nobody (no firm) can drive to the future on cruise control.[1] Toffler further suggests that leaders need to anticipate social, technological, political, cultural, and religious shocks and their impact on organizations.[2] It has become paramount for firms to learn as much as possible about the environment within which they compete if they are to survive and prosper. However, mere awareness of the environment is not enough; firms must act upon this awareness; they must adapt and change to remain competitive.

THE EXTERNAL ENVIRONMENT

Developing effective strategies, operations, and polices requires a parallel study of a firm's anticipated future environment. The environment may be envisioned both as remote and immediate, or task. The remote environment, which has only an indirect impact on the organization, consists of external factors such as:

1. Economic fabric of the world, country, or region of firm operations
2. Political and legal factors
3. Social and demographic features and trends
4. Technology
5. Physical environment of resources, weather, climate, and earth changes

The immediate or task environment influencing the future of a firm consists of the following entities that interact with the firm on a day-to-day basis:

1. Customers and potential customers
2. Competitors
3. Labor forces/unions
4. Suppliers
5. Creditors
6. Regulatory agencies at various levels of government

PREDICTING THE FUTURE

Anticipation of future events and their effect upon a firm's continued viability is paramount to the firm positioning itself for the future There is no escaping the inherent need for management to adequately prepare for changes that will influence their future operating environment. It is common for business people in smaller companies to say, "We can't predict the future and, anyway, our problems are in the present." Many of the present problems are there because the business person did not attempt to look ahead and take action at an earlier point in time! Because companies operate within dynamic environments, events and influences will change over time, and operations must be adjusted accordingly. This is an ongoing process. Managers should anticipate how the environment will change. Complaining about inadequate data or information is not a valid excuse for failing to address this important step. To lessen surprises, firms should engage in the practice of vulnerability analysis to forecast possible, even if remote, evolutionary and revolutionary environmental changes. Three of the more popular techniques are cross-impact analysis, trend impact analysis, and the Delphi technique.

> *Cross-impact analysis:* Using this technique, managers should select about 25 events that could come to pass in either the remote or task environments that could have a significant impact on the organization. Then, estimate the probabilities that each will occur and when, and follow this with an assessment of the impact on the

future of the business. A U.S. hospital might select events such as legislative enactment of national health care, a cure for cancer, or perfection of organ cloning technology. A manufacturing firm might forecast factors such as having their largest customer declare bankruptcy, which could cancel accounts receivable, disrupt supply channels, and lessen the overall product demand or they might forecast a total breakdown in their incoming logistics systems.

Trend impact analysis: Trend impact analysis is similar to a cross-impact analysis with the exception that the events forecasted result from identified environmental trends. After event trends are identified and forecasted, the probability of the trend continuing and the event occurring is determined, and the event's impact on the business's future is predicted. Continuing with the hospital example, a hospital might use trend analysis to develop a demand prediction for the continued decline in cardiac bypass procedures and the increase in cardiac radiological treatments. A distribution firm might identify a trend among its major suppliers of slowly reducing the number of distributors and increasing the size of its own sales force.

Delphi technique: The Delphi technique embraces both the collective wisdom of a group and a group's tendency to influence individual members and bring about a compromise. Care should be taken to only include individuals who are experts on the topic being investigated. The technique is based on the concept of successive iterations. Participants will be asked to develop their best predictions of some future state. Everyone's answers will be transcribed and shared with the panel of experts who, after having an opportunity to digest everyone's individual responses, will once again be asked to share their predictions. The process continues until the panel has reached a consensus. The process can be an inexpensive method of generating informed but subjective predictions. Its value is dependent on the quality of the participants, and it is to a degree subject to the behavioral errors normally associated with group-think.

Regardless of the technique utilized to anticipate future events, a forecasted event must be defined in enough detail that were it to materialize, the firm would recognize the occurrence and be able to react accordingly. The forecasted recognition point that indicates the event is either about to happen or is happening is known in contingency planning as the *trigger point.* When the trigger point is reached, the firm should implement whatever response action that has been preplanned and is required by the contingency plan. Environmental event forecasting assists organizations to maintain a competitive edge and its importance should not be minimized.

OPPORTUNITIES AND THREATS

One of the oldest and most accurate clichés is that beauty is in the eye of the beholder. The same can be said with regard to the events that take place in the dynamic environment in which firms operate. Whether a neutral event is an opportunity or threat for any given firm is dependent on two primary factors. The first factor is the firm's ability to recognize the event. If the event is significant and goes unnoticed, chances are near 100 percent that the event will eventually pose a survival threat to the unaware firm. The second factor is the firm's ability to react in a positive way to the event itself. The ability to react in a positive way is completely dependent on the firm's ability to apply the required resources that will transform a neutral environmental event into an opportunity for the firm. Thus, firms must have a complete understanding of the resources they control and the ability to redeploy resources as necessary.

Opportunities

Neutral environmental events present both opportunities and threats to firms. Opportunities should be identified as those that are either immediate or long-term. Immediate or short-term opportunities often result from management's recognition of opportunities that had previously gone unnoticed. Sometimes, this recognition results from spontaneous or serendipitous insights; although at other times, the recognition is the result of creatively focusing management's attention. A few examples of immediate opportunities are:

1. Previously unrecognized needs of individuals, companies, or government
2. New applications of current products and services
3. Sudden trends in growths of demand (for example, designer jeans)
4. New method of distribution
5. New manufacturing process or substitution of materials
6. New and better method for improved customer service

Immediate opportunities are those for which a company is presently prepared. In other words, a company must have a special competence or a competitive advantage that allows it to pursue a program to achieve greater sales and profits. A competitive advantage is an edge or strength a firm has over rivals; it is a strategic measure of business success.

However, long-term opportunities must be identified in terms of both the environment and the firm's capability to reshape itself if necessary. Without a clear understanding of their resources, capabilities, and strengths, a firm's ability to grasp and exploit its opportunities is severely limited. Preparing a firm to take advantage of some future opportunity is the focus of strategic management.

Threats

Failure to recognize neutral environmental events that will affect the firm will eventually and inevitably make their presence known in the form of a threat (Figure 5.1). By the time a firm recognizes environmental threats, the company may be in mortal danger. Many immediate threats are consequences of an internal firm focus, which promotes a culturally driven status quo maintenance approach to resource and operations management. Other immediate threats may result from past strategic errors and poor application of organizational resources. Today's dynamic business environment is changing and becoming more complex at an ever-increasing rate. Those firms that fail to adapt either cease to exist entirely as a result of a dramatic collapse, or somehow continue to operate in a state of life-support, bleeding resources until they fade quietly from the scene.

Pressures from investors, Wall Street analysts, and executive compensation plans have often diverted management attention from firms' long-term viability to short-term profitability. The nearsightedness of the short-term focus has often caused management to sell out the future for short-term performance. Some of these actions have brought widespread media attention to both unethical and illegal actions taken by managements, as in the case with "Chainsaw" Al Dunlap, CEO of Sunbeam Corporation. Sunbeam's management team under Dunlap's leadership wrongly recorded product sales in advance of actual sales to bolster income to inflate the stock price. The inflated stock was then used as currency in acquisitions. Upon discovery and revelation of the accounting irregularities, the stock plummeted, the corporate officers perpetrating the fraud were fired, and the firm eventually declared bankruptcy. Al Dunlap, himself, was publicly

U.S. tile makers were slow to identify environmental opportunities in the floor-covering market and failed to take adaptive actions. From the postwar period to the mid-1970s demand for ceramic tiles increased modestly, suggesting a mature market. But in more recent years, consumer tastes have shifted from linoleum to decorative ceramic tiles for new housing construction and home improvements. More often than not, these tiles are being imported. European, Japanese, and Korean tile makers have succeeded in capturing a larger share of this growing market than domestic producers. Some established U.S. tile makers have been driven out of the business. The remaining U.S. producers are now struggling to catch up on style and technology. For instance, U.S. Ceramics has invested over $100 million into new plant and equipment in recent years.

Figure 5.1   Failure to recognize threats.

admonished for his behavior and fined $500,000 by the Securities and Exchange Commission (SEC). Unfortunately, Sunbeam is not an isolated case of business fraud in the United States. Since Sunbeam, others to have surfaced have included such giants as Enron and Arthur Andersen, Cendant Corporation, Tyco International, and WorldCom.

Accepting the fact that executive and corporate greed is ugly and unacceptable, the fact is that the major destroyer of value and whole companies comes down to simple incompetent executive management. Firms don't end up in bankruptcy courts unless the management has made many strategic mistakes. Although the vast majority of executives of even bankrupt firms act wholly within the law, they are guilty of malpractice when it comes to strategically running their business. Examples of these firms are way too abundant and include Winn Dixie, Kmart, United Airlines, and U.S. Air. In fact, if the corporate bankruptcies from 2001 and 2002 are added together, firms would be seeking protection from over 600 billion dollars in liabilities. Further, the majority of firms that enter bankruptcy either don't emerge or emerge only to fail again.

Although, both opportunities and threats are, in fact, only neutral environmental events whose explicit affects are determined by a firm's capability to respond in a positive manner, a few of the rather commonly identified sources of environmental threats include:

1. Competitors
2. Changes in customer wants or needs
3. Dwindling resources and rising prices
4. Governmental legislation
5. Inflation
6. Recession
7. International political and monetary relationships
8. Technological breakthroughs

Constraints

Constraints imposed by the external environment require careful attention to uncover and identify. Legal constraints may be obvious, but political constraints are often more subtle. In the latter case, politicians or government agencies may be inclined to mobilize public opinion or introduce new legislation if a company exceeds certain bounds by raising prices, closing down plants, polluting the environment, or compensating foreign officials in international trade.

Constraints to growth may be present because of the lack of natural resources, well-established competitors, declining productivity, declining GDP, or a deteriorating transportation system. Other constraints may include the cost of capital, equipment, or union labor. Political instability in countries where a company does business is another constraint in today's dynamic world.

INDUSTRY ANALYSIS

Industry analysis is most often presented as part of the environmental analysis as it is here because it is, in fact, external to the firm. However, because the firm is part of the industry in which it competes, its relationship with the industry is reciprocal in nature as it both influences and is influenced by the industry. Of all the external environmental factors that influence the viability of a firm, direct competition from within one's own industry is the most significant. All firms desire to exist in conditions where the demand for their product or service is greater than the available supply. However, in the modern world economy, it is very unlikely that market conditions of demand exceeding supply can ever be more than a temporary aberration. The reason is simply that where unfulfilled demand exists, firms will enter the market and seek to fill that demand.

Structure–Conduct–Performance (SCP) Model

The SCP model depicted in Figure 5.2 is very useful in explaining the competitive nature of an industry. The *structure* of the industry refers to the number of firms competing within the industry, the extent of product or firm differentiation, and the capital intensity of the industry. The *conduct* refers to the competitive behavior of the firms within the industry. *Performance* refers to the performance of the individual firms within the industry and, thus, the industry as whole. A simplistic way of viewing and understanding the SCP relationships is to utilize a three-layer continuum (Figure 5.3).

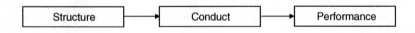

Figure 5.2   Structure–Conduct–Performance (SCP) model.

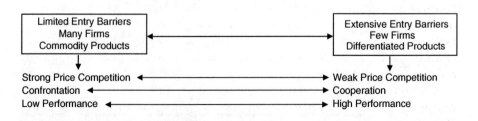

Figure 5.3   Vertical view of SCP.

As shown in the preceding text, the easier it is for firms to enter the market, the greater the number of firms competing, the more likely the products are to become undifferentiated, which leads to price competition and reduced profits for all competing firms.

Porter's Five Forces

Michael Porter, developer of the industry five forces model posits that "a good strategy is concerned with the structural evolution of the industry as well as the firm's own unique position within that industry."[3] Porter's five forces industry analysis model identifies five forces that firms must consider when deciding if an industry is attractive. The five forces are:

Rivalry among firms: Competition is the single most influential force in an industry. When the existing firms in the industry are highly competitive, profits tend to be squeezed. Coke and Pepsi have very strong rivalry between themselves in the soft drink industry. This duopoly has prevented any other major players from entering this industry. However, the very strong competition between the two major players also may be viewed as a very warped method of cooperation to prevent new competitors from entering the market.

Relative power of suppliers: The supply-chain relationship is a game of who has the power. Firms must balance the added costs of maintaining relationships with multiple suppliers, with the risk exposure incurred from the dependency on a single key supplier (Figure 5.4). When organizations have multiple suppliers whose products lack marketable differentiation and supply is greater than demand, the organization has more control than the suppliers. This simply results from the organization having more choices and, further, it is not dependent on any one supplier. This provides the organization with greater flexibility to negotiate a favorable contract and reduces the

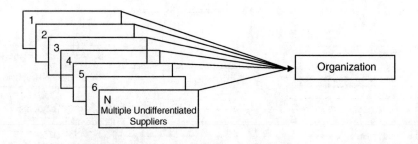

Figure 5.4 Multiple suppliers.

suppliers' ability to negotiate. However, there are at least three caveats that need to be noted. First, if the supplier has successfully differentiated the product, there may not be suitable substitutes. Second, if the vendor has successfully built in heavy product switching costs, changing suppliers could be too expensive. And last, supply must exceed demand; if it does not, the suppliers will likely have the flexibility to negotiate the favorable terms. Maintaining relationships with multiple suppliers also reduces vendor-associated risks: risks that include system-related breakdowns, labor issues, and natural disasters. Spreading the risk over multiple vendors reduces the impact that any one supplier can have on the firm and is in keeping with portfolio risk-management techniques.

Relative power of customers: Again, the relationship between the organization and its customers is an act of balancing sales and customer service costs with risks (Figure 5.5). All things being equal, it is far more profitable to service one or two large customers than it is to service many small ones. However, there are many examples of firms that have focused their efforts on supplying only a handful of key customers, only to have the rug pulled out from underneath them either by the customer or by an environmental event or organizational blunder that affected the customer negatively, and, consequently, the organizations supplying them. As depicted, the organization is not dependent on a single customer, and thus has the negotiation power to deal independently with any one of the customers.

New entrants: The pursuit of new opportunity motivates many organizations to enter new markets. New entrants may be either altogether new firms, entrepreneurial ventures, or well-established firms entering new markets through new ventures or established firms entering through a merger or acquisition. If the industry is very attractive in terms of profits, low entry barriers, and either a growing

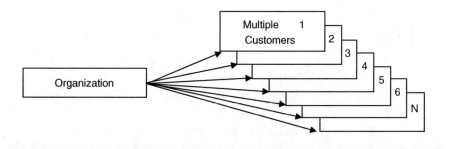

Figure 5.5　Multiple customers.

or underserved market, more firms will seek to compete in the industry. If the industry has low profits, fierce competition, or a declining market, fewer new firms tend to enter the industry. Established firms seek to repel new entrants by creating or reinforcing barriers to entry. Barriers may include contrived as well as real barriers. The four major railroads in the Unite States aren't concerned with new entrants because there is a real barrier, which can't be breached — the barrier of land right-of-ways. It is highly unlikely that a would-be entrant could ever gain the right-of-ways necessary to establish a railroad and then be able to compete economically. Where natural or real barriers to entry do not exist, firms attempt to establish contrived barriers. These may include strategies of overbuilding capacity, company information leaks regarding new projects, and developing expensive switching costs for customers. Nevertheless, if profits appear high enough, new entrants are likely to show interest.

Substitute products: Finally, Porter identified the threat of substitute products as an industry factor that should be analyzed. For example, contact lenses were substituted for eyeglasses, thus reducing the demand for eyeglasses. Subsequently, lasik surgery has become a substitute for both eyeglasses and contact lenses. Today, radiological procedures are replacing open-heart surgery, just as high-frequency sound procedures have replaced surgical procedures for kidney stones. Technological advances have reduced the need for frequent business travels. Companies can call on their customers via satellite links or videoconferencing rather than making personal visits.

Does the presence of Porter's five forces within an industry enhance the industry's attractiveness or detract from it? The nondifferentiated, mass-produced, graduate student approved answer "it depends" is in fact the correct answer. It depends on whether you are a current or perspective member of the industry. If you are a current member, high barriers are viewed as positive; if not a current member of the industry, high barriers will deter a firm from entering and will be viewed as negative and loathsome.

Importance of Industry Analysis

Understanding the industry is a very important part of strategy; however, understanding your own business and the environmental impact is equally important. Neither the industry, firm, nor environment can, by itself, provide a picture of what a firm will likely face in the future; but the three combined become a powerful tool.

▼▲▼

IBM

IBM is a classic example of a company caught off guard by changes in its industry.[4] IBM was the major player in the mainframe computer market and on the leading edge of the computer industry in the 1980s. Their ability to respond quickly to the personal computer market extended their brand recognition from the corporate board room to the household living room. Yet in the 1990s, clone manufacturers flooded the market with low-cost personal computers. PCs became a commodity product, primarily sold on price. IBM chose not to compete on price, attempted and failed at successfully differentiating its product, and thus lost ground to competitors. IBM, losing money selling its desktop computers through retail outlets, discontinued the use of the retail distribution channel for all but its higher margin laptop computers.

▼▲▼

SEARS

Sears, Roebuck and Company (Sears) is an example of a firm, once a dominant player in the retail industry, that lost its way. An abridged version of the Sears story follows. Sears was America's store in the 1950s, 1960s, and 1970s. An extremely successful mail-order retailer, Sears opened major retail outlets in the suburbs throughout America and even satellite retail outlets in rural America, which promoted its catalogue sales. Not only did Sears sell everything, including houses, cars, soft goods, household appliances, work tools, and everything in between, but also financed everything they sold. America shopped at Sears because Sears sold everything and, importantly, almost anyone could finance purchases directly with Sears: the one-stop approach. Sears had various finance plans, one called "easy pay" and another that was a revolving charge. Sears might be said to have pioneered the 21 percent interest rate, which was the unknowing model for their own collapse.

During these good times, Sears was earning a great deal of money from its retail operations, and much more from its credit operation. Sears had developed a competitive advantage derived from the symbiotic relation between its retail and finance, with many of its customers choosing Sears to shop at because it was one place where they could finance. During this time of high performance, Sears diversified into insurance, investment banking, credit cards, and real estate.[5] However, Sears failed to understand its own business and the roots of its success. Further, its financial success blinded Sears to the changing retail environment and, in particular, to the threat that the bank credit card posed with its widespread introduction to the American culture in the 1960s and 1970s. No longer was the American shopper tied to store credit; instead they had portable credit, which they could use in many outlets. Not only had Sears' competitive advantage, based on the retail–credit relationship, been destroyed by noncompetitors, but Sears also naively refused to accept the outside bank credit cards for payment, fearing that they would lose their credit income. Finding itself sliding closer and closer to the brink of financial disaster, Sears sold its profitable Allstate Insurance Company and cut its losses by divesting itself of its marginal and losing diversification ventures.

Ultimately, the firm downsized and attempted to refocus on the retail industry, its core business. However, it is unlikely that Sears, once traded on the New York Stock Exchange under the trading symbol **S**, ever again will become a power player in the retail industry. In what would seem to be a double desperation play, Kmart, another retail giant, which recently emerged from Chapter 11 reorganization, acquired Sears for an $11 billion stock swap; the new merged company is to be known as the Sears Holding Company. Even though the market seems to love this merger, its real value remains to be seen. Can two losers be combined to make one winner, or was this marriage just another corporate blunder? That question will be addressed in the next edition of this text.

------------------------------ ▼▲▼ ------------------------------

AT&T Universal Card

Once upon a time, AT&T could have been said to be the "king of the hill" in the telecommunications industry, and then the Federal Trade Commission rained on AT&T's parade, threatening to break up the firm and its monopolistic control of telecommunications. Upon threat of forced dissolution, AT&T broke itself up and separated itself into the mother firm, AT&T long distance, the Baby Bells, and other various entities such as Lucent Technologies and American Transtech. On its own, and slightly reeling from ego deflation, it realized that size may matter after all; AT&T sought business opportunities in which it could invest and had some special competence. The decision was made to enter the bank card business. It had billing, calling center, customer service experience, and one valuable, rare, and inimitable resource to exploit. That unique resource was a mailing, contact list of literally every head of household with a telephone in the United States.

To achieve its goal of entering the crowded and competitive credit card industry, AT&T Universal Card Services (UCS) analyzed the firms in the industry. There were over 6000 firms that issued credit cards in the United States at that time; but UCS was able to jump into the top ten credit card issuers, was third in the total number of accounts, and was second in the amount of dollars customers spent.[6] The company was able to achieve these outstanding results by comparing its operations to the strongest competitors. It set internal goals and measured performance against these standards, rewarding its staff with performance bonuses for achieving the standards.

Unfortunately for AT&T, the first executive management team for UCS didn't seem to use profit or any other beneficial income-related performance measure in determining its performance. Subsequently, it built a large customer base, won the Malcolm Baldrige National Quality Award, and received a great deal of outside recognition for its efforts, wrote off a lot of bad debts, and added chaos to an already distressed industry. UCS's strategy of preapproving unsolicited accounts, mailing cards, elimination of annual card fees, and other low-cost, market-share-driven behavior helped to turn the bank card industry into a commodity market. As a postscript, AT&T abandoned the industry by selling Universal Card Services to Citibank in 1997 for $3.5 billion in cash, a substantial discount to accounts receivable outstanding.

Firms must understand the industry in which they currently operate or plan to enter. Industry participants that don't fully grasp the SCP model will employ perverse and destructive behaviors by industry behavioral standards. These behaviors likely will negatively affect the performance of the industry and all those participating in the given market. Sears didn't understand the true nature of its competitive advantage and certainly never realized the threat that would come from the retail industry's acceptance of the bank card. IBM, the one-time leader in the personal computer industry and promoter of open architecture machines, never expected personal computers to be sold as commodities where their product was undifferentiated from the others, even with the IBM brand. And after a grand entrance to the bank card industry, AT&T chose to exit the industry a mere seven years later. One would have to assume that even with their high-profile industry analysis conducted before they entered, the industry just did not meet their expectations.

SUMMARY

A firm's strategy should not only be developed systematically and be based on the resources and competencies that it possesses, but strategy must also be grounded by the constraints imposed by the industry and the environment. Once the firm has established a successful strategy, it must be maintained by adjusting its strategy as the industry and environment evolve. This requires executive management to (1) understand the source of their success and (2) develop systems that facilitate the continuous monitoring of the changes taking place around them. The firm's relationship with the environment must remain stable or improve, or improve over time; otherwise, the firm's significance will fade.

REFERENCES

1. Gibson, R., *Rethinking the Future,* Nicholas Brealey Publishing, London, 1997, 1.
2. Toffler, A., Foreword in *Rethinking the Future,* Nicholas Brealey Publishing, London, 1997, x.
3. Porter, M., *Competitive Advantage,* The Free Press, New York, 1985, 6.
4. Bourgeois, L., III, Duhaime, I., and Stimpert, J., *Strategic Management, A Managerial Prospective,* Dryden Press, Fort Worth, 1999, 5-6.
5. Ibid.
6. AT&T Universal Card Services Summary of 1992 Application for Malcolm Baldrige National Quality Award, AT&T UCS, Jacksonville, FL, 1993, vii.

6

INFLUENCERS OF CORPORATE STRATEGY

LIFE-CYCLE INFLUENCE

The corporate strategy that a firm may choose to implement, to a large extent, is determined by the life cycle of the firm. It appears that organizations resemble organic systems in more than one way. The open systems model of organizations, previously discussed, survived by taking inputs from the external environment, processing those and returning the processed inputs to the external environment to gain more resources for continuation of the process. The second and equally relevant resemblance is that a product (the output of an open system), the firm (the open system itself), and the industry in which the firm operates all seem to have a life cycle that resembles that of an organic life cycle. An organic system begins with birth, progresses through a growth stage before reaching maturity, which is followed by decline in vitality, and then finally succumbs to death. The primary difference among the product, firm, and industry life cycles is simply the unit of analysis. Otherwise, they share many similarities.

Product Life Cycle

All products have a life cycle; some seem to extend to infinity in one form or another based on their basic importance to sustaining either human life or civilization, and others have life cycles that go from introduction to decline rapidly.

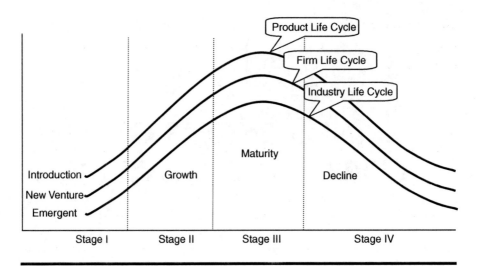

Figure 6.1 Life cycle model.

Introduction Phase

The product life cycle depicted in Figure 6.1 shows the life cycle beginning with the introduction phase. The introduction phase should be considered to represent the development of a truly new product by a firm or a significant modification of an already existing product to the point that it is perceived by the public as a new product. The introduction phase is owned by innovative firms that invest in new product development and by entrepreneurs who enter a market with a new product.

The firm that introduces the new product will seek a first-mover advantage. This advantage allows the firm to develop a reputation and following before other firms join the competition with similar products. Firms seek to develop a market for their new product through advertising and promotion and often utilize a price-skimming strategy to earn as much from the product as possible while it is developing a market. Price skimming introduces the product at a price well above what will eventually become the product's price in the mature market. New products appeal to early adopters, who are motivated to purchase the product because it is new and offers unique advantages, and to those who are not as price sensitive as those consumers who will eventually adopt the product in its latter stages. Price-skimming strategies also assist the firm to limit demand during a product's initial introduction. Although most firms will desire to get their new products to market as quickly as possible to begin to generate revenue, generally speaking, the initial ability of firms to produce in large quantities is limited; price skimming introduces a product, generates revenue, limits current product demand, and develops future demand.

Growth Stage

During the growth stage, firms seek to enlarge the market and capture more customers. This requires a firm to evolve its pricing strategy from one of skimming to one of penetration pricing. Firms are likely to encounter competition from firms that have followed with similar products, and the firm must either successfully differentiate its product from the new entries or move to a low-cost strategy selling at the market price and while still making more than their competitors. Investments are usually made in both marketing and production. Firms market heavily at this stage to build their demand and move toward production efficiencies that enable them to produce at a higher rate and enjoy the advantages of scale and the shorter learning curve. Increasing the volume should have the effect of reducing per-unit production costs, should spread the overhead over more units of output, and gain human effectiveness as employees gain experience manufacturing the new product.

Maturity Stage

As the product enters the mature stage, the demand for the product stabilizes and ceases to expand. At this point, the firm invests in production, distribution, and marketing improvements that enhance its ability to maintain or improve its market position. As the market is no longer growing, the firm will generally face the prospect that the overall supply of product will be greater than the demand for the product. This will create an environment that will be conducive to price competition and the general commoditization of the product. Falling prices will lead to falling profits and the need for a strong focus on efficiency. The goal of a firm manufacturing a product that is in its mature life cycle is to extend the mature cycle and gain dominance in the market through some form of differentiation.

Decline Stage

As a product enters the decline stage of the life cycle, the demand for the product begins to diminish. Unless new uses for the product that might reverse the decline are found, it is very likely that manufacture of the product will eventually cease. Certainly, a firm finding itself dependent on a product in the decline stage would be well advised to look elsewhere for its future.

Firm Life Cycle

Closely tied to product life cycle is the firm life cycle. Firms have a life cycle. They begin as a new venture, proceed through a growth stage that is followed by maturity and eventual decline. However, as previously mentioned in Chapter 1, many new ventures fail early on and take a shortcut to decline and failure without ever successfully establishing themselves. A firm's life-cycle stage is also difficult to determine from a mere survey of its activities. Is Wal-Mart a mature firm or is it a growth firm? Wal-Mart continues to build new and larger stores and to increase its revenues; however, its location on the growth curve is uncertain. An argument can be made that when a firm begins to pay dividends or return invested capital to its owners that it has reached the maturity stage even though it continues to get larger.

New Venture

Start-up ventures seek to establish their legitimacy and provide a product or service to meet the needs of an identified customer. New ventures are characterized by capital investment, which many a time includes the "sweat equity" or effort of the owner-operator and low revenues and profits. Depending on the scale of the venture, the actual capital invested will vary from a few thousand dollars to millions of dollars, but regardless of the actual dollars invested, the investment is generally significant to the investors, and many of the failures can be traced to a lack of financial capital. The primary strategy employed by start-up ventures is investment and development of its revenue-generation capabilities.

Growth Stage

Firms that survive the new-venture stage move into a growth stage. Firms in the growth stage continue to invest heavily in building capabilities and developing customers and markets for products and services. Little, if any, profits are available, at least initially, to return to investors as most profits are reinvested in the firm to support continued growth. Firms seek market penetration and focus on generating revenue. Growth strategies may include horizontal growth, vertical integration, related diversification, and unrelated diversification.

Most often, the start-up venture utilizes horizontal-growth strategies first. Horizontal growth can result from internal expansion or through acquisition of similar firms producing the same products or services; thus, it is a firm conducting business as normal, but producing more and serving more customers. However, horizontal growth and the expansion of the market base also is sometimes utilized by mature firms as well. CSX's acquisition of the Conrail system was an example of a mature firm utilizing this growth strategy.

Firms that choose to grow through vertical integration are either integrating backward toward their suppliers or forward toward the final consumer of their products or services. A firm utilizing vertical integration is motivated either by a desire to secure critical access to its supplies, or to its customers, or to acquire the profits that are being earned by the acquired firm. Shell Oil Company, which participates in exploration, drilling, refining, and distribution, is an example of a fully integrated firm.

Firms that utilize related diversification are motivated to grow via acquisition or internal development of a different but related activity. The activity must be such that the acquiring firm can utilize its core competencies or unique capabilities in the new business. PepsiCo, parent company of Pepsi, Frito-Lay, and Tropicana, is an example of a firm that successfully utilized the related diversification strategy. Primarily, the relatedness of the three firms resides in the distribution systems and customers.

Firms may also utilize unrelated diversification as a growth strategy. Many large firms could be singled out as examples of those having grown via unrelated diversification. General Electric (GE) owns many unrelated businesses. The GE family of companies is diversified to the point that GE almost could be described as a mutual fund in itself; however, it is difficult to visualize GE as a firm in its growth stage although many of its subsidiaries are.

Maturity Stage

Mature firms manage for profits. The firm no longer has growth as its primary goal. Firms generally enter a period of stability and concentrate their efforts on becoming more efficient in doing what they do. Again, it is difficult to identify exactly when a firm enters maturity. On occasion, they purposefully pause their expansion to figuratively "catch their breath" or regroup, thereby strengthening their internal systems before returning to a growth strategy. The pause strategy can be beneficial for a firm, but may also cause it to lose momentum. At other times, firms may implement a "proceed slowly" plan. Proceeding slowly requires firms to slow their growth under controlled circumstances, but not to stop. The rationale here is that it is easier to regain growth momentum if the inertia of a dead stop doesn't have to be overcome. At other times, firms may choose to do nothing, that is, make no changes, which can be a very dangerous position for a firm to take. Doing nothing will lead to stagnation and put the firm in jeopardy of losing its connection to the constantly evolving environment.

Decline Stage

It is difficult to identify exactly when a firm enters the maturity stage of the life cycle, but determining when a firm begins to decline is even more difficult. Identification of entry into this life-cycle stage is difficult from several perspectives. First, it is often difficult to determine if a downtrend in firm vitality is a temporary slump or the initial phase of a long-term decline. Second, it is sometimes difficult to determine if the cause of the downtrend is rooted in internal or external causes. Finally, entering the decline stage of the life cycle is not something that is psychologically easy to accept and when accepted, can become as disruptive to a firm as a mid-life crisis can become to an individual.

Strategies that can be enacted by firms in the decline stage include turnaround, captive company, exhaustion, divestiture, liquidation, and bankruptcy. The goal of most CEOs is to grow a large successful firm, and this goal often seems to be tied directly to the ego of the CEO. Managing a firm in the decline stage of a life cycle can be very different than managing one in any other life-cycle stage. The CEO of a firm in its decline stage needs to be acutely aware of the firm's position and must fully evaluate how it, as a resource, can be exploited to maximum benefit; not every declining firm can be turned around. However, the *turnaround* strategy is usually the first considered, even if not attempted. The natural response to an ailing patient is to attempt to heal him or her and return them to a state of health; it is the same for a firm. However, modern medicine is only capable of extending life to a point; after which, regardless of the money spent on life support, the patient will die when removed from the life-support system. The same is true for organizations; many just can't be saved, regardless of the money spent to revive, reorganize, or restructure; the eventual outcome remains unchanged. Bankruptcy, although listed as a separate strategy, is often used to facilitate a turnaround strategy.

A firm may seek to implement a *captive company strategy* if it can tie itself closely to another firm that utilizes its services. This equates to having only one customer and becoming totally dependent on that customer, or unofficially becoming a part of your customer's firm. In utilizing the captive company strategy, a firm reduces or eliminates all nonessential activities. These activities would include all sales and marketing related expenses and possibly even engineering and design, thus reducing the internal costs of doing business.

Exhaustion is another strategy that can be employed to manage a firm in decline. Here, the decline may be widely recognized, eliminating its attractiveness to would-be suitors. In addition, there may be no, or only a limited, salvage market for the assets the firm controls, eliminating the attractiveness of applying a liquidation strategy. In this situation, the exhaustion strategy might provide for the maximum return to firms. Exhaustion is squeezing the last bit of profit from the firm as a going concern. Consider the dray horses that pull the carriages through Central Park in New York, the old town in Saint Augustine, Florida, and the Vieux Carre in New Orleans; if they were to be closely inspected, they would be found to be old and broken down, but still capable of pulling the carriage, at least for a period of time. They are worth more alive and working than they are any other way. Basically, only minimum maintenance is provided to these animals and when one is no longer profitable, it is "put down."

A very popular strategy is *divestiture*. Divestiture is the selling of a firm as an ongoing entity. Employees stay employed and the community maintains economic assets instead of gaining an economic liability created by closing a firm. Divestiture should not be equated to failure; it can be, but isn't always. Many entrepreneurs grow businesses for the express purposes of eventually selling them. Also, it is possible that under a different management, the assets may be put to better use, and the new business is rejuvenated.

Liquidation, once considered the option of last resort, has developed almost a cult following since the corporate takeover craze of the 1980s. Liquidation is the strategy of choice when the firm is worth more dead than alive. That is to say that the sum of its parts is worth more than the firm as whole or as an ongoing concern. A firm that finds itself in this position should always liquidate itself; to do anything else will probably lead to a continued drain of firm resources that could otherwise be returned to the investors, and even an escalation in its decline.

Liquidation also seems to have been officially adopted as a strategy in some industries, and unofficially implemented in still others. Real estate investment trusts (REITs) are examples of such firms. Timber REITs, such as Rayonier, are in the liquidation business. They are slowly liquidating their timber and timberlands and returning the investment through dividends to the owners. The management of Sears Holding Company, formerly Kmart management, has been closing and liquidating assets at an amazing rate. They have been liquidating both former Kmart and Sears locations, and the trend is likely to continue. CSX Railroad has been liquidating many of its land holdings to add to its operational bottom line. Care should be utilized when using a liquidation strategy as an ongoing strategy as opposed to using it as an end-game strategy.

Finally, *bankruptcy* is sometimes used as a strategy. Most often, it seems to be used as a framework for attempting an organizational turnaround. Firms file for bankruptcy protection from creditors and, many times, contract relief from labor unions. In essence, filing for bankruptcy is an acknowledgment that management has not been effectively utilizing the firm's resources and has dug itself a hole that it cannot climb out of. The sad reality is that most firms that actually emerge from bankruptcy as new revitalized firms collapse again within the first few years of reorganization. Many of these would have been better off to simply liquidate themselves. Where is Dr. Kevorkian when he is needed?

Industry Life Cycle

The final life cycle that is discussed is the industry life cycle. Here, the unit of analysis is the industry or the aggregate of all those firms competing with similar products within the same market. Automobile producers in aggregate comprise the automobile industry; airlines in aggregate comprise the airline industry, etc. The industry life cycle is very similar to the firm life cycle. Its beginning point is the emergent stage, followed by a growth stage, followed by maturity, which is then followed by decline. Regardless of the stage of life that an industry is in, the firms within the industry and the products the firms manufacture can be at any life stage within their own life cycles. To clarify, the steel production industry in the United States is well down the slope of the decline stage; however, the individual firms operating within this declining industry may well be in the growth stage of their firm's life cycle and further may be introducing (introduction stage) a new product. Even in overall unprofitable industries, there are opportunities for individual firms.

Extension of Life Cycle

Although it appears that the decline stage at one time or another is inevitable, the pervasive influence of the global economy has created many new opportunities for actually extending product, firm, and industry life cycles. Life-cycle extensions have been created by developing new markets for products that have run their course in their original markets, but are new and in demand in the newly opened markets. Firms and complete industries have migrated to countries where they can begin anew.

GLOBALIZATION INFLUENCE

The global arena impacts all firms even if they compete in only one country. Firms vary in their scope of competition. It may be global, national, regional, state, or local. However, all firms are affected by multinational competition. This is because a firm's rivals may be producing in large quantities for worldwide sales, or are outsourcing functions to reduce costs. Many previous domestic players from the United States, Europe, and Japan have become major international competitors in the last decade. Examples include Digital Equipment Corporation (DEC), Electrolux, a producer of household appliances, and Komatsu, an earth moving company that now rivals Caterpillar.[1] Each developed its international dominance by focusing on a narrow niche initially. The companies focused on one specific product in one specific market, and developed a strong competitive niche in that market. Over time, they expanded into more products and more geographic locations, ultimately providing a global challenge to traditional multinational firms.

Internationalization can help firms to reduce costs and increase their knowledge by increasing economies of scale and exposing the firm to new markets and opportunities. Domestic players that wish to become globally competitive or to increase their domestic scope have choices in terms of growth. The company can develop new locations by building its own facilities or it can make acquisitions of existing firms. Buying an existing firm is a much quicker way to extend your competitive reach. The company purchases a business that already produces products or services and has customers. More than 22,000 acquisitions occurred during the 1980s and more than $3 trillion was spent on acquisitions in 1999 alone. The number of acquisitions continues to grow each year as more European firms invest in the United States because of the North American Free Trade Agreement (NAFTA). U.S. and Asian firms continue to make acquisitions in Europe because of the European Union (EU). These regional trade agreements have a strong impact on internationalization of firms.

Yet, John Naisbitt, author of *Megatrends 2000*, has predicted a new breed of multinationals in that huge multinational firms will no longer dominate the global economy. There is a new kind of bigness, known as *big networks*, rather than large organizations.[2] These arrangements are driven by strategic alliances between firms rather than one large firm. Firms of all sizes are utilizing interfirm networks. These networks permit flows of knowledge across borders. Naisbitt's point is that firms can now create quality anywhere in the world; so, competitive differentiation comes from swiftness to market and innovate. Firms can locate facilities in many locations around the world depending on their needs for raw materials, competitive wages, transportation costs, and government receptivity.

Host-government receptivity is a critical factor in deciding where to locate international facilities. The potential for nationalization of corporate assets or the milder forms of control, such as local content requirement and local ownership, have a major impact on multinational companies. Local content requirement is when the host government dictates that the multinational firm must purchase a certain percentage of its components locally. This serves to create additional jobs and increase the skills and knowledge of the host country workforce. In many locations, 100 percent ownership by the multinational firm is not possible. Either the government or a local citizen must be a partner in the company.

There are three types of international strategy. Firms that need to achieve economies of scale and high levels of efficiency use a global strategy. Basically, the product is almost universal around the world, and therefore can be produced in large volume at a few locations and shipped to other countries. Companies in the pharmaceutical or aviation industries have fairly standardized products that can be produced in strategic locations and transported to other countries.

Alternatively, many firms need to customize their products and services because of local variations. These firms use a multidomestic strategy whereby the product is modified in each local market. Country managers become much more influential in the product design, marketing, and advertising decisions. Economies of scale are not possible on a global basis because each country's market requires slightly different products and services.

Bartlett and Ghosal identified the third strategy.[3] This new breed of global competitor is known as a *transnational firm*. These firms must master global efficiency, multinational flexibility, and worldwide learning to remain competitive. There are few true transnational firms in existence.

Regardless of where firms choose to operate, there are activities they can undertake to improve effectiveness of internal operations. Achieving consistent delivery of products and services that meet or exceed the customers' expectations is one way to improve effectiveness. Operations can also be improved by comparing the firm to other firms using the same processes.

INTEGRATING LIFE CYCLE AND PORTFOLIO ANALYSIS

Portfolio analysis is a technique that has been utilized by financial analysts for many years. Portfolio analysis has assisted financial analysts to systematically evaluate the risks and returns of individual investments that together become the investment portfolio. About 50 years ago, the Boston Consulting Group (BCG) proposed its two-dimensional "market attractiveness matrix," now commonly referred to as the BCG matrix. The four-cell BCG matrix is based on the life-cycle model, and thus is an alternative method of depicting the life cycle. Following the lead of the BCG, GE, with assistance from McKinsey and Company, developed a nine-cell analytical tool that considered business strengths and industry attractiveness factors. The GE matrix includes many more factors, but still is no better than the subjective estimates on which they are based. Figure 6.2 combines the life-cycle stages with the BCG matrix; the same can be done with the GE matrix.

Mergers and Acquisitions Influence

The total value of mergers and acquisitions worldwide was over $3 trillion dollars in 1999.[4] Many of these deals have not been successful. For example, AT&T purchased NCR for $7.4 billion in stock in 1991 only to spin it off in 1995 in a deal valued at only $3.4 billion. Likewise, Novell

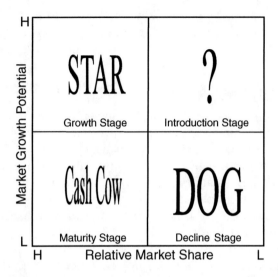

Figure 6.2   Boston Consulting Group matrix.

purchased WordPerfect for $1.4 billion in 1994 only to later sell WordPerfect to Corel for $124 million plus a licensing pact in 1996. Finally, Quaker Oats bought Snapple for $1.7 billion in 1994 and, three years later, sold it for a mere $300 million. There are always great expectations in creating these larger organizations but few of them are realized. One of the primary reasons that mergers and acquisitions are not successful is that managers fail to analyze the differences between these firms. They analyze technology but underestimate the systems and people differences. The integration after the deal has closed takes much longer and is much more expensive than estimated. To date, only the acquired company's stock performs well. Kidder Peabody (KPMG) analyzed 700 of the most expensive mergers from 1996 to 1998 and found that 53 percent actually reduced shareholder value.[5] Managers should consider that bigger is not always better.

Why do most mergers not live up to expectations? Simply because the reason for merger pursuit is often based primarily on CEO ego and the CEO's need to buy something new. Everyone has heard of new car fever; a consumer becomes sensitized and focused on the purchase of a new car to the point that reason no longer comes into play. The term obsession is appropriate to describe this behavior. CEOs would seem to suffer from an obsession to buy new operations in much the same way that the average person may become obsessed with a new car. When this happens with a CEO, it is likely that due diligence and rational evaluation will take a vacation until after the deal has been done. This behavior often results in CEOs committing their gravest error — that of paying too much and then trying to justify it by rationalizing the synergies that are expected to be derived from the merger. If a firm pays too much for an acquisition, they will never get that money back.

ORGANIZATIONAL LEARNING AND CULTURAL INFLUENCE

Learning in organizations is a goal for many companies, yet few have developed these competencies. Most firms want to be able to improve their processes and procedures. Many managers believe that upgrades in technology are a form of learning. However, Peter Senge, author of *The Fifth Discipline*, feels that only the most superficial changes are being brought about by technology.[6] Organizations are doing what they have always done, only faster. Business process reengineering (BPR) is one of the recent managerial trends of the late 1990s. BPR is based on ignoring current processes and designing what should be done without consideration of any existing processes and procedures.[7] Yet, dropping new technologies into old infrastructures will not necessarily provide productivity breakthroughs. Many companies have tried reengineering their systems and processes to streamline operations. Reengineering was popularized by Michael Hammer and James Champy in their best-selling book, *Reengineering the Corporation*.[8] Yet, few of the companies that have tried reengineering have improved their overall profits because learning requires changing both people and process habits.

In keeping with the goal of strategic management for firms to create a sustainable competitive advantage, which is not easily imitated, firms should integrate cross-functionally to create a unique position. To achieve a sustainable competitive advantage, a firm must develop core competencies, which are not easily imitated. There must be a vision driving all of these cross-functional activities and processes. System-based advantages are not copied as easily as product-based advantages. Product features are copied almost as quickly as they are introduced and are unlikely to ever provide a firm with a sustainable competitive advantage. In addition, individual employees seldom lead to a competitive advantage, and where they seem to, it is usually the organizational systems that underlie, stimulate, and nurture the human activity that should be credited.

Learning involves the acquisition of new information, the dissemination of this knowledge, and the ability to develop common understanding of its applications. Learning may involve unlearning of old routines as employees tend to do what they have always done. It is very difficult to get people to change habits from established routines. Individuals must scan information from outside the organization in the external environment and bring useful knowledge into the firm. Knowledge must be shared and become the new way of doing things to remain competitive. Sharing knowledge occurs when people are genuinely interested in helping one another develop new capacities for action. Many things that a firm needs to learn actually come from outside its industry.[9] Organizational networks and internationalization are two important sources of learning.

How can firms develop a proactive culture? In part, corporate culture is influenced by national culture. Hofstede empirically identified five dimensions of national cultural differences. These dimensions are individual–collective, masculinity–femininity, power distance, uncertainty avoidance, and time orientation.[10] National cultural orientations determine societal and individual norms about acceptable behaviors.

Corporate culture is about the implicit shared values among a group of people.[11] Healthy cultures develop when leaders value the various players in the organization. Likewise, initiative and leadership are truly valued and encouraged at every level of the organization. The corporate culture that develops, usually through the initial influence of the founder or CEO, can promote or discourage change.

Culture has been defined in many ways, but one succinct definition is the way that work gets done.[12] There are acceptable and established routines for all processes and procedures in most organizations. The "we've always done it this way" syndrome can be problematic. Many American firms have run into difficulty in trying to implement change, such as total quality management (TQM), reengineering, and restructuring, because of the inertia caused by corporate culture. Cultures can be changed and modified, but it may take two to five years, depending on the size of the firm, with strong direction from top management.

Corporate cultures also influence international mergers and acquisitions. Compatibility of both corporate and national cultures becomes critical in successfully implementing a merger or acquisition. Differences in culture have been the downfall of many mergers and acquisitions, although overpayment, incompatibility of technology, and differences in customer preferences are also contributing factors to the high failure rate of mergers and acquisitions, both domestically and internationally.

REFERENCES

1. Bartlett, C., and Ghoshal, S., *Transnational Management*, 3rd ed., McGraw-Hill, Boston, 2000, 257.
2. Naisbitt, J., From nation states to networks, *Rethinking the Future*, Nicholas Brealey Publishing, London, 1997, 213.
3. Bartlett and Ghoshal, op cit. 253.
4. Deogun, N. and Lipin, S., Cautionary tales: When the big deals turn bad, *Wall Street Journal*, December 8, 1999, C1.

5. Kotler, P., Mapping the future market place, *Rethinking the Future*, Nicholas Brealey Publishing, London, 1997, 208.

6. Senge, P., *The Fifth Discipline: The Art and Practice of the Learning Organization*, Doubleday, 1993.

7. Kubeck, L., *Techniques for Business Process Redesign: Tying It all Together*, John Wiley and Sons, New York, 1995.

8. Hammer, M. and Champy, J., *Reengineering the Corporation: A Manifesto for Business Revolution*, Harper & Row, New York, 1994.

9. Hamel, G. and Prahalad, C., *Competing for the Future*, Harvard Business School Press, Boston, 1995.

10. Hofstede, G., *Culture's Consequences: International Differences in Work-Related Values*, Sage, Beverly Hills, CA, 1980.

11. Kotter, J. and Heskett, J., *Corporate Culture and Performance*, Free Press, New York, 1999.

12. Trompenaars, F., *Riding the Waves of Culture*, Free Press, Chicago, 1994.

7

ORGANIZATION DESIGN AND STRUCTURE

Paul A. Fadil

One of the most fundamental challenges that all organizations confront early in their life cycle is the creation and subsequent enhancement of a sustainable structure. The correct organizational structure is absolutely imperative for strategy formulation and implementation. An organization's structure determines a place for each position and department, and provides the integration necessary for the organization to function. Managers who develop these organizational structures face numerous alternatives and obstacles in designing a framework that best suits their specific corporate needs. To continuously improve organizational performance and effectively serve its stakeholders, an organization's structure must be constantly evaluated and updated. To this end, a well-designed structure contributes positively to the attainment of an organization's goals and objectives, and facilitates a high level of operational effectiveness.

DEFINING, DESIGNING, AND CHARTING AN ORGANIZATION STRUCTURE

An organization's structure is considered an intangible entity. No one has ever seen one, and its existence is only reflected in an organizational chart. Thus, neither determining an organization's structure nor defining the concept of organization structure is an easy task. Mintzberg defines *organization structure* as "the sum total of the ways in which the organization divides its labor into distinct tasks and then achieves coordination among them." Although this definition focuses on differentiation (the division of labor) and integration (coordination), two very important aspects of organizational structure, it is somewhat limiting in its scope.

A more complete definition of structure is given by Daft, who reduces organization structure down to its most basic elements and then explains each one individually as follows:

1. It designates formal reporting relationships, hierarchy levels, and span of control.
2. It identifies the grouping together of individuals into departments.
3. It includes the design of systems to ensure effective communication, coordination, and integration of efforts across departments.

The three components identified and defined by Daft illustrate both the vertical and horizontal factors of the organization structure. The first two elements of this description deal with vertical communication and structural framework, whereas the third component focuses on horizontal communication and integration across departments. Therefore, an organization structure is vital in determining how labor activities are controlled and coordinated, as well as how people are grouped and allocated throughout the corporation.

An important distinction that should be made at this point is the difference between organization structure and organization design. Whereas organization structure focuses on the differentiation of labor throughout the organization and its subsequent integration, organization design centers on the decisions and actions by managers that result in a structure. In other words, the managerial decision-making process necessary to formulate and develop a structure is called *organizational design*. Upon completing the organization design, an organizational chart depicting the formal organization structure is derived.

An organization chart illustrates how people, processes, and tasks are structurally grouped and shows the formal reporting relationships that exist in an organization (Figure 7.1). Each place on the organizational chart is typically occupied by an individual, and each horizontal level represents a level of authority. As companies grow larger in size, many charts are needed to fully understand how employees are grouped and how each position is integrated into a cohesive whole. It is very important to note that the organization chart presents only the formal structure designed by company officials. The informal structure, albeit nebulous and undefined, does have an impact in many organizations. Although we may briefly mention the informal organization structure when its influence is important, for the most part, this chapter will focus only on the formal organizational structure, as well as the decisions and evaluations that are necessary to design an effective one.

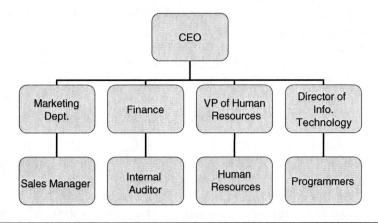

Figure 7.1 Organizational chart.

ORGANIZATION DESIGN DECISIONS

As previously stated, when designing an organizational structure, certain decisions must be made. These decisions will determine the actual size and shape of the structure, while developing the communication channels for the organization. The factors that must be considered when creating an organizational structure include: span of control, division of authority, division of labor, and integration. The consequences of these decisions all contribute to shaping each organization's structure to suit its unique environment.

Span of Control

One of the first decisions to be made by managers designing an organizational structure is to determine how many subordinates should report to a specific supervisor in each department. This concept is called the span of control. Simply put, this decision comes down to, "How many subordinates can a single supervisor oversee?" If a supervisor can oversee five subordinates, he or she is said to have a span of control of five. As the number of subordinates under a supervisor increases, the supervisor develops a wider span of control. Conversely, a decreasing number of subordinates will lead to a narrower span of control.

Central to deriving a supervisor's span of control is the determination of how efficiently a manager can integrate and coordinate the tasks of his or her subordinates. Although researchers have suggested that the best number of subordinates reporting to a single supervisor is between five and seven, in today's complex organizations, other factors have to be taken into account when deciding on the appropriate span of control. For example, two issues that greatly impact span of control are professionalism and informal reporting relationships.

The professionalism factor within individual departments greatly influences the supervisor to subordinate ratio. Higher levels of education usually lead to more self-supervision and, subsequently, ease the burden on a supervisor. Therefore, supervisors in a professional setting, with a department of highly educated subordinates, should have a much wider span of control. For example, college departments at larger universities routinely have 30 to 40 full-time and adjunct professors under a single department head. It is therefore very clear that a high level of professionalism can lead to a very wide span of control.

A second variable that impacts a supervisor's span of control to a major extent is the organization's informal reporting relationships. In modern organizations, task forces and other cross-functional work teams are popular organizational methods of dealing with unexpected environmental issues and change. Consider a manager who has a span of control of eight subordinates, but also chairs two task forces and a cross-functional committee. The members of the task forces and the committee who report directly to the chairperson (the manager) must be included under the manager's span of control to accurately gauge his or her managerial performance. Although these informal reporting relationships vary in frequency and intensity, a manager must respond to them as seriously as he or she would respond to one of the formal subordinates. Thus, the span of control for managers in modern organizations is not as easily determined as it was a few years ago.

The major impact that span of control has on the shape of the organizational structure is in the height of the organization. If an organization tends to have departments with wide spans of control, the organizational structure will be relatively flat. A flat organization is one with very few layers in its hierarchy, where many employees report to a specific supervisor and many supervisors report to a specific manager. On the other hand, tall organizations have many more layers in their hierarchy due to relatively narrow spans of control. This also increases the supervisor to subordinate ratio at all levels of the organization, thereby giving the organization more managers to monitor employee performance and thereby increasing managerial control.

Division of Authority: Vertical Differentiation

Managers designing an organization structure must make decisions regarding the levels of vertical differentiation in an organization. Specifically, they must create a hierarchy by classifying people and positions according to rank and authority. Positions at the top of the hierarchy (CEO) possess more authority than positions at the bottom of the hierarchy (first-level supervisor).

Vertical differentiation reflects the division of authority throughout the organization. Specifically, vertical differentiation focuses on the authority differences at various levels of the organization's structure and emphasizes the reporting relationships that link these positions to others above and below them in the hierarchy. An organization's vertical differentiation can be easily assessed by counting the number of horizontal levels given on the organizational chart. These reporting relationships, or vertical linkages, establish a transparent chain of command and facilitate effective communication from the top to the bottom of the organizational chart. The extensive use of vertical linkages also dictates a very strict hierarchy, a well-established chain of command, and many rules within the organization. To conclude, a vertically differentiated organization is created for control and efficiency.

DIVISION OF LABOR: HORIZONTAL DIFFERENTIATION

Dividing labor throughout the organization is another challenge that the managerial design team must face. Determining the role of each position and department in the organization structure is extremely important for an organization to function effectively. Specifically, each position must have a description that illustrates both its role and purpose. Each department must formulate a group of activities that guide both the employees and the managers toward organizational goals and objectives. This division of labor into separate tasks, and the subsequent grouping of these tasks into distinct departments, is known as *horizontal differentiation*.

A high number of separate and distinct departments reflect not only a high level of horizontal differentiation but also a high level of task specialization. Horizontal differentiation facilitates the specialization of tasks, thereby enabling the employees in the organization to develop unique skills and become more productive. Specialization reflects how narrowly the tasks are divided and assigned throughout the organization structure. The specialization of labor in complex organization structures is at the very center of horizontal differentiation.

Horizontal differentiation and job specialization are extremely applicable in today's organizational environment. As mom-and-pop stores give way to larger, more developed organizations, the extensive division of labor in these organizations requires high levels of specialization. In these modern organizations, positions have become much more focused and specific. Highly specialized organizations that have narrowly defined tasks must hire well-trained employees to perform these advanced activities.

Unique, specialized skill sets are now required to perform highly specific tasks and functions required by these organizations.

High levels of horizontal differentiation can be considered an organizational advantage because it facilitates superior organizational learning and environmental adaptation. Many companies, however, have found that extreme levels of specialization may cause communication and coordination problems, as well as interdepartmental conflict. Often, highly specialized departments operate as a separate entity from the organization. They not only achieve their objectives independently of other departments, but they also compete with these same departments for scarce resources. These problems must be addressed by developing integrating factors and horizontal communication linkages throughout the organization structure.

INTEGRATION: COMMUNICATION AND COORDINATION

The final design challenge for the managerial design team is to determine how to facilitate communication and coordination across positions and departments in the organization. The process of coordinating people and activities throughout the organization is called *integration*. How an organizational structure pulls together its differentiated tasks will critically impact its effectiveness.

Just as organizations differentiate the work that must be done, they must also find a way to plan and coordinate their efforts to ensure organizational success. Managers must develop integrating roles and mechanisms to overcome communication and cooperation barriers that come into existence between departments. These roles and mechanisms can include, but are not limited to, direct contact, liaisons, task forces, teams, and an organizational integrator. Each of these integrating factors will now be defined individually.

Direct Contact

Direct contact between managers and employees of different departments will expose these individuals to the challenges that other departments face. Establishing these personal relationships should give employees a more organizational, as opposed to a departmental, orientation. Managers and employees from different sectors in the organization will work together to solve problems that may affect them individually in different ways. Without direct contact, employees in different departments would be ignorant of the far-reaching impact some of their actions may have on their organizational counterparts in different departments. Therefore, direct contact gives employees across departments an opportunity to work together to solve common problems and share expertise.

Liaison

A liaison is an individual in a department who acts as a bridge between his or her department and another department. For example, an individual working in the finance department with a major in marketing could serve as a liaison between the finance and marketing departments in the organization. The people who hold this role in a department serve as the main representative of their department when dealing with other particular units in the organization. Eventually, liaisons learn the flexibility necessary to coordinate and plan with other departments.

Task Force

The integrating factors of direct contact and liaisons usually link only two departments. When a more complex integrating mechanism is needed to coordinate a greater number of organizational units, a task force is employed. A task force is a temporary team made up of individuals spanning several departments, brought together to solve a particular problem or perform a specific function. After their duties are successfully completed, task forces will disband. Task force members are then responsible for taking the information gleaned from the task force back to their formal departments for evaluation. Task forces are especially effective integrating mechanisms for temporary issues; for more substantive, long-range issues, organizations must rely on teams.

Teams

When a task force's problem becomes a long-term strategic situation, the task force must become permanent. A permanent task force is called a *team* or a committee. Project teams are one of the strongest integrating factors. These cross-functional teams coordinate activities across departments over a long period of time. A major project or a substantive change in the organization could require a special team to coordinate the organization's departments. Teams provide the opportunity for people from different departments of the organization to meet and work together toward a common goal. The camaraderie that is built on a successful team could last for years, as well as consistently pay dividends in future cooperative efforts. Thus, teams are important assets in an organization's constant efforts to integrate its operations.

Organizational Integrator

The most direct solution to the communication and coordination problems that exist because of extreme levels of horizontal differentiation is to create a position whose only purpose is integrating the departments of the organization. An organizational integrator is located outside the departments that he or she is responsible for and therefore does not report to the managers in the departments that are being coordinated. Acting as a project manager, the organizational integrator must communicate with several individuals across several departments, even though he or she has no formal authority over them. As organizational integrators have tremendous responsibility coupled with very little authority, communication skills are a must. If an organization has many people acting as integrators, it can create an integration department to oversee the integrative process.

STRUCTURAL DIMENSIONS

Once the design of the organization structure is complete, an understanding of the unique attributes of the structure is required to evaluate both its fit and overall effectiveness. Nearly every firm reorganizes at some point in its life cycle and subsequently alters its structure to take advantage of new opportunities in the environment. As managers assess their company's structure, they will observe specific dimensions that characterize their organization. If they choose to change these dimensions, a slight or large-scale restructuring is usually necessary. The four major dimensions that organizations examine to determine the effectiveness of their structure are centralization, formalization, standardization, and complexity.

Centralization

Centralization describes where the decision-making authority rests in the organization. An organizational structure that facilitates decision making and authority at the top of the hierarchy is considered centralized. An organizational structure that forces managers to delegate authority and decision making to all levels of the organization is considered decentralized. On either side of the centralization continuum, one will find advantages and disadvantages.

The major advantage of centralization is that it provides upper-level managers with a large amount of control. Top managers can make decisions that will keep the organization focused on its goals, while moving it forward to accomplish current and future strategic objectives. The disadvantages of centralization, however, are reduced employee morale (due to motivation, efficacy, and control issues) and top management work overload (due to continuously being involved in the day-to-day operational issues).

Decentralization facilitates flexibility, decreases reaction time to environmental changes, and empowers lower- and mid-level managers, by providing them with the authority and responsibility necessary to make critical decisions. It significantly increases morale, while allowing managers to be held accountable for their decisions. Unfortunately, these advantages come at the expense of planning, integration, coordination, and control. An effective organization design team weighs the pros and cons of centralization and decentralization and, hopefully, capitalizes on the strengths of both approaches. This will allow the organization's top managers to maintain focus on the organizational goals, while allowing those closest to the situation the freedom to make important decisions.

Formalization

Formalization is the degree to which written rules and procedures are utilized to guide employee actions. A formal organization is one where written rules are extensive, work goals and job descriptions are intensely specified, and violations of these rules are strictly enforced. An example of a formal organization is the U.S. military, where written manuals and verbal commands not only guide employee behavior, but these employees have absolutely no authority to break or even question the rules. The major goal of formalization is to standardize operating procedures to such a point that employee behavior becomes predictable and these procedures eventually become second nature. In other words, a high level of formalization typically ensures a high level of standardized behavior.

Standardization

Standardization is the degree of routine and predictable actions that result from formalization. Employees conforming to a given set of rules and procedures, so that their behaviors are similar and predictable in many specific situations, reflect a highly standardized organization. Managers, in turn, gain a high level of control over their employees because their work activities are predictable. Standardization also reduces the need for a large number of supervisors, because formal rules and procedures replace them by acting as written monitors of employee behavior. Organizations that value similarity and control, such as fast-food franchises and sales companies, strongly endorse standardization within their organization structure.

Complexity

Complexity is the consequence of dividing both labor and authority. Specifically, complexity represents the number of different positions and departments, as well as the number of authority levels in an organization.

Organizations that are larger tend to be more complex than smaller firms that do not have as much differentiation and tend to have more complex challenges than your typical mom-and-pop establishment. Thus, complex firms tend to put a higher value on learning and adapting as opposed to maximizing efficiency and control. Therefore, complex organizations are much more difficult to control and coordinate than simple ones, and they require more effort and attention in integration than their smaller, simpler counterparts.

ORGANIZATIONAL STRUCTURE AND THE ENVIRONMENT

Each design and dimensional choice made by a managerial team as they construct the organizational structure has tremendous consequences on the actions of the employees of the organization. It would be foolhardy, however, for the design team to completely ignore the specific environment where the organization will operate. In 1961, Burns and Stalker observed several industrial corporations and determined that the external environment and the organization's structure were interrelated. They identified two types of organizational structures that were at opposite sides of a continuum, namely, the mechanistic and the organic. Each of these structures was proven effective when operating in an environment conducive to their structures.

The Mechanistic Structure

The mechanistic structure is designed to encourage employees to act in a predictable, standardized way. The rules and regulations in the mechanistic organization practically standardize employee behavior to the point where each individual is considered a part of an overall machine. Standardization in the mechanistic structure is the chosen method of control. This structure is considered optimal in environments that are both stable and predictable.

Some characteristics of mechanistic organizations include:

Highly specialized, defined tasks — each employee completes a specialized task by working individually and separately.

Centralized decision making — the decision making is done at the top of the organization.

High formalization — tremendous amount of rules.

High standardization — behaviors are predictable due to the use of standard operating procedures.

High levels of vertical communication — these create a clear chain of command.

The Organic Structure

The organic structure is at the other end of the continuum. The organic structure is designed to encourage flexibility and environmental responsiveness. In rapidly changing environments, an organizational structure must be flexible, loose, and adaptive. Managers at the lower levels of the structure must have the authority to make important decisions if they are to effectively respond to the environmental challenges. If there were a reliance on rules and high-level decision making, the speed of the environmental changes would paralyze the organization. Organic structures tend to be learning, adjustable entities that can adjust quickly, based on environmental opportunities and threats. Therefore, this structure is considered optimal when the organization is exposed to high levels of environmental uncertainty.

Some characteristics of organic organizations include:

Common tasks — employees complete common tasks that contribute to the overall organization.

Decentralized decision making — the decision making is done at lower levels in the organization because of emphasis on reaction speed.

Low formalization — very few rules.

Low standardization — employees must be able to react to unique situations.

High levels of horizontal communication — integration is very important as several task forces and teams are present.

STRUCTURAL DEPARTMENTALIZATION

The organization process that structurally combines jobs and tasks into specific groups is called *departmentalization.* Jobs must be grouped into departments to facilitate coordination and integration. This grouping also affects employees as they must work together to achieve common objectives in the department. The most important question of departmentalization is how the departments are organized. The most accepted types of departmentalization are functional and divisional, either by product or geography. Any two of these departmentalization structures can be combined to form a matrix structure. All four of these designs will now be discussed in further detail.

Functional Departmentalization

The most widely utilized form of departmentalization is by functional grouping. In a functional structure, individuals are grouped together based

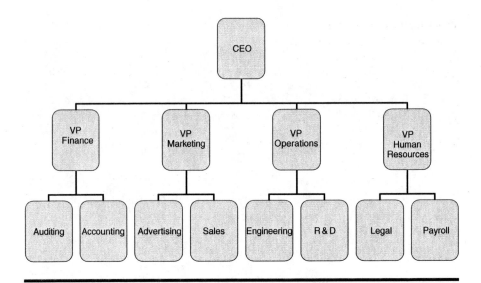

Figure 7.2 Functional departmentalization.

on the similarity of their tasks. Each of the functions in an organization can become a particular department, and workers performing the function's activities can be grouped into that department. For example, some of the functions in a hospital include: surgery, pediatrics, nursing, physical plant, pharmacy, human resources, and food service. These functions serve as a guideline for grouping workers. In a traditional corporation, the departments might include such functions as marketing, operations, finance, accounting, and legal aspects. Although the functions that appear as departments vary from organization to organization, this functional grouping facilitates the emergence of core competencies where organizations can consolidate significant competitive advantages.

Some of the strengths of functional structure are that it promotes expertise, economies of scale, efficiency, and achievement of functional goals. Some of the weaknesses of this structure include slow response to environmental uncertainty, foregoing organizational goals for departmental goals, poor communication and cooperation across departments, and an ignorance of organizational issues that do not concern the department. Organizations that tend to perform effectively with a strict functional structure tend to have only one or very few products, when operating in a stable environment (Figure 7.2).

Divisional Departmentalization by Product

As organizations grow and produce a more diversified set of products, a divisional structure will better suit their needs. A divisional or product structure is one in which the organization is structured around product groupings. The products that drive the departmentalization are also the organization's outputs. Specifically, all aspects of a particular product or product line are placed in one division. Within these separate divisions, a set of support functions exist to service each product or product line. For example, automobile companies tend to build divisions around different makes and models of their cars. Each division has its own marketing, finance, and operations departments and could be considered a freestanding entity.

The divisional departmentalization method is synonymous with organizational growth. Most of the larger companies throughout the United States employ a divisional structure because it allows them to build a separate organizational unit around each product. If the products in an organization's inventory are considerably unique, the company will now be able to market, finance, and manufacture each product while centering their efforts on maximizing the competitive advantage in each self-contained division. Some of the strengths of divisional departmentalization are environmental responsiveness, increased control over outputs, internal divisional cooperation, and easier identification of profitable divisions. Some of the disadvantages include: no functional economies of scale, decreased coordination and communication between divisions, loyalty to separate divisions instead of the organization, and standardization across product lines becoming virtually impossible. Organizations that tend to perform effectively with a strict divisional structure tend to have large product lines while operating in a highly uncertain, unstable environment (Figure 7.3).

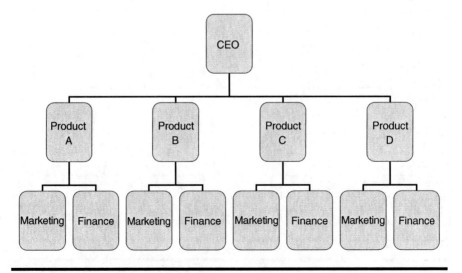

Figure 7.3 Product division structure.

Divisional Departmentalization by Geography

The third design method for departmentalizing the organization is by geographic area. Specifically, a geographic divisional structure is one where divisions are organized according to the different areas where the organization operates. This organizational method groups the firm's customers by regions of the country or world (Figure 7.4). An example of companies that would consistently employ a geographic structure is in sales corporations. Sales organizations divide their operation areas into sectors, and then allocate distinct territories for their salespeople to cover these sectors. The salespeople then report to district managers who are responsible for sales throughout the entire sector. Each sector of an organization's operating environment may have different needs, desires, or tastes. By dividing the corporation according to geographic areas, these sections can be adequately served, and their idiosyncrasies duly noted.

The geographic departmentalization design is also synonymous with extensive growth. Because large companies have national and international customer bases, the geographic structure allows the firm to group all activities in a given region under one manager. This provides an extra degree of control when an organization's physical operations are spread throughout the country or the world. As in the divisional departmentalization, the self-contained geographic unit has its own functional support and can create value independent of the rest of the organization. Summarizing, the geographic structure allows the organization to focus on specific customer needs in a particular geographic area. As the geographic

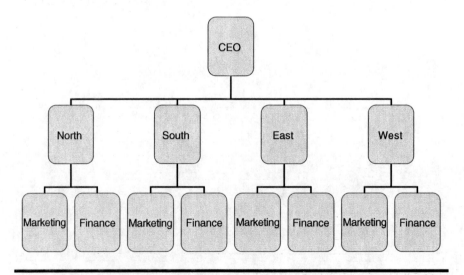

Figure 7.4 Geographic division structure.

structure is very similar to the divisional structure explained above, the strengths and weaknesses of the geographic structure mirror those of the divisional structure. The only difference lies in the unit, that is, the geographical division versus the product division.

Matrix Structure

An organization employing the matrix structure seeks to combine two of the previously mentioned designs. A company may seek to become multifocused by combining the functional and divisional structure, or functional and geographic structure, at the same time. Specifically, matrix organizations achieve this multidimensionality by overlaying one structure on top of another. This structure seeks to glean the advantages from the functional structure, while maintaining the innovation of a divisional structure. For example, even though an organization may be strictly divided along functional lines, managers who need production assistance for their special divisions could tap employees from different departments to assist in their efforts. These employees will now report to two bosses, the functional manager and the product manager, both of whom have equal authority over the employees in their departments. This dual authority hierarchy is a distinctive characteristic and, some would say, major weakness of the matrix structure.

The matrix structure utilizes teams and task forces extensively to coordinate activities, thereby forcing integration on the organization and allowing it to meet the dual demands of its customers and environment (Figure 7.5). These structures need to be carefully monitored to maintain

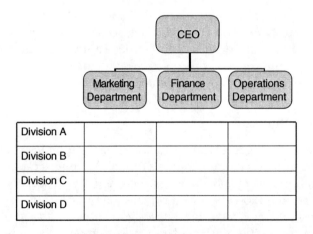

Figure 7.5 Matrix structure.

their effectiveness. The matrix structure is at its best when the organization needs to maximize its human expertise for specific projects by coordinating its functional experts. This structure is at its worst, however, when authority lines become blurred and employees get frustrated with the demands being placed on them by two separate bosses. To counter this problem, managers must spend a lot of time coordinating and cooperating with each other, while ensuring that the organization's goals are at the forefront of all decisions.

STRUCTURE AND STRATEGY

Strategy is defined as the manipulation of the relationship of an organization and its environment to better achieve the organization's goals and objectives. The relationship between strategy and structure is important in determining the overall effectiveness of the organization. For example, if one were implementing a low-cost leadership strategy to increase market share and focus on efficient production, a more mechanistic structure with tight controls would be preferred. On the other hand, a differentiation strategy would call for a more organic, horizontal structure to respond to changes in the environment. If management does not focus its strategy around the strengths of the organization's structure, or fails to acknowledge the significant relationship between these two organizational factors, the organization will be at a serious competitive disadvantage and its overall performance will suffer.

Regardless of an organization's strategy, structure, or their respective interrelationship, one important point must be made clear: an effective strategy greatly depends upon the organization's structure. Actually, an organization's structure drives strategic decision making, not the other way around. Strategies can only be formulated and implemented once a sound organization structure is in place. In fact, to formulate and implement a successful strategy, the organization's structure must act as the strategy's foundation and the genesis of its objectives and therefore an organization's strategy must be tailored to fit its structure.

CONCLUSION

The design of an organization's structure is an important challenge that many managers face. An organization's formal structure is clearly illustrated in an organizational chart. Managers face numerous decisions in determining an organization's span of control, division of authority, division of labor, and integration during the design process. Although these decisions create the visible design of the organization's structure, there are other structural dimensions to consider. These dimensions include the centralization of decision making, the formalization of rules, the standardization of behaviors, and the complexity of the overall structure. In conjunction with the design principles, these dimensions assist in determining if the organization's structure will be mechanistic or organic. The managers must then decide how the organization will be departmentalized. The organization will either be grouped by functional department, by division (either by geographic area or product), or by a matrix structure that combines any two of these departmentalization techniques. Now that the structure of the organization is in place, the managers can proceed to formulate the competitive strategy that best fits the organizational structure and successfully interacts with the operating environment.

SELECTED READINGS

Burns, T. and Stalker, G., *The Management of Innovation*, Tavistock Publications, London, 1961.

Daft, R., *Organization Theory and Design*, Thomson South-Western, Mason, OH, 2007.

Gibson, J., Ivancevich, J., and Donnely, J., *Organizations: Behavior, Structure and Processes*, Irwin McGraw-Hill, 2000.

Hatch, M.J. and Cunliffe, A., *Organization Theory: Modern, Symbolic and Postmodern Perspectives*, Oxford University Press, 2006.

Hodge, B.J. and Anthony, W., *Organization Theory: A Strategic Approach*, Allyn and Bacon, Needham Heights, MA, 1991.

Jones, G., *Organizational Theory, Design and Change*, Prentice Hall, Upper Saddle River, NJ, 2004.

Mintzberg, H., *The Structuring of Organizations*, Prentice Hall, Englewood Cliffs, NJ, 1979.

8

STRATEGIC MARKETING ISSUES

Young-Tae Choi

Marketing fundamentals are key elements necessary for firms to compete in the current complex and dynamic market situations. Technological advances and the global economy have changed the firm's business practices. The Internet and increasing global competition in domestic and foreign markets have reshaped the way firms conduct businesses for markets and consumers. Consumers shop online, have access information on prices, features, or quality of products or services, and enjoy a large selection of products and services. These circumstances inevitably necessitate the firms understand current strategic marketing concepts and issues and develop new ways of strategic thinking and planning in marketing to be successful.

THE MARKETING CONCEPT

Over the decades, the concept of marketing has changed and evolved from the selling and delivery process of products and services between buyers and sellers to an exchange process that satisfies the needs of individuals and organizations. Recently, the American Marketing Association defined marketing as "an organizational function and a set of processes for creating, communicating, and delivering value to customers and for managing customer relationships in ways that benefit the organization and its stakeholders."[1] Although marketing as an organizational function has typically been involved in creating, promoting, and delivering products or services to consumers and businesses, the definition emphasizes the importance of marketing for the overall success of the entire organization and its members. The focus on customer relationship management (CRM) requires organizations to be customer-centric by identifying customers and their needs, and by maintaining the positive, long-term relationships to survive in today's dynamic, competitive market environment.

Regardless of the various changing marketing orientations, the focal point in marketing is the customer; customers are at the center of all marketing activities. The essence of marketing activities is to satisfy customers. Organizations develop the product or service to meet current or potential customers' needs and expect to receive the price charged for the product or service in exchange from customers. This successful exchange between customers and organizations is mutually beneficial by satisfying each other's needs.[2]

Marketing activities are typically involved in the "marketing mix," commonly referred to as the "4 Ps of marketing" — product, price, promotion, and place (distribution) — to satisfy customers. What product or service should be produced, what price to charge, how to promote and distribute the product or service, and how and where the product or service should be made available are all marketing decisions. Because all of the decisions critically impact the success of the organization, marketers should make conscious, organized, and planned efforts to develop an effective marketing mix that sustains long-term customer relations and generates both customer satisfaction and organization profits.

MARKETING MIX AND STRATEGIES

These can be itemized as follows:

Product and Marketing Strategies

Firms manufacture products or services to satisfy customers' needs. A product is a physical item that customers can see, touch, and feel; an automobile, a notebook computer, and a toothbrush are product examples. Product strategies include not only the development of a tangible item but also the creation and maintenance of branding and packaging of the item to stimulate its purchase. Branding involves the building of the image or perception of the product on the customer, by creating a name, trademark, logo, or other unique symbol of the product. Branding generates value, recognition, and quality of the product that can differentiate it from competitors' products. Therefore, marketers need to develop and maintain effective branding strategies for the product's long-term success. Packaging involves designing and producing a container and a graphic design for a product (e.g., color, texture, shape, and graphics). Packaging basically protects the product during transportation from the manufacturer's warehouse to the final customer and maintains its contents for a certain period of time. Packaging also can be a means of communication with customers about the functions of the product (e.g., how the product works or nutritional information). Packaging helps customers to use the product conveniently, thus creating additional value. Effective packaging thus positively influences development of the product image, or brand, or even the company.

Product transactions usually occur in industrial or consumer markets. Industrial markets exist in a business to business (B2B) environment. The transactions of products in this environment take place between businesses, including government. The purchases made by an organization are either integrated into the organization's product/services, used to manufacture the product, or support its commercial operations. Consumer markets are characterized by transactions where consumers buy products/services for personal use. One example of consumer markets is a retail grocery market where consumers purchase groceries for their family's consumption.

As a variety of factors pertaining to customers, competitors, and market conditions may change over time, firms need to develop new products, extend or modify existing ones, or eliminate the products that no longer satisfy the needs of customers or bring any more profits. Products provide a basic tool for firms to differentiate themselves from other competitors. However, products also progress through life cycles as humans do and, therefore, firms should adjust and adapt their marketing strategies to be successful in the market, regardless of the particular life-cycle stage of the product.

The product life cycle (PLC) has four stages; introduction, growth, maturity, and decline. The PLC begins with the introduction stage whereby a new product is introduced into the market. The introduction stage is generally characterized by low sales that are unlikely to reap profits. Firms are in a position to cover the large expenses associated with the promotion and distribution of the new product. The successfully introduced product moves into the growth stage. Here, sales rapidly increase as many customers become aware of the product and demand increases along with profits for the firm. Although firms may enjoy first-mover advantages, such as higher market share and brand recognition with the product, competitors enter the market and competition intensifies. Therefore, in the later stage of growth, profits begin to decline and firms may face tough competition. To remain competitive, firms can intensify the brand loyalty of customers by emphasizing the brand or product benefits, developing different market segments, modifying product features, or offering lower prices. During the maturity stage, the profits continue to fall and customers begin to switch to other brands. Weaker competitors are squeezed out of the market, whereas other firms try to maintain their market share. Promotion and advertising strategies are likely to be based on maintaining sales and profits. Firms may engage in price wars and can step up services/product quality to differentiate them from competitors. The decline stage is characterized by rapidly falling sales that drastically erode profits. Intense competition from firms marketing similar or substitute products may cause customers to switch to other brands; and, because in the decline stage a product drains firm resources, marketers must either decide whether the product should be dropped from the market or find a way to extend its life. Arm & Hammer is one company that has done an exceptional job of rejuvenating demand for its product.

Firms need to understand where the product stands, in regard to its overall life cycle, to develop appropriate marketing strategies. Marketing strategies should reflect the product's stage in the life cycle. For example, if a product has been around for a long time and has achieved its potential in the market, promotional efforts can emphasize new benefits of the product or brand. As market segments change, firms may use different distribution channels to reach their customers (e.g., the Internet) to appeal to new market segments. Product modifications, such as adding features or change in packaging, can also be used to appeal to new segments.

Pricing and Marketing Strategies

Firms receive a certain value, usually expressed as money, from customers in return for their offerings. Price strongly influences the purchase of a product or service and is considered as a surrogate measure of quality for many consumers — if it costs more, then it is of higher quality. Pricing decisions, therefore, require careful consideration of many factors. Firms should clearly consider the following pricing objectives: what is the goal of pricing strategies for firms? Is the goal penetrating the market, increasing market share, or maintaining the status quo? Firms should also consider fixed and variable costs when they manufacture the product. Other considerations can include the demand for offerings given the price level, the purchasing power of potential customers, and competitors' pricing strategies for similar offerings.

One of the most important pricing strategies for marketers is pricing for innovative products. They often use price skimming in which prices are set relatively high for buyers. This pricing strategy is used to maximize the firm's profits because the product is very new to the market, as was the case with early marketers of video games and Sony camcorders. On the other hand, firms may choose to use penetration pricing, whereby prices are set below those of competing brands. Penetration pricing may appeal to many customers, achieve a high market share in a short period of time, and prevent potential competitors from entering the market. Other pricing strategies include everyday low prices (EDLP), where prices are set low on a consistent basis (e.g., Wal-Mart's pricing strategies), odd pricing (e.g., $14.95 instead of $15), which makes customers perceive that they purchase the product at a lower price, and price-bundling, which allows customers to purchase a package at a cost less than the sum of the prices of the individual products or services (e.g., members of a health club can purchase a package of classes, aerobics, weight-loss training, and massage services at a lower price than if the services were purchased individually). Firms also may use going-rate pricing, which follows competitors' prices. In this case, a firm might charge the same, less, or more than major competitors' prices for their offerings (e.g., gas prices).

Price is the only P that generates revenue for firms, which requires them to consider diverse factors in setting appropriate prices for their offerings. In setting pricing strategies, firms need to refine and modify the initial pricing strategies because they also need to be adjusted to the changing market or industry circumstances.

Promotion and Marketing Strategies

Marketers communicate with customers to determine how to find target customers, how to reach them, what they want, how to effectively provide information on products or services for them, and how to develop and maintain a long-term relationship with them. Marketers use various promotional tools such as advertising, sales promotion, personal selling, and public relations to communicate with customers and stimulate the customers' demand for products or services. Depending on their marketing strategies, firms choose different promotional tools, such as advertising, personal selling, sales promotion, or public relations (PR). Even firms in the same industry often use different types of promotional tools. Firms also blend different types of promotional tools to effectively promote their offerings and approach customers.

Advertising is any paid form of nonpersonal communication about a firm and its products or services delivered to the firm's target market segments through mass media, such as the Internet, TVs, magazines, direct mail, newspapers, radios, outdoor signs and displays, and billboards. Advertising can reach target audiences repeatedly in a short period of time (e.g., TV commercials and the Internet) with low cost per audience but the overall costs may be very high (e.g., TV commercials).

Personal selling is a person-to-person communication that persuades customers to purchase a firm's products or services. The cost to reach each customer may be higher than that of advertising, but personal selling is a more direct approach to reach an individual or individuals than advertising. Thus, personal selling allows the firm to get instant feedback from customers, which enables it to easily adjust its offerings or messages to target more customers. Direct interaction with customers requires the firm to hire motivated people with a sales attitude, refined communication skills, and flexibility to achieve success.

Sales promotion is a short-term communication with customers, based on incentives, to stimulate quick sales for the product or service. The incentives include coupons, rebates, sweepstakes, free samples, reduced price, and contests. Marketers spend more money on sales promotion than on advertising, because sales promotion has proven to be more effective than advertising. The sales promotion expenditure has been steadily increasing and appears to be a faster growing promotion area.[3]

PR involves communications that are used to create favorable relationships between a firm and its stakeholders, such as customers, employees, suppliers, stockholders, the media, communities, and government agencies. The firm tries to maintain positive relationships with the stakeholders through annual reports, press conferences, brochures, and sponsorships for certain events, because the stakeholder affects the firm's long-term survival and success. Many firms have a PR department or an individual who monitors public opinions, so as to build a favorable public awareness or image or to minimize any negative publicity against them. Alternatively, publicity, although free of charge, cannot be controlled; it may be positive or negative.

As communication media have diversified through the Internet, cable TV, network TV, direct mail, e-mail solicitation, newspapers, and magazines, marketers have begun to realize the importance of integrated marketing communications (IMC). The purpose of the IMC is that a firm integrates and coordinates all of its marketing communication channels to deliver a uniform and consistent message to customers. The IMC allows the firm to synchronize its promotions and unify the firm's brand images and messages to facilitate communication between the firm and its customers for building successful and long-term relationships.

Distribution (Place) and Marketing Strategies

The last marketing-mix variable involves distribution (place) or marketing channels through which products or services become available for end users. Many industrial products are sold through direct channels (i.e., the manufacturer $\rightarrow$ the end user) whereas most consumer products or services are distributed or sold through marketing intermediaries (e.g., wholesalers or retailers). The intermediaries facilitate and control the flow of products or services between the manufacturer and the final purchaser. Wholesalers buy and resell products to other wholesalers, retailers, and other ultimate customers who buy for resale or business use. For example, McKesson Corporation is the largest drug wholesaler in the United States, which sells medicines to retail drug stores like Walgreens. Retailers, such as JC Penny, Best Buy, and Wal-Mart primarily sell products to final customers. Many wholesalers have faced survival challenges in recent years because many consumer product manufacturers have tried to bypass wholesalers and sell directly to retailers (e.g., Wal-Mart and The Home Depot). Technology development has also enabled retailers to carry out many of the traditional functions of wholesalers such as ordering, storing, delivery, stocking of products, and gathering market and customer information.

When delivering products to final consumers, firms face the problem of how to move products to them. They are therefore involved in logistics, the process of moving raw materials and finished products to final buyers. In other words, logistics is concerned with the physical flow of products through marketing channels. The functions of logistics generally include sales forecasting, order processing (i.e., the receipt and movement of the sales order), inventory management, warehousing, materials handling, transportation, and customer service. The functions can be performed by a manufacturer, a wholesaler, a retailer, or can be outsourced to a third party logistics firm like FedEx. The ultimate purpose of logistics is to deliver products to end customers in the cheapest way while maintaining quality service, because logistics functions account for about half of all marketing costs.[4] As logistics relates to various channels, such as suppliers, manufacturers, wholesalers, retailers, warehousers, and transportation firms, cooperation between these members is essential to establish an effective logistics system.

CURRENT STRATEGIC MARKETING OUTLOOKS

Different marketing outlooks include:

International Marketing

Technological developments (e.g., the Internet) and global media, such as MTV, *The Wall Street Journal, Business Week, The Economist,* the growth of the World Trade Organization, new emerging markets (e.g., China, Russia, and Brazil), and the increasing acceptance of free market systems, have provided opportunities for firms to market their products or services on a limitless basis in foreign countries. Thus, many firms develop and perform marketing activities across international boundaries to take advantage of increasing market opportunities. For example, Starbucks has more than 1500 stores in more than 30 countries outside North America and is expected to expand their markets in more countries.[5] However, the trend toward globalization is a two-edged sword in that it also poses challenges for firms to compete against foreign firms, both domestically and internationally. The current competition U.S. car makers face against foreign car makers in the United States and other country markets is a well-known example.

Once a firm decides to commit to international markets, it first has to determine the mode of entry. Foreign market entry modes include: exporting, licensing, franchising, international joint ventures, international strategic alliances, and foreign direct ownership. Exporting is still the sole alternative for many firms to market their products in foreign countries. Firms can handle their own exports, or export products through independent intermediaries such as export management companies. Firms become involved in international marketing via licensing in which the licensee, foreign or domestic, acquires a license to use patent rights, trade rights, or technologies in return for royalties or fees for the licensor. Franchising is currently the fastest growing and most successful mode of entry, whereby the franchiser provides the name, products, logo, service systems, and other business-related technologies to the foreign franchisor who provides market knowledge, financial, and personal commitment to conduct business (e.g., McDonald's in Japan). An international joint venture (IJV) and an international strategic alliance (ISA) involve a partnership between a domestic firm and a foreign firm or governments to cooperatively pool and utilize the participants' resources. The difference between the IJV and the ISA is that the participants in an IJV share ownership. For example, Prudential UK has a 33 percent stake in a planned fund-management joint venture with China International Trust & Investment Corporation. The participants in an ISA generally do not share ownership but only exchange their resources. An example is the Oneworld Alliance between American Airlines, British Airways, Qantas, Cathay Pacific, and Canadian Airlines. A foreign firm can buy part or full ownership of a local firm or build a new facility to have direct ownership of the firm. Hyundai Motor Company built a manufacturing facility in Alabama to become one of many foreign automobile manufacturers who have built automobile manufacturing plants in the United States.

Another important issue in international marketing is whether a firm should standardize or adapt its marketing mix when it enters a foreign market. Differences in politics, cultures, technology, the level of economic development, trade or business regulations, the level of income, exchange rate, labor issues, financial systems, business practices, languages, and customs make the firm adapt their mix strategies to foreign markets or customers. However, the global homogenization of customers' preferences and tastes often allows firms to use more of a standardized marketing mix strategy. Whether firms use customized (multidomestic) or standardized (global) marketing strategies, the success of such strategies depends more on how they maintain the balance between the customized and standardized strategies, given the overall market strategies, objectives, capabilities, resources, and foreign market situations.

Services Marketing

Services industries account for almost 80 percent of the U.S. gross domestic product (GDP) and about 80 percent of employment. The importance of service industries in the U.S. economy is expected to continue to grow in the future. Services industries include transportation and public utilities, education, finance, insurance, real estate, hotels, airlines, health care, and Internet-based services.

Services, defined as deeds, processes, or performances, have distinctive characteristics different from those of products.[4] First, services are more intangible and cannot be touched, felt, or tasted, which makes display or communication of services difficult. Second, services are more heterogeneous because no two services are exactly the same as they are mostly performed by humans. For example, the performance of the same service provider may differ from time to time and no two customers are the same because each customer may have different expectations of services. The heterogeneous characteristic of services suggests that the delivery of consistent quality service may be challenging for firms. Third, services are more simultaneously produced and consumed because most services are sold and then produced and consumed at the same time, whereas most products are manufactured, sold, and then consumed. The simultaneous production and consumption characteristic of services indicates that mass production of services is difficult and that the service provider plays a critical role in the success of services. Lastly, services are more perishable because services cannot be stored, saved, or returned. For example, an empty airplane seat cannot be resold and a bad haircut cannot be undone. The perishability of services makes it difficult to synchronize supply and demand for such services.

One important new trend is that technology has significantly shaped new practices in service industries. For example, the Internet — through services such as eBay.com, Amazon.com, and Google.com — ATMs, automated airline ticket kiosks, self-checkout counters, and online banking allow service firms to effectively and efficiently deliver services for many customers despite privacy issues, a phobia of technological services by some customers, and a lack of human interactions between service firms and customers.

Despite the growing importance of service and technology infusion into service delivery systems, the American Customer Satisfaction Index

(ACSI) has exhibited generally lower scores for services compared to those of products, which indicates that many customers still perceive low quality of services in general.[6] The low indices imply that customers are generally not satisfied with the services they receive from service firms. The inherent characteristics of services and increasing customers' expectations of high-quality services, due to the excellent services they received from some firms, may contribute to customers' perceptions of the overall low service quality. Therefore, the indices suggest that there is much room for service firms to improve their service quality.

Service quality is the customers' perception of how well a service meets or exceeds their expectations and has multiple dimensions.[7] The most well-known dimensions are:

Reliability — the ability to perform promised services dependably and accurately

Responsiveness — the willingness to help customers and to provide prompt services

Assurance — the employees' knowledge or competence to convey trust and confidence in services

Empathy — the caring and individual attention by service providers

Tangibles — the physical evidence of services such as facilities, personnel, equipment, and ambient conditions such as color, music, and temperature

It is well known that quality services enable service firms to retain customers for a long period of time, which, in turn, positively affects lowering operating costs, increasing the volume of customers' purchases, providing the ability to charge higher prices, and achieving positive word-of-mouth among potential customers. High-quality services bring profits to service firms.[8] Thus, service marketers need to understand what customers expect and then develop quality services that meet their expectations to remain successful and competitive in the market.

Electronic (E) or Internet Marketing

The development and expansion of Internet-related technologies have offered new opportunities for many firms. The increasing number of Internet users provides potential opportunities for marketers domestically and internationally. For example, approximately 186 million Americans used the Internet in 2004 and the number is expected to rise to 247 million in 2009.[9] Approximately 935 million people in the world used the Internet in 2004 and the number is expected to reach 1.6 billion in 2009.[10] The U.S. online retail sales are expected to grow from $172 billion in 2005 to

$329 billion in 2010.[11] The 25 percent Internet-based sales growth from 2002 to 2003 outpaced the total retail growth that was 4 percent for the same period.[12] To meet the increasing Internet-based businesses, the advertising spending on the Internet is expected to account for approximately 10 percent in 2010 compared to 5 percent in 2004.[13] Many large firms such as Anheuser–Busch, Procter & Gamble, and Verizon have already begun to move portions of their advertising budgets from TV to the Web.

The Internet provides a lot of benefits to marketers and customers. One of the important benefits of marketing via the Internet is the interactivity between marketers and customers. Marketers provide visible information about the products or services on the Web, whereby customers can easily learn about them, thus shaping customers' perceptions and expectations of products or services. Customers also can provide quick feedback on products or services to firms, enabling them to adjust their offerings to meet customers' needs or demands in a relatively short period of time. Customers also have better access to the prices of products and can compare prices more easily than before to find the best value for them.

The Internet, however, still poses challenges for marketers; privacy concerns related to improper use of personal information, spam e-mails to customers, the protection of intellectual property rights, and how to cope with "the digital divide" must still be addressed. Marketers not only need to address the above issues but also need to come up with appropriate Internet marketing strategies to keep pace with the very dynamic and rapidly changing nature of the Internet.

CUSTOMER RELATIONSHIP MANAGEMENT (CRM)

One of the key activities that marketers should understand is how to effectively manage positive relationships with customers. Firms focus on CRM to have quality relationships with customers. CRM consists of the firm's activities to build, retain, and sustain long-term relationships with customers, whereby it tries to improve profitability in the long run.[14] To have an effective CRM system, the first task for the firm is to maximize the collection of customer information. Internet and information technology enable the firm to easily target specific customers, learn about their unique needs, analyze their behavior, and provide the best value to them. An effective CRM mainly depends on technologies based on advanced databases and analytical tools to analyze customer data and provide better products or services. For example, data mining, which is involved in specialized statistical software programs, allows a firm to uncover and predict customer behavior and purchase patterns. The firm can then tailor its marketing strategies to meet the customers' specific needs. Web sites or call centers are also examples of CRM systems that are used to support customer services, whereby the firm manages positive relationships with customers.

Although sophisticated statistical analytic software and information technologies play a critical role in the success of CRM implementation, it is not just the software or technologies that drive the building, maintaining, and sustaining of customer relationships. CRM means more than harnessing a technology-based customer database. CRM is the overall firm commitment to the development of proactive customer relationship strategies that are combined with other business strategies. The purpose of CRM is to provide satisfaction for customers. CRM is more than the simple reduction of marketing costs and more efficient interactions with customers; it is the building of a long-lasting customer-centric orientation within the firm.

SOCIAL MARKETING: LEGAL AND ETHICAL ISSUES IN MARKETING

A firm's primary task is to determine the needs, wants, and interests of target customers and to deliver their desired needs to them, but the firm must ensure that its marketing activities are socially responsible, within the law, and ethically acceptable by the general society. Such marketing activities, involve, but are not limited to, promoting deceptive advertising, distributing illegal or pirated products, and selling health and safety-related products such as alcohol, tobacco products, guns, and hamburgers. Some people advocate that marketers should accept social and ethical responsibility. They argue that business or marketing must maintain a balance between customers' wants and needs and customers' long-term welfare.

In assuming the responsibility for consumers' welfare, firms are involved in social marketing, "the use of marketing principles and techniques to influence a target audience to voluntarily accept, reject, or abandon a behavior for the benefit of individuals, groups, and society as a whole."[15] One of the social marketing strategies is a demarketing strategy, which is used to reduce demand for products or services.[16] The antitobacco campaign targeting youngsters or warnings that address the safe and sane consumption of alcohol are the examples of a demarketing strategy. Some marketers also engage in green marketing, which highlights the environmentally friendly aspects of their products as with hybrid cars, to address the concerns of social responsibility of firms.

Marketers need to be aware of ethical standards when conducting marketing activities. Although the activities of marketers may not be legally wrong, marketers should also understand ethical standards accepted by industries, government, customers, special interest groups, and society in general, to make sure that their decisions and actions are acceptable to them. It is important for firms to understand that unethical marketing practices can jeopardize either their short- or long-term business success.

REFERENCES

1. www.marketingpower.com, accessed on December 2005.
2. Pride, W.M. and Ferrell, O.C., *Marketing: Concepts and Strategies*, Houghton Mifflin Company, Boston, MA, 2006.
3. Ibid.
4. Zeithmal, V.A., Bitner, M.J., and Gremler, D.D., *Services Marketing: Integrating Customer Focus Across the Firm*, 4th ed., McGraw-Hill/Irwin, New York, 2005.
5. http://www.starbucks.com, accessed on November 2005.
6. http://www.theacsi.org, accessed on December 2005.
7. Parasuraman, Z. and Berry, L.L., A conceptual model of service quality and its implications for future research, *Journal of Marketing*, Fall 1985.
8. Zeithmal, V.A., Bitner, M.J., and Gremler, D.D., *Services Marketing: Integrating Customer Focus Across the Firm*.
9. http://www.etforecasts.com/products/ES_intusersv2.htm, accessed on January 2006.
10. Ibid.
11. http://www.madma.org/madma/oct05forrester, accessed on December 2005.
12. http://www.census.gov/eos/www/papers/2003/2003finaltext.pdf, accessed on December 2005.
13. http://www.clickz.com/stats/sectors/advertising/article.php/3569616, accessed on December 2005.
14. Crosby, L.A. and Johnson. S.L., Customer relationship management, *Marketing Management*, Fall 2002.
15. Kolter, P., Roberto, N., and Lee, N., *Social Marketing: Improving the Quality of Life*, 2nd ed., Sage Publications, Thousand Oaks, CA, 2002, p. 5.
16. Kotler, P., *Marketing Management*, Prentice Hall, Upper Saddle River, NJ, 2000, p. 6.

9

FINANCIAL STATEMENTS

Cheryl Frohlich

Every graduate of a university business school plans, some day, to manage his or her own division in a company. For some, the graduate's aspirations may expand to manage an entire company or to own a business. Whatever the career aspiration may be, the one undeniable fact is that, in business, an understanding of financial statements is essential for success.

One needs to understand (1) the current and the future state of the economy to understand what is likely to happen to the market and (2) the economic factors that affect stock prices. Given the forecasted economic relationship, then one may use the second step of fundamental analysis, industry analysis, to determine which industry will succeed and then, finally, what companies within the chosen industry will do well.

The ability to analyze the financial statements of a company not only reveals the company position but pinpoints its strengths and weaknesses. It is through magnifying the strengths and correcting the weaknesses that the future success of the company can be enhanced. The financial analysts make recommendations to the investment community, based upon their analysis of financial statements. Individuals who are investing (investors) make judgments about the company's securities. Investors look for growth in their securities whereas lenders (management of financial institutions) prefer to examine the company's stability and the cash flow. Furthermore, the financial analysts' review of the financial statements highlight areas in which management may expend further attention to improve the performance of the company.

MACROECONOMIC ANALYSIS

Macroeconomic analysis is the study of the economy as a whole, including the causes of the business cycle. Macroeconomics ignores the demand and supply for individual goods and instead looks at the demand and supply of all goods. The main tool of macroeconomics is the aggregate demand and supply diagram as shown in Figure 9.1. The quantity on the horizontal axis is the total output of the whole economy, whereas the vertical axis is the price of the output. The aggregate demand curve is the total amount of goods demanded in an economy (the total amount of goods that people want to buy). Aggregate demand equals the sum of consumption, invest-ment, government, and net export expenditures that people want to make. The aggregate demand curve shows that aggregate demand rises when the price level falls. Aggregate supply equals the sum of the money supply, transaction demand, and the speculative demand for money. The aggregate supply curve shows that the aggregate supply falls when the price level rises. Equilibrium results when companies produce the quantity of goods that people want to buy (aggregate supply equals aggregate demand). Both the aggregate demand and supply will shift because of changes in the amount demanded by customers. As a result, the price and the quantity demanded will change.

Economic indicators are at the center of a feedback mechanism oper-ating through economic activity, economic policy, and investor behavior. These indicators measure how the economy is currently performing and suggest how it will perform in the future. Stocks and bonds normally move in different directions. When the economy is expanding (growing), stock prices usually increase whereas bond prices decline.

This activity would suggest that the stock market should go up if the Gross Domestic Product (GDP) goes up. However, the important issue is

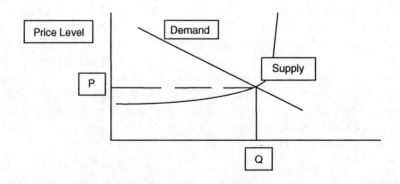

Figure 9.1 Aggregate supply and demand (short-run).

not whether it goes up, but how the movement relates to the expectations in the market. Upward movements that are larger than expected will generally increase stock prices, whereas upward movements less than expected will tend to lower stock prices. If the expectations are fully realized, there should be no change in stock prices because the market has already fully discounted the movement in GDP. Thus, the markets react only to unanticipated news.

One notable departure from the pattern that stocks and bonds move in different directions is the reaction to inflation. Unanticipated good news about inflation (lower than expected) drives the interest rate down and has a positive effect on both the stock and bond market. The basic question is: How do the stock and bond markets react to improvements in each of the economic indicators? The final column in Table 9.1 shows the "conventional wisdom" about how prices react to good news about an indicator. In general, good news about any of the indicators related to expenditure drives stock prices up and bond prices down.

Table 9.1 Predicted Market Price Response to "Good News" to Movement of Economic Indicators

Name	Supply (s) or Demand (d) Factor	Predicted Market Price Response to "Good News"[a]
Nominal GDP	D	Bonds — down Stocks — up
Real GDP	D	Bonds — down Stocks — up
Consumer price index (CPI)	S/D	Bonds — down Stocks — up
Unemployment rate	S/D	Bonds — down Stocks — up
Disposable personal income	S	Bonds — down Stocks — up
Personal consumption expenditures	D	Bonds — down Stocks — up
Net (disposable personal income minus personal consumption expenditures)	S	Bonds — down Stocks — up
Personal savings rate	S	Bonds — down Stocks — up

Table 9.1 (continued) Predicted Market Price Response to "Good News" to Movement of Economic Indicators

Name	Supply (s) or Demand (d) Factor	Predicted Market Price Response to "Good News"[a]
Consumer sentiment	S/D	Bonds — down Stocks — up
Light-weight vehicle sales — automatic and light trucks	D	Bonds — down Stocks — up
Retail and food services sales	D	Bonds — down Stocks — up
Durable good sales	D	Bonds — down Stocks — up
New one-family housing sold	D	Bonds — down Stocks — up
Total: new privately owned housing units starts	D	Bonds — down Stocks — up
Housing permits	D	Bonds — down Stocks — up
Manufacturing and trade inventories	D	Bonds — down Stocks — up
Industrial production index	D	Bonds — down Stocks — up
Producer price index	D	Bonds — down Stocks — up
Spot oil prices — West Texas intermediate	D	Bonds — down Stocks — up
Money balances (M-2)	S	Bonds — down Stocks — up

[a] Market response as an indicator about probable security price reaction to good news about the indicator. Good news means the news is better than perceived or indicated. Bond yield is the opposite of a bond price reaction.

Source: From St. Louis Federal Reserve economic database Fred (http://research.stlouisfed.org/fred2/). With permission.

STOCK AND BOND VALUATIONS

To understand why stocks and bonds react in opposite directions with unanticipated news in the economy, one needs to reflect on the basics of bond and stock valuations. Valuation of stocks is more complicated because good news will likely affect both the numerator and denominator of the formula. The denominator behaves as it does in the bond formula — good news will increase interest rates, which lower value. Thus, bond prices are lowered with good news. However, good news about the economy means that companies will earn more, implying they will pay higher dividends in the future. This indicates that the numerator will increase with good news, driving up the value of the stock. Thus, in the stock valuation formula, there are two effects which work in opposite directions. Which one of these effects dominates? Conventional wisdom on Wall Street is that the effect on the numerator is usually stronger than the denominator, so that stock prices rise on good news. One notable departure from the pattern that stocks and bonds move in different directions is the reaction to inflation.

Most companies are influenced by economic expansions and contractions in the business cycle. An economic analysis helps one to estimate the future performance of the company during the subsequent business cycles. Subsequent to the economic changes within a country, an industry effect is significant. Industries affect the companies within them differently, but the relationship is always significant. The industry effect is strongest for industries with homogenous products. One should examine the industry's performance relative to aggregate economic activity. How does the industry react when the economy is expanding?

INDUSTRY EFFECT

The potential value of industry analysis can be seen by assessing the performance of different industries over time. Over a long time period, the Standard and Poor's monthly stock price index shows industries perform differently over time. An implication is that stock performance may be affected by the industry. Therefore, industries that are performing consistently over time should be acquired. However, one must question whether an industry's performance can be predicted reliably on the basis of past success. An industry's performance rankings may be inconsistent over time (uptrends and downtrends in the economy).

Furthermore, are industry classifications clear-cut? Industries cannot be casually identified and classified. A company's diversified line of business may cause classification problems. Industries continue to become more mixed in their activities and less identifiable with one product or service. Industries are classified by a standard industrial classification (SIC) code. The SIC code is based on census data and on the basis of what is produced. SIC codes have 11 divisions that have several major industry groups, designated by a two-digit code. The larger the number of SIC digits, the more specific the breakdown. The North American industry classification system (NAICS) has replaced the SIC codes, as this system uses six digits.

When one analyzes an industry, it may be done by its life-cycle stage. The life-cycle stages are the pioneering stage, expansion stage, stabilization or maturity stage, and a decline stage. In the pioneering stage, a company will experience rapid growth in demand and may attract other companies and venture capitalists. It is difficult to identify likely survivors during this stage. The expansion stage is where survivors from the pioneering stage are identified. These companies' operations are more stable and dependable. Considerable investment funds are attracted and dividends are likely to become payable. These companies have financial policies that are firmly established. The stabilization or maturity stage includes companies where growth has begun to be moderate. The costs of these companies are stable rather than decreasing and these companies tend to focus on sales, market share, and investment in the industry. The marketplace is full of these types of competitors. The pioneering stage offers the highest potential returns but also the greatest risks. Investors interested in capital gains should avoid the stabilization or maturity stage. As a result, the expansion stage provides the most interest to investors with growth that is rapid but orderly.

Once an investor has decided what the economy is going to do and, given the forecasted economic state, has determined in which industry they wish to invest, the next area that an investor would examine is the individual companies within that industry. They would examine the financial statements of the companies besides the common-size statement.

INDIVIDUAL COMPANIES

There are several types of financial statements, but the three that are discussed here are the balance sheet, the income statement, and the common-size statement. These can be examined from a historical perspective. The historical record of sales' and earnings' growth and price performance should be considered. Although the past cannot be simply extrapolated into the future, it does provide context.

BALANCE SHEET AND INCOME STATEMENT

The balance sheet shows the financial condition or financial position of a company on a particular date. It is a summary of what a company owns (assets) and what it owes to others (liabilities) and to internal owners (stockholders). Assets are recorded on the balance sheet at the price the company paid for them (historical cost). The liabilities are amounts the company owes its creditors, and the stockholders' equity is the difference

Table 9.2   Balance Sheet

Assets			Liabilities		
Cash	$2,000		Accounts payable	$4,500	
Accounts receivable	7,000		Accruals	1,500	
Inventory	4,000		Current liabilities		$6,000
Current assets		$13,000			
Fixed assets			Long-term debt	$7,000	
Gross	$6,000		Long-term liabilities		$7,000
Accumulated depreciation	(1,000)		Equity	5,000	
Net		$5,000	Total capital		$5,000
			Total liabilities and equity		$18,000
Total assets		$18,000			

between total assets and liabilities. The income statement presents revenues, expenses, net income, and earnings per share (EPS) for an accounting period. The income statement in the common-size statement form is a statement of ratios of the income statement line items to net sales revenue. The balance sheet in the common-size statement form is a statement of ratios of the balance sheet items relative to total assets. Common-size financial statements allow trends in financial performance to be detected and monitored more easily than with financial statements showing only dollar amounts. The common-size statement facilitates operating comparisons over time and between companies of different sizes. More details are provided near the end of this chapter.

First let's look at the balance sheet. The balance sheet shows the total assets equated to total liabilities plus net worth (equity). The balance sheet is arranged in order of decreasing liquidity. The balance sheet is also referred to as the statement of condition or statement of financial position. A simple example of a balance sheet is provided in Table 9.2.

Assets

Assets can be further classified as current and fixed assets.

Current assets: Current assets are due within a year. They include cash, accounts receivables, prepaid expenses, and inventory. Cash includes such items as checking accounts and currency. Accounts receivable includes such items as anything that is due from sales on credit.

Inventory includes the raw materials, work-in-process, and finished goods.

Fixed assets: Fixed assets are those items that are long-lived and depreciated. The value is stated as net of their accumulated depreciation.

Current Liabilities

Current liabilities are due within a year. Basically, accounts payable and notes payable are the main constituents of the current liabilities. Accounts payable are due from purchases on credit and reflect the terms of sale. Notes payable are current maturities on long-term debt.

Long-Term Debt

Bonds and loans are long-term debt. This debt generates an interest expense. With increasing interest expense there is an increased risk of failure.

Equity

Equity is the direct investment by owners paying for the stock. Under the equity section, one would find the par value of the stock and the paid-in-excess accounts. As earnings arrive they are applied to the retained earnings account.

Our next review will be to examine the income categories of ratios. They are:

1. Liquidity
2 Activity — asset/liability management
3 Debt management — financial leverage
4 Profitability
5 Market value

One must remember that ratios do not provide answers but they do help one to consider the right questions. We will start with the liquidity ratios.

Liquidity Ratios

Any company that intends to remain a viable business must have enough cash on hand to pay its bills as they become due. In other words, the company must be liquid. The liquidity ratios are quick measures of a company's ability to provide sufficient cash to conduct business over the next few months.

This section discusses four different liquidity ratios: the current ratio, the quick ratio, the adjusted quick ratio, and the cash-flow liquidity ratio.

Current Ratio

$$\frac{\text{Current Assets}}{\text{Current Liabilities}} = X$$

Current assets are cash and any assets that can be converted into cash within a normal operating period of 12 months. Some analysts eliminate prepaid expenses and supplies from the numerator because they are not a source of cash. Current liabilities are any financial obligations expected to fall due within the next year. The current ratio captures the ability to convert (sell) current assets at $1.00/X to meet current liabilities (i.e., if X equals 1.5, then current assets must be liquidated at 67 cents on the dollar). If the industry average of the current ratio is 2.00, then the average company in the industry must convert only $.50 ($1.00/2 = $.50) of each dollar of current assets into cash to meet short-term obligations.

Cash-Flow Liquidity Ratio

$$\frac{\text{Cash} + \text{Marketable Securities} + \text{Cash Flow from Operating Activities}}{\text{Current Liabilities}} = X'$$

The fact that a current ratio is below the industrial average does not mean that the company would consider closing its doors. Nor does it mean that the company's creditors are less protected than creditors of companies within the industry that have a higher current ratio than the one just computed. This ratio only provides one standard for measuring liquidity. One must continue looking at the liquidity ratios to determine if the company has a problem.

Quick Ratio

$$\frac{\text{Current Assets} - \text{Inventories}}{\text{Current Liabilities}} = Y$$

This ratio is often called the acid test because it provides a more stringent measure of liquidity than the current ratio. Inventories are often a company's least-liquid current assets. The quick ratio captures the ability to convert (sell) current assets (less inventory) at $1.00/Y to meet current liabilities (i.e., if Y equals 1.5, then current assets must be liquidated at 67 cents on the dollar). As Y becomes smaller they must be liquidated at full value.

If the liquidity of a company's receivables is doubted, one may wish to prepare an aging schedule. To construct an aging schedule, one would need to know what are the company's selling terms and its receivables. If a company expected to be paid within 30 days, then, if the aging schedule indicated that the majority of the receivables were over 30 days, it would indicate many accounts are past due. However, the crucial point is when one considers the percentage of accounts that are over 90 days past due.

Adjusted Quick Ratio

$$\frac{\text{Current Assets} - \text{Inventories} - \text{Accounts Receivable over 90 days}}{\text{Current Liabilities}}$$

If the adjusted quick ratio is significantly different from the quick ratio, it may indicate a collection problem. However, the data required to prepare an aging schedule, which is necessary to determine those account receivables over 90 days, is not available to outside analysts. Therefore, the aging schedule is primarily for those within the organization.

Asset and Liability Management Ratios

One objective is to determine how a company's resources can be best distributed among the various asset accounts. If a proper mix of the company's cash, receivables, inventories, plant, property, and equipment can be achieved, the company's asset structure will be more effective in generating sales revenue.

Asset management ratios indicate how much a company has invested in a particular type of asset relative to the revenue the asset is producing. By comparing asset management ratios to industrial norms, one can determine how efficiently the company is allocating its resources. The accounts receivable turnover is the number of times that net sales divided by account receivables occurs.

Account Receivable Turnover: $\dfrac{\text{Net Sales}}{\text{Accounts Receivable}} = \text{X times}$

If the account receivable turnover computed X times is greater than the industry norm, then the company has lower sales for the amount of account receivables carried. This could indicate a problem in sales or account receivable policies.

The average collection period is the average number of days an account receivable remains outstanding. It is normally determined by dividing the company's year-end receivables by the average daily credit sales.

$$\textbf{Average Collection Period: } \frac{\text{Accounts Receivable}}{(\text{Annual Credit Sales}/365)} = \text{X days}$$

The average collection period determines how long resources are tied up in receivables. If X is less than the industry norm, then the company may have a too restrictive credit policy. If the average collection period X is greater than the industry norm, then the company may have problems with collection or the company may have a too lenient credit policy.

An average collection period that is substantially above the industry norm is usually not desirable. However, an average collection period far below the industry norm may indicate that the company's credit terms are too stringent and are hurting the company's sales.

Although the cost of sales is usually listed in the income statement, the average inventory has to be calculated. This can be done in a number of ways. The day's inventory may be calculated or the average inventory may be determined. If the company has seasonal sales, then the average inventory can be calculated by adding each month-end value for inventory and dividing by twelve.

$$\textbf{Inventory Turnover Ratio: } \frac{\text{Cost of Goods Sold}}{\text{Average Inventories}} = \text{X times}$$

To calculate the day's inventory, the following formula may be used:

$$\textbf{Days Inventory: } \frac{365}{((\text{Cost of Goods Sold}/\text{Inventory}) \text{ Ratio})} = \text{X days}$$

To calculate the average inventory, the following formula may be used:

$$\textbf{Average Inventory: } \frac{\text{beginning} + \text{ending}}{2}$$

If your company has seasonal sales, then the average inventory may be determined as follows:

Seasonal Sales Average Inventory:

$$\frac{\text{Add Month-End Inventory}}{12} = \text{X times}$$

If the calculated X times or days is less than the industry norm, then the company may be carrying too much inventory or the inventory may be obsolete, damaged, or slow-moving. If the calculated X is greater than the industry norm, then there may be problems with restocking, which may cause loss of sales.

Although the next ratio is not always seen within the normal text, it is one that is very good at determining the ability of the company to make payments on its accounts. It is termed days payable and is computed by taking the Cost of Goods Sold, divided by the Payables, to produce a ratio. By dividing 365 by this ratio (Cost of Goods divided by the Payables) the number of days that the payable is outstanding is obtained.

$$\textbf{Days Payable:} \quad \frac{365}{((\text{Cost of Goods Sold/Payables}) \text{ Ratio})} = \text{X days}$$

If the computed X days is greater then the industry norm, then there may be problems with the company stretching payables, which may cause vendors to put the company on a cash on delivery (COD) basis.

The fixed-asset turnover ratio indicates the extent to which a company is using its existing property, plant, and equipment to generate sales.

$$\textbf{Fixed-Asset Turnover Ratio:} \quad \frac{\text{Net Sales}}{\text{Net Fixed Assets}} = \text{X times}$$

The balance sheet figures that show a company's property, plant, or equipment are affected by several factors, such as:

- The cost of the assets when acquired
- The length of time since acquisition
- The depreciation policies adopted by the company
- The extent to which fixed assets may be leased rather than owned

Therefore, it is possible for companies with virtually identical plants to have significantly different fixed-asset turnover ratios. Thus, this ratio should be used primarily within a company to determine yearly comparisons.

The total-asset turnover ratio indicates how effectively a company uses its total resources to generate sales. Typically, if this ratio is not at an industry norm, one would use it as a flag indicating the need to look at other activity ratios.

$$\textbf{Total-Asset Turnover Ratio:} \quad \frac{\text{Net Sales}}{\text{Total Assets}} = \text{X times}$$

If the X times is less than the industry norm, then the company may be using assets less efficiently and, therefore, one may need to look at other activity ratios.

Debt Management Ratios

Debt management ratios measure the company's debt level using ending balances relative to the company's assets, equity, and income. These ratios indicate a company's capacity to meet short- and long-term debt.

Balance-Sheet Approach

The debt ratio measures the proportion of a company's total assets that are financed with creditors' funds.

$$\textbf{Debt Ratio: } \frac{\text{Total Debt}}{\text{Total Assets}} = Y$$

If Y equals 0.58, then 58 percent of assets are financed by internal debt. The higher the ratio, the lower the protection creditors have in the event of bankruptcy. If the debt ratio = 85 percent, then the total assets value can decrease by 15 percent before creditors are at risk. If Y is greater than the industry norm, then the company is borrowing more than the norm of the industry and the company's cost will be higher. A company's ability to maintain a high debt ratio depends upon the debt ratio growth and the stability of cash flows.

Debt-to-equity measures the riskiness of the company's capital structure in terms of the relationship between creditors and investors. In other words, it relates the amount of a company's debt financing to the amount of equity financing.

$$\textbf{Debt to Equity: } \frac{\text{Total Debt}}{\text{Total Equity}} = Y$$

If Y equals 1.5, then 150 percent debt financing is used compared to equity (for every $1 of equity raise $1.50 in debt) financing. The greater the ratio, the company's debt suppliers have a lower margin of safety compared to those companies within the industry with a lower ratio.

Income Statement (Debt Coverage Ratios)

The debt coverage ratios measure the company's ability to service debt with operating income and cash flows. The first of the debt coverage ratios will be the times interest earned ratio.

It measures the interest charges relative to the company's ability to pay them.

$$\textbf{Times Interest Earned Ratio:} \quad \frac{\text{EBIT}}{\text{Interest Charges}} = \text{X times}$$

If the times interest earned ratio is 3.65, the company's annual interest payments are covered 3.65 times by the company's current earnings.

A variation on times interest earned ratio to achieve a better measure of the company's cash flow is the cash coverage ratio.

$$\textbf{Cash Coverage Ratio:} \quad \frac{\text{EBIT} + \text{Depreciation}}{\text{Interest}} = \text{X times}$$

The fixed charge coverage ratio is a variation on the times interest earned ratio to include lease payments as fixed financial charges equivalent to interest. It measures the number of times a company is able to cover fixed charges.

Fixed Charge Coverage Ratio:

$$\frac{\text{EBIT} + \text{Lease Payments}}{\text{Interest} + \text{Lease Payments} + \text{Preferred Dividends Before Tax} + \text{Before Tax Sinking Fund}} = \text{X times}$$

Lease payments are added back into the numerator because they were deducted as an operating expense to calculate operating profits. They are similar to interest expense in that they both represent obligations that must be met on an annual basis.

If X equals 1.65 times, then the fixed charges can be covered 1.65 times by EBIT and lease payments. If X is less than the industry norm, the company is operating at a higher level of risk and will have problems in securing credit.

The cash flow adequacy ratio measures how well a company can cover annual payments such as debt, capital expenditures, and dividends from operating cash flow.

Cash Flow Adequacy Ratio:

$$\frac{\text{Cash Flow from Operating Activities}}{\text{Average Annual Long-Term Debt Maturities}} = \text{X times}$$

Profitability Ratios

Profitability ratios, using average balances, measure the profitability of a company relative to the company's sales, assets, and the owners' investment (equity-owners). It also measures how effectively a company's management generates profits on sales, assets, and owners' investments.

Gross profit margin measures the relative profitability of a company's sales after the cost of goods sold has been deducted. This gross profit margin reveals how well the company is making decisions relative to its pricing and control of production costs.

$$\textbf{Gross Profit Margin:} \quad \frac{\text{Sales} - \text{Cost of Goods Sold}}{\text{Sales}} = Y$$

If Y is equal to .2463, then the company's gross profit margin is 24.63 percent. The gross profit margin is the company's return before payment of operating expenses, interest, or taxes. If Y is less than the industry norm, there are problems in either the pricing policies or in the production methods. Further investigation into the company would be demanded by such a revelation and the activity ratios would be analyzed next.

The net profit margin measures how profitable a company's sales are after all expenses, including taxes and interest, have been deducted.

$$\textbf{Net Profit Margin (return on sales):} \quad \frac{\text{Earnings After Taxes}}{\text{Sales}} = Y$$

Some analysts also compute and examine an operating profit margin ratio. It measures the profitability of a company's operations before considering the effects of financing decisions. As the ratio is computed before considering interest charges, this ratio is often more suitable for comparing profit performance of different companies.

$$\textbf{Operating Profit Margin:} \quad \frac{\text{EBIT}}{\text{Sales}} = Y$$

By using this ratio, it separates financing decisions from performance. It is usually more suitable for comparing the profit performance of different companies. If Y is less than the industry norm, the company is likely to have problems controlling total expenses or determining pricing policies.

The cash flow margin measures the ability of the company to convert sales into cash and is defined as follows:

$$\textbf{Cash Flow Margin:} \quad \frac{\text{Cash flow from Operating Activities}}{\text{Net Sales}}$$

The return on investment (ROI) measures a company's net income in relation to the total assets and is defined as follows:

$$\textbf{ROI:} \quad \frac{\text{EAT}}{\text{Total Assets}} = Y$$

The ROI is also the net profit margin times the total asset turnover and is defined as follows:

$$\textbf{ROI:} \quad \frac{\text{EAT}}{\text{Sales}} \times \frac{\text{Sales}}{\text{Total Assets}} = Y$$

If Y is less than the industry norm, then the company has problems. These problems are either low activity ratios or a low profit margin.

The return on equity measures the rate of return that the company earns on the stockholders' equity.

$$\textbf{Return on Equity (ROE):} \quad \frac{\text{EAT}}{\text{Stockholders' Equity}} = Y$$

$$\textbf{ROE = ROI} \times \textbf{Equity Multiplier} = \frac{\text{EAT}}{\text{Sales}} \times \frac{\text{Sales}}{\text{Total Assets}} \times \frac{\text{Total Assets}}{\text{Equity}} = Y$$

If Y is less than the industry norm, then the company has problems with low activity ratios, low profit margins, or debt leverage.

Market Value Ratios

Market value ratios measure the market's opinion of the stock as an investment, based on its price, using ending balances. The financial ratios discussed in the previous four groups are all derived from accounting and income statements provided by a company. The market-based ratios for a company should parallel the accounting ratios of the company.

The price/earnings ratio (P/E) is the amount investors will pay for each dollar of earnings. It is based primarily on expected growth of the company.

$$\textbf{Price/Earnings Ratio (P/E):} \quad \frac{\text{Market Price per Share}}{\text{Current Earnings per Share}}$$

The P/E increases as the risk of a company drops. The P/E increases as earnings grow. If the P/E is less than the industry norm, such problems as higher risk or lower growth are occurring.

The market price to book value ratio identifies the going value of the company as perceived by investors. The ratio is affected by the accounting treatments used by a company in such vital areas as inventory valuation and depreciation. Therefore, comparisons between companies may be misleading.

$$\textbf{Market to Book Value Ratio (P/B):} \quad \frac{\text{Market Price per Share}}{\text{Book Value per Share}}$$

The higher the rate of return a company is earning on its common equity relative to the return required by investors, the higher will be the P/B ratio.

$$\textbf{Book Value:} \quad \frac{\text{Total Common Stockholders' Equity}}{\text{Number of Companies Outstanding}}$$

$$\textbf{Stockholders' Equity:} \quad \text{Total Assets} - \text{Total Liability}$$

Dividend Policy Ratios

The two primary dividend ratios, the payout ratio and the dividend yield ratio, yield insights regarding a company's dividend strategies and its future growth prospects.

The payout ratio indicates the percentage of a company's earnings that are paid out as dividends. It is defined as follows:

$$\textbf{Payout Ratio:} \quad \frac{\text{Dividend per Share}}{\text{Earnings per Share}}$$

Companies with stable earnings are more likely to pay out larger dividends than companies that have more volatile earnings. Also, companies that have large, continuing high return investment projects may be less likely to pay out large dividends because of their need to use the capital to finance these projects.

A stock's dividend yield is the expected yearly dividend divided by its current stock price. It is defined as:

$$\textbf{Dividend Yield:} \quad \frac{\text{Expected Dividend per Share}}{\text{Stock Price}}$$

The returns received by an investor in common stock are the sum of the dividend yield and the expected growth in the company's earnings, dividends, and stock price. Stocks with low dividend yields often indicate high expected future growth, whereas high dividend yields, such as the ones that utility companies use, are frequently signs of low future growth prospects.

COMMON-SIZE FINANCIAL STATEMENTS

A common-size balance sheet shows the company's assets and liabilities and stockholder's equity as a percentage of total assets. A common-size income statement lists the company's income and expense items as a percentage of net sales. Common-size financial statements allow trends in financial performance to be more easily computed and monitored than using the financial statements that show only the dollar amounts. Common-size statements are helpful in detecting and monitoring financial trends.

SUMMARY

We have now completed looking at the analysis of the current and future state of the economy and the economic factors that affect the stock prices. Furthermore, we have recalled what one must do to analyze the industry and to determine which industry will succeed given the forecasted economy, and then, finally, what companies within the chosen industry will do well.

As we said at the beginning of the chapter, the ability to analyze the financial statements of a company not only reveals the company's position but pinpoints its strengths and weaknesses. It is through magnifying the strengths and correcting the weaknesses that the future success of the company can be enhanced. The financial analyst makes recommendations to the investment community based upon his or her analysis of financial statements. The financial analyst's review of the financial statements highlights areas in which management may spend further attention to improve the performance of their companies.

SELECTED BIBLIOGRAPHY

Lasher, W.R., *Practical Financial Management*, 4th ed., Thomson and South-Western, Cincinnati, OH.

Moyer, R.C., McGuigan, J.R., and Kretlow, W.J., *Contemporary Financial Management*, 9th ed., Thomson and South-Western, Mason, OH.

Reilly, F.K. and Brown, K.C., *Investment Analysis Portfolio Management*, 7th ed., Thomson and South-Western, Cincinnati, OH.

Wessels, W.J., *Economics*, 3rd ed., Barrons, Hauppauge, NY.

Weston, J.F., Besley, S., and Brigham, E.F., *Essentials of Managerial Finance,* 11th ed., The Dryden Press, Orlando, FL.

10

PRODUCTION AND OPERATIONS MANAGEMENT

Antony Paulraj

Production and operations management relates to the creation of goods and services through effective use of people, material, and machines. In the past, when the field was related primarily to manufacturing, it was called production management. Later, the name was expanded to production and operations management (POM) or more simply, operations management (OM), to include service industries as well. POM is the business function that primarily plans, organizes, coordinates, and controls the resources needed to produce a company's goods or services. It is further considered as the central part or "hub" of every company, whether it (1) is large or small, (2) provides a physical good or a service, and (3) is for profit or not for profit. Without operations, there would be no goods or services to sell to customers. Accordingly, every company has a production/operations function. In fact, the other organizational functions exist to provide support to the production/operations function. The marketing function provides promotions for the merchandise and information on customer requirements, and the finance function provides the required capital investments. It is the operations function, however, that plans and coordinates all the resources needed to design, produce, and deliver the merchandise to the various retail locations.

Although the specific nature differs among enterprises, the main principles and functions of POM are the same. It is responsible for orchestrating all the resources needed to produce the end product. Among others, it includes designing the product; deciding what resources are needed; acquiring resources; arranging schedules, equipment, and facilities; planning and controlling production; managing inventory; controlling product quality; and measuring performance. In general, POM is responsible for all aspects of the process of transforming inputs into outputs. Specifically, it must ensure that the transformation process is performed efficiently and that the output is of greater value than the sum of all inputs. Thus, the role of operations is to create or add value. The greater the value added, the more productive a business is. An obvious way to add value is to reduce the cost of activities in the transformation process. Activities that do not add value are considered superfluous and must be eliminated. In addition to value added, production/operations must also be efficient. In other words, all activities must be performed well, and at the lowest possible cost. In summary, an important role of operations is to analyze all activities, eliminate those that do not add value, and restructure processes and jobs to achieve greater efficiency.

Of all the business functions, operations are the most diverse in terms of the tasks performed. Production/operations managers hold crucial positions in every firm. The head of the operations function in a company usually holds the title of vice president of operations, vice president of manufacturing, or director of supply-chain operations and generally reports directly to the chief operating officer or the chief executive officer. Middle-level manager positions, including manufacturing manager, operations manager, plant manager, quality control manager, etc., fall directly under the vice president level. These managers perform a variety of tasks, such as designing products and processes, ensuring quality, monitoring inventory, and delivering services. Thus, there are many job opportunities within OM that offer high salaries, interesting work, and excellent opportunity for advancement.

OM is a highly important function in today's dynamic business environment. Accordingly, there are numerous issues, concepts, and techniques associated with the field of OM. In this chapter, we will survey some of the contemporary themes that make OM an exciting and interesting topic for aspiring managers and those who want the challenge of leadership. These topics include:

■ Product and service design
■ Process selection
■ Just-in-time and lean systems
■ Supply-chain management
■ Quality management

PRODUCT AND SERVICE DESIGN

The objective of any organization is to provide products or services to its customers. Organizations can gain a sustainable competitive advantage through designs that bring new ideas to the market quickly while simultaneously doing a better job at meeting customer requirements.[1] Product design brings together personnel from diverse functions, such as marketing, design and engineering, production, finance, and others, to think and plan strategically. It is highly creative and can lead to renewed success for the company. On the other hand, if neglected, it could badly ruin the company's current image. *Product design* defines the characteristics of a given product, such as its appearance, the materials it is made of, its specifications, and performance standards. *Service design* defines the service, including the entire service concept. As with a tangible product, the service concept is based on meeting customer needs. Service design adds to the esthetic and psychological benefits of the product. It also focuses on service elements of the operation, such as promptness, friendliness, ambiance, and image among others.

Certain steps are pertinent in the development of a new product. They are idea generation, product feasibility screening, preliminary design and testing, and final design. Improving the design process involves completely restructuring the decision-making process and the participants in that process. The concept of functional silos should be completely replaced with new cross-functional alliances and modes of interaction. This can be achieved only through (1) multifunctional design teams; (2) concurrent engineering; (3) design for manufacture, assembly, and robustness; (4) quality function deployment; and (5) collaborative design. In this section, some of the tools and techniques that aid in the product development process are briefly discussed. The final subsection focuses on the design issues specific to service operations.

Concurrent Engineering

Concurrent engineering (CE) can be defined as the integration of interrelated functions at the outset of the design process so as to minimize risk as well as to better meet customers' needs. It brings many people together in the early phase to simultaneously design the product and the process.[2] In the traditional sequential product-design process, also called the "over-the-wall" approach, there is little or no cross-communication among various functions, and information generated from one activity is handed off to the next only after its completion. The commonly encountered problems with this traditional approach are increased effort, development time, and cost. On the contrary, CE overcomes these obstacles by taking into account the inherent interdependencies that exist between product and process design. Multifunctional teams, concurrency of product/process development, integration tools, information technologies, and process coordination are among the key elements that enable CE to improve performance. Though it is more challenging to coordinate, the potential benefits of a CE process are considerable. It helps to improve the quality of early design decisions and thereby reduces the length and cost of the design process. It enables many organizations to improve their product development, production, product support, and customer relationships. Evidence suggests that when a CE approach is appropriately designed and implemented, organizational performance improves significantly, resulting in lower cost, improved product quality, reduction in cycle time and time-to-market, and improved utilization and coordination of human resources.

Quality Function Deployment

Quality function deployment (QFD) is the complete process that uses a structured and systematic method to transform the voice of the customers into the design, components, manufacturing, and cost of product or service.[3] QFD uses a series of matrix diagrams that resemble connected houses to convert customer requirements into product design characteristics including technical specifications. It has six sections: a customer requirements section, a competitive assessment section, a design characteristics section, a relationship matrix, a trade-off section, and a target-value section. Each section's important outputs (HOWs), generated from its inputs (WHATs), are converted into the next section as its inputs (WHATs). Therefore, each section can be described by a matrix of WHATs and HOWs, which is easy and convenient to deal with in practice. The first section of QFD, usually called the "house of quality," is of fundamental importance in the QFD system, because it is in this section that the customer needs for the product are identified and then, incorporating the company's competitive priorities, converted into appropriate technical requirements to fulfill the customer needs. The house of quality has been found to be very useful in increasing cross-functional communications because it neatly connects the market requirements, which the customer values, with the design characteristics that the engineers must consider. Thus, a design can be developed that will meet the needs of the market while still considering all the design trade-offs required. QFD can also be applied to service industries in much the same way as manufacturing. Its purpose is based on satisfying demand and creating value with customers. There are several benefits to using QFD. Besides requiring fewer resources than other quality tools, QFD can (1) improve a company's processes, products, or services; (2) produce a faster outcome; (3) give definition to the design process; (4) facilitate interfunctional cooperation; (5) help a team stay focused; and (6) allow for easy management and peer review of design activities.

Design for Manufacture, Assembly, and Robustness

When designing products, we generally think of how to please the customer. However, as illustrated earlier, we also need to consider how easy or difficult it is to manufacture as well as assemble the product. Otherwise, it would be difficult or too costly to manufacture and assemble the product.[4] Design for manufacturing (DFM) is an approach that deals with (1) simplification of the product design and (2) manufacture of multiple products using common parts, processes, and modules. Design simplification reduces the number of parts and features of the product whenever possible.

A simpler product is easier to make, costs less, and gives higher quality. Products are usually designed one at a time without much regard for commonality of parts or modular properties that can aid production while still meeting customer needs. Modular design makes it possible to have relatively high product variety and low component variety at the same time. The core idea is to develop a series of basic product components, or modules, that can be assembled into a large number of different products. Modular design, a prerequisite to mass customization, offers a fundamental way to change product-design thinking. Instead of designing each product separately, the firm designs products around standard component modules and standard processes. The approach will still allow for a great deal of product variety, but the number of unnecessary product variations will be reduced.

Design for assembly (DFA) is a set of procedures for reducing the number of parts in an assembly, evaluating methods for assembly, and determining an appropriate assembly sequence.[5] It provides guidelines for (1) choosing between manual and automated assembly, (2) avoiding part tangling in feeding operations, (3) finding the fewest assembly steps, and (4) determining the most foolproof sequence of assembly.

Customers subject products to extreme operating conditions and at the same time expect them to function normally. A product that is designed to withstand extreme variations in environmental and operating conditions is said to be robust or to possess robust quality. Superior quality is derived from products that are robust, and robust products are a result of robust design.[6] The various conditions that cause a product to operate poorly can be grouped into controllable and uncontrollable factors. From a designer's point of view, the controllable factors are design parameters such as material used, specifications, and form of processing. Uncontrollable factors such as length of use, maintenance, and settings are under the user's control. The underlying objective of the design for robustness is to choose values of the controllable factors that react in a robust fashion to the possible occurrences of uncontrollable factors.

Designing Services

The two basic features that make service organizations different from manufacturing are (1) intangibility of the product manufactured and (2) high degree of customer contact. Because of the unique nature of services, service design is more comprehensive and occurs more often than product design. Service design starts with the service concept, which defines (1) the target customer, (2) the desired customer experience, (3) how a firm's service is different from others, and (4) how a firm will compete in the marketplace. From the service concept, a service package is created to meet customer needs. The service package is a grouping of features that are purchased together as part of the service. The three critical elements of the service package are (1) the physical goods, (2) the sensual benefits, and (3) the psychological benefits.[7] Effective service design recognizes and defines all the components of a service package. It not only focuses on the tangible aspects, but also considers the sensual and psychological benefits, which are the deciding factors in the success of the service. The service package should be designed to precisely meet the expectations of target customers. From the service package, specifications are developed for performance, design, and delivery. Performance specifications outline the requirements of general and specific customers. Performance specifications are converted into design specifications, which typically describe (1) the activities to be performed; (2) skill requirements and guidelines for service providers; (3) cost and time estimates; (4) facility size, location, and layout; and (5) equipment needs. Delivery specifications outline the steps required in the work process, including the work schedule, deliverables, and the locations at which the work is to be performed. Taking the time to design a service carefully, through direct customer participation, helps to prevent disagreements between customer and service provider and results in higher levels of customer satisfaction.[8]

PROCESS SELECTION

In the previous section, we discussed product design in detail. Though product design is important, it cannot be considered in isolation from the selection of the process that would be used to create the product. In this section, we will briefly discuss the issues involved in process design. A process is a group of related tasks with specific inputs and outputs. Process design defines the tasks that need to be done and further specifies how they need to be coordinated among functions, people, and organizations. Process selection decisions are strategic in nature and they require a long-term perspective and a great deal of cross-functional coordination.[9] These decisions further tend to be capital intensive and cannot be changed easily. Therefore, the firm is committed to the process choice for many years to come. In this section, we will discuss traditional forms of production processes and other modern concepts including mass customization and process reengineering. The section ends with a discussion on advancements in manufacturing technology.

Types of Processes

All processes can be grouped into two broad categories: intermittent and repetitive operations. The most common differences between intermittent and repetitive operations relate to the amount of product volume produced and the degree of product standardization. Intermittent operations are used to manufacture a variety of products with different processing requirements in lower volumes. To be able to manufacture products with different processing requirements, intermittent operations tend to be labor-intensive rather than capital-intensive. Equipment in this type of environment is more general purpose to satisfy different processing requirements. Given that products with different processing requirements are produced in lower volumes, it is usually not cost-effective to invest in automation. Intermittent operations can be further divided into project processes and batch processes. Project processes are used to make a unique product exactly to customer specifications. These processes are used when there is high customization and low product volume, because each product is different. Batch processes, also referred as job shops, are used to manufacture small quantities of products in batches or lots. The volume of each product is still low and subsequently requires a high degree of customization.

Repetitive operations are used to manufacture one or a few standardized products in high volume. To efficiently manufacture a large volume of one type of product, these operations tend to be capital-intensive. Often, these operations rely heavily on automation and technology to improve efficiency and increase output. Repetitive operations can be further divided into line processes and continuous processes. Line processes, also known as mass production, are used to manufacture more standardized products in larger quantities than batch production can economically handle. This process is capital-intensive and highly repetitive, with specialized equipment and limited labor skills. Continuous processes are used for very-high-volume product that is very standardized. The system is highly automated and is typically in operation continuously 24 hr a day. Firms that operate in this fashion are referred to as process industries. Pharmaceutical drugs and petroleum refining are examples of these types of industries.

Processes Planning

Process planning determines how a product is manufactured or a service provided.[10] First, it decides which components will be produced within a firm and which components will be purchased from an outside supplier. This preliminary sourcing decision is called make-or-buy and rests on the evaluation of multiple criteria, including cost, capacity, quality, speed, reliability, and expertise. Another critical decision is to decide whether the product is made/bought-to-order (MTO) or made/bought-to-stock (MTS). An MTS process can provide faster service to customers from available stock and lower costs than an MTO process. But, the MTO process has higher flexibility for product customization. Although the MTS process is measured by service level and efficiency in replenishing inventory, the MTO process is measured by its response time to customers and the efficiency in meeting its customer orders. Recently, assemble-to-order (ATO) processes have gained significant prominence. The ATO process, also known as build-to-order, produces subassemblies in advance of demand and puts them together at the last minute to satisfy customer demand. ATO is a hybrid process of MTO and MTS. After deciding that a part is produced or service provided in-house, specific equipment decisions can be made. Alternatives include using, replacing, or upgrading existing equipments, adding extra capacity, or purchasing new equipments. Any alternative that involves an outlay of funds is considered a capital investment and is usually large and can have a significant impact on the future profitability of the firm. Accordingly, these decisions are carefully analyzed using effective quantitative techniques and require approval from top management.

Process Analysis

Process analysis is the systematic explanation of all aspects of a process to make it faster, more efficient, less costly, or more responsive to the customer. The basic tools used for process analysis are process flowcharts, process diagrams, and process maps. Process flowcharts look at the manufacture of a product or delivery of a service from a broad perspective. The details of each process are not necessary for this chart. However, the time required to perform each process and the distance between processes are often included. These charts provide a standardized method for documenting the steps in a process and may be used to analyze the efficiency of a series of processes and suggest necessary improvements. Process diagrams detail each step of a process in a simple graphic form. More complex process diagrams are often called process maps. For service operations, flowcharting is called service blueprinting. It shows how the customer and service providers interact at each step of the service-delivery process. Each horizontal row on the blueprint is for a specific person, the customer, or one of the service providers. Service blueprinting is a very good way to show all points of interaction between the customer and one or more service providers. In total, the service blueprint shows the cycle of service from beginning to end.

Mass Customization

With the advent of advanced technologies, including flexible manufacturing, mass customization has gained prominence. Traditional mass production is built on economies of scale by means of a high volume standardized product with few options. On the other hand, mass customization depends on economies of scope, which reflects a high variety of products from a single process. Therefore, mass customization comes from a different economic basis, a common process rather than a common product.[11] Customers are integrated into the value creation by defining, configuring, matching, or modifying an individual solution. Customization demands that the recipients of the customized good transfer their needs and desires into a concrete product specification so as to facilitate a different product for each customer. But, mass customization is customization at approximately the same cost as mass production. This is a stringent requirement and means that some products cannot be mass-customized because the cost would be higher. The four forms of mass customization are: modular production and ATO, fast changeover (zero setup time between orders), postponement of options, and mass-customized services. Modular production provides a variety of options using an ATO process. Postponement facilitates delayed product differentiation by keeping the product in generic form as long as possible and postponing completion of the product until specific customer preferences are known.

Business Process Reengineering

Processes are planned in response to new facilities, products, technologies, markets, or customer expectations. These processes need to be analyzed on a continuous basis to look for possible improvements. When continual improvement efforts have been exhausted and performance expectations still cannot be reached with an existing process, it is time to completely redesign or reengineer the process. Business process reengineering (BPR) starts with the entire business and identifies critical processes required to meet the customers' needs. Then, these critical processes, many of which cut across organization boundaries, are analyzed in detail. As a result, core business processes are redesigned and integrated using specific just-in-time techniques and other information technology enablers to better serve the customer. BPR is the fundamental rethinking and radical redesign of business processes to achieve dramatic improvements.[12] BPR is most successful in organizations that can articulate a clear vision and strategic motivation for change, listen without bias to their customers, view their system as a set of processes overlapping functional areas, and rethink and simplify how value is provided to their customers.

Manufacturing Technology

Advances in technology have had the greatest impact on process-design decisions. These advances have enabled firms to manufacture products faster, with better quality, and at lower cost. More importantly, because of the significant outlay of money, technology adoption defines the future capabilities of a firm and sets the stage for competitive interactions. Technology has led to increased automation of processes. Machines such as automated guided vehicles (AGV), automated storage and retrieval systems (AS/RSs), and computer numerically controlled (CNC) machines have improved the operations of almost any business.

Flexible manufacturing systems (FMS), programmable machining system configurations that incorporate intelligent software and hardware, have led to improved economies of scope of many firms. As evident from the definition, this is a system of automated machines like computer-controlled machines or robots, automated handling devices for moving, loading, and unloading, and a computer-control center. These systems are designed to combine flexibility and efficiency so as to handle changes in work orders, production schedules, and tooling for several families of parts/components with relative ease. The objective of a FMS is to make possible the manufacture of several families of parts on the same production process, with shortened changeover time.

FMS has become the technology of the past. One popular concept is that the factory of the future will use computers for every aspect of the production process, including new product introduction, process design, forecasting, and production and inventory control. The crux of the factory of the future is not fewer people but a factory centered on computer integrated manufacturing (CIM). Considerable flexibility is provided in CIM factories through the use of computer-aided design, computer-aided manufacturing, robotics, and computerized routing and scheduling. But CIM factories are still more the exception than the rule. Although many factories make extensive use of computers, they are not fully integrated.[13]

When the CIM system is extended to include accounting, order entry, and sales information, it becomes an enterprise resource planning system (ERP), which encompasses the entire business. When operations transactions are computerized, they can be fed directly to the accounting and finance system. Likewise, the information system in operations can be integrated with marketing and human resource systems (HR). When operations, finance/accounting, marketing/sales, and HR systems are integrated through a common database, the ERP system is completed. The ERP system will track transactions from their origin to the customer to order entry through operations and accounting until the transaction is completed. Also, all decisions made in one function will be apparent to other functions and reflected in their information systems.

JUST-IN-TIME AND LEAN SYSTEMS

Shortened product life cycles, ever-demanding customers, and advanced information systems have placed intense pressure on manufacturers for increased variety, quick response, and shortened cycle times. This pressure, in turn, is transferred down the supply chain. Though one way to ensure a quick turnaround is by holding inventory, the inventory costs can easily become prohibitive. Therefore, the appropriate way is to make the production system lean and agile to adapt to changing customer demands. Collaboration along a supply chain can work only if the participants coordinate their production processes and operate with the same rhythm. Companies have supposedly found this rhythm in a well-renowned, yet difficult to implement philosophy called *just-in-time* (JIT). The JIT system was developed at the Toyota Motor Company in Japan. The roots of the JIT system can be traced to the Japanese environment.[14] Owing to a lack of space and natural resources, the Japanese view scrap and rework as waste and thus strive for perfect quality.

Types of waste can include material, such as excess inventory to protect against uncertain deliveries by suppliers of poor quality. Other types of wastes include time, energy, space, or human activity that does not contribute to the value of the product or service being produced. JIT is both a philosophy and an integrated system for production management that evolved slowly through a trial-and-error process over a span of more than 15 years. For JIT to work, many fundamental elements including, flexible resources, cellular layouts, pull production system, *kanban* production control, small lot size, quick setups, uniform production levels, quality at the source, total productive maintenance, and supplier networks must be in place. In the following paragraphs, some of these key elements are briefly discussed.

Pull Production System

Traditional manufacturing operations are push-type systems. They are based on the assumption that it is better to anticipate future production requirements and plan for them. These systems produce goods well in advance so as to have the products in stock when demand occurs. Thus, products are pushed through the system and stored in anticipation of demand, often resulting in overproduction because anticipated demand may not materialize. On the contrary, JIT uses a pull system to move products through the facility. Communication for demand in JIT starts with the last workstation in the production line or with the customer and works backward through the system. Each station requests the precise amount of products that is needed from the previous workstation. If products are not requested, they are not produced. In this manner, no excess inventory is generated. Even though the concept of pull production seems simple, it can be difficult to implement because it is so different from normal scheduling procedures. After many years of trial and error, *kanbans* were introduced to exercise more control over the pull process on the shop floor.

Kanban Production Control

Kanban is the method of production authorization and materials movement in the JIT system. Kanban is the Japanese word for a marker (card, sign, plaque, or other device). A kanban contains basic information such as product name, part number, quantity that needs to be produced, preceding station (where it came from), and subsequent station (where it goes to). Sometimes, the kanban is color-coded to indicate raw materials or other stages of manufacturing. Kanbans do not make the schedule of production; they maintain the discipline of pull production by authorizing the production and movement of materials. When workers need products from a preceding workstation, they pass the kanban and the empty container to that station. The kanban authorizes the worker at the preceding station to produce the amount of goods specified on the kanban. There are many different types and variations of kanbans. The most sophisticated is probably the dual-kanban system used by Toyota, which uses two types of kanban cards: production cards that authorize production and withdrawal cards that authorize withdrawal of materials. Kanbans can also be used outside the factory to order material from suppliers. The supplier brings the order (i.e., a filled container) directly to its point of use in the factory and picks up an empty container with a supplier kanban to fill and return later.

Quick Setups

To produce economically in small lot sizes, JIT has found ways to reduce setup times.[15] Reducing setup time is important because it increases available capacity, increases flexibility to meet schedule changes, and reduces inventory. As setup time approaches zero, the ideal lot size of one unit can be reached. Though zero setup time is next to impossible, firms are trying to achieve single setups. Single setup refers to a setup time that has a single digit in minutes. One-touch setups are also being pursued, which refers to a setup of less than 1 min. These low setup times can be achieved by two steps: internal and external setups. Internal setup requires the machine to be stopped for the setup to be performed. External setup can be performed while the machine is still running. Almost all setups in traditional manufacturing systems are internal. With JIT, much of the setup process has been converted to external setups. This requires engineering ingenuity and cleverly designed fixtures and tools. In a number of companies, the workers even practice the setup process and try to increase their speed.

Quality at the Source

For the JIT system to work seamlessly, quality has to be extremely high. Because there is no extra inventory to buffer against defective units, producing poor quality items cannot be an option. In pursuit of zero defects, the company seeks to identify quality problems at the source, to solve them, and never to pass on a defective item. To achieve this, the workers, not inspectors, are given the responsibility for product quality. To go along with this responsibility, the workers are also given the unparalleled authority of *jidoka* — the authority to stop the production line if quality problems exist. To perform jidoka, each worker can use a switch to activate call lights or to halt production. The call lights, called *andons*, flash above the workstation and at several andon boards throughout the plant. Green lights indicate normal operation, yellow lights show a call for help, and red lights indicate a line stoppage. Visual control of quality, such as the andons, often leads to what the Japanese call a *poka-yoke*. A poka-yoke is any foolproof device or mechanism that prevents defects from occurring.

Finally, quality in JIT is based on *kaizen*, the Japanese term for continuous improvement. As a practical system for production, created from trial-and-error experiences in eliminating waste and simplifying operations, JIT continuously looks for ways to reacting faster to customer demand. Continuous improvement is not something that can be delegated to a department, staff, or experts. It is a highly complex undertaking that requires total employee involvement — the participation of every employee at every level. The essence of JIT success is the willingness of workers to spot quality problems, halt production when necessary, generate ideas for improvement, analyze processes, perform different functions, and adjust their working routines.

Total Production Maintenance

An important aspect of quality management of JIT is maintenance. Machines cannot operate continuously without stoppages. Breakdown maintenance activities can be performed when a machine breaks down and needs to be restored to its original operating condition. To avoid unexpected machine stoppages, a company can also invest in preventive maintenance, which is regular inspections and maintenance designed to keep machines operational. Though preventive maintenance is costly, the costs are significantly smaller than the cost of an unexpected machine breakdown. But, even with preventive maintenance, breakdowns still occur. Therefore, JIT requires more than preventive maintenance; it requires total productive maintenance (TPM). TPM combines the practice of preventive maintenance with concepts like zero defects and total employee involvement. It allows the machine operators to maintain their own machines with daily care, periodic inspections, and preventive repair activities. In addition to operator involvement and attention to detail, to achieve the goal of zero breakdowns, TPM also requires management to take a broader, strategic view of maintenance.

Supplier Networks

With JIT, a company respects its suppliers and focuses on building long-term supplier relationships. Because the traditional approach of competitive bidding and buying parts from the cheapest supplier is contradictory to the JIT philosophy, JIT companies are emphasizing working closely and cooperatively with a limited number of suppliers who are trustworthy. The number of suppliers is typically smaller than in traditional systems, and the goal is to shift to single-source suppliers that provide an entire family of parts for a given manufacturer. A close relationship means that supply-chain members share information, risks and rewards, can fully rely on each other, and are willing to maintain the relationship for the long haul. With a long-term relationship, a supplier acts as a partner rather than a one-time seller. The building blocks of such a relationship are cost and information sharing. The manufacturer shares information about forecasts and production schedules, allowing the supplier to see what is going to be ordered. The supplier, in turn, shares cost information and cost-cutting efforts with the manufacturer. Both parties help each other and together reap the benefits for a win–win situation.

JIT in Services

It is easy to imagine that JIT is applicable to the manufacturing firms. But, it would not be thought of being applicable to service organizations. JIT is an all-encompassing philosophy that includes eliminating waste, improving quality, continuous improvement, increased responsiveness to customers, close supplier relationships, and increased speed of delivery. Therefore,

JIT philosophy is equally applicable to service organizations as well. In fact, we can readily observe the basic elements of JIT being applied in service organizations. Trucking firms, railroads, and delivery services have used JIT philosophy to increase the reliability and speed at which their services are performed.

SUPPLY-CHAIN MANAGEMENT

A supply chain, a sequence of business processes and activities from suppliers through customers, covers all the activities associated with the transformation of goods and services from raw materials through to the end user. To achieve maximum effectiveness, the business processes must operate in alignment with a company's product-development process. Supply-chain management (SCM) focuses on managing the flow of goods and services and information through the supply chain to attain the level of synchronization that will make it more responsive to customer needs while lowering costs.[16] Traditionally, each member within a supply chain was managed as a stand-alone entity focused on its own goal. However, in today's highly competitive global environment, the ability of a firm is characterized by the combined capabilities of all the members in the supply chain. Therefore, it is imperative to synchronize all supply-chain members to gain competitive advantage.

Synchronization of activities across the supply chain requires that the channel members are able to increase coordination both within and across firms. Seamless coordination can be achieved only through trust and the willingness to share information. It is the informal and timely flow of information among customers, suppliers, distributors, and manufacturers that characterizes the contemporary SCM. Coordination can also be increased in several ways, including cross-organizational teams, partnerships with customers and suppliers, better information systems, and a non-power-based, flatter organizational structure.[17] Each of these drivers enables diverse organizations to work together towards a common goal rather than narrowly defined departmental or firm goals. In the following sections, some of the key drivers of SCM are briefly explained.

Information Exchange

Information is an essential link between all supply-chain members including suppliers, manufacturers, distributors, and customers. Information systems enable the efficient flow of real-time, online communication throughout the supply chain. Research has shown information technology to be an effective means of promoting collaboration between collections of firms, such as groups of suppliers and customers organized into networks. In particular, it can facilitate collaborative planning among supply-chain partners by sharing information on demand forecasts and production schedules that dictate supply-chain activities. Furthermore, information technology can effectively link customer-demand information to upstream supply-chain functions (e.g., manufacturing, distribution, and purchasing) and subsequently facilitate "pull" (demand driven) supply-chain operations. More than ever before, today's information technology is permeating the supply chain at every point, transforming the way exchange-related activities are performed and the nature of the linkages between them.

Interorganizational information systems may be simple electronic data interchange (EDI) systems for exchanging data, such as purchase orders, advice of delivery notices, and invoices, or may involve more complex transactions, such as integrated cash management systems, shared technical databases, internet, Intranet, and extranet. EDI is not just an electronic-ordering system. It facilitates the integration of stocking, logistics, materials acquisition, shipping, and other functions to create a more proactive and effective style of business management and customer responsiveness, and thereby improve competitive advantage. It helps in sharing information about markets, materials requirements, forecasts, inventory levels, production and delivery schedules. ERP encompasses functions such as HR planning, decision-support applications, distribution and manufacturing, SCM, sales and marketing, etc. ERP systems can be considered as an information technology infrastructure that is able to facilitate the flow of information between all supply-chain processes in an organization. The ERP systems represent an optimum technology infrastructure that, when integrated properly with a process-oriented business design, can effectively support SCM systems.

Given that the Web is a flexible, interactive, and relatively efficient medium through which various business partners and consumers can communicate, the potential that it offers for improvement of efficiency in the channel functions is enormous. In addition, innovations in technologies such as intranets and extranets are critical in integrating and coordinating cross-functional teams across organizational boundaries. Extranets connect enterprises to their partners, and the Internet links the enterprises to their customers and other agencies. Intranets merge the advantages of Internet with those of local area networks to provide support for electronic connections between intraorganizational partners and electronic access to operational data. Intranets use Web-based and Internet technology to easily and inexpensively share data across a private network and are capable of providing information in a way that is immediate, cost-effective, easy to use, rich in format, and versatile. This allows all the firms to have the same demand and supply data at the same time, to spot changes in demand or supply problems immediately, and to respond in a concerted fashion.

Role of Purchasing

The growing importance of SCM has led to an increasing recognition of the strategic role of the purchasing function. Purchasing has evolved from a mere buying function into a strategic function and has recently been recognized as a critical driving force in the strategic management of supply chains. It is crucial to the usage of a limited number of suppliers, because the latter compromises the leveraging ability of the buying firms, and therefore requires an entirely different management style. Numerous firms with strategic purchasing are able to reduce the number of primary suppliers and allocate a majority of purchased material to a single source. Firms that conduct long-term planning and consider purchasing to be strategic are more likely to build long-term cooperative relationships with their key suppliers.[18] Purchasing can and does play a crucial role in the cross-functional team assigned to the concurrent design of the firm's products. It also helps orchestrate the participation and involvement of key suppliers in new product development.

Strategic Sourcing

In the past, firms commonly contracted with a large number of suppliers. Recently, a significant shift has occurred from the traditional adversarial buyer–seller relationships to the use of a limited number of qualified suppliers. Moreover, supplier contracts have increasingly become long term, and more and more suppliers provide customers with information regarding their processes, quality performance, and even cost structure. A closer long-term relationship with a limited number of suppliers means that channel participants share risks and rewards and are willing to maintain the relationship over the long term for mutual benefits. Through such long-term relationships, the suppliers also become part of a well-managed chain and have a lasting effect on the competitiveness of the entire supply chain. Collaborative working relationships can (1) foster and deepen trust and cooperation, (2) facilitate knowledge development and exchange, (3) enable exchange partners to detect and address operational issues early in the production process, and (4) enhance a firm's ability to respond effectively to the needs of its customers. Establishing close relationships with a limited number of suppliers, when properly and selectively used, has been directly linked to improved performance. Many companies have achieved substantial cost savings by reducing the number of suppliers in their supplier base and deepening the relationships with remaining suppliers.

Logistics

Logistics has experienced a surge of interest with the renewed attention to SCM. When narrowly defined, *logistics* includes traffic management and distribution management. Traffic management is the selection and monitoring of external carriers (trucking, railroads, airlines, shipping, and courier companies). Distribution management is the packaging, storage, and handling of products at receiving docks, warehouses, and retail outlets. The driving force behind distribution and transportation in today's highly competitive business environment is speed. Seamless coordination requires real-time information about schedules, capacity, and other transportation-specific information. Therefore, firms are making full use of information technology to speed up the distribution process, including EDI, bar code technology, and the Internet, to provide quick response to customers.

Distribution centers typically incorporate the warehousing or storage functions. Several recent trends are changing the way warehouses and distribution centers are managed. To handle the new trends and demands, companies employ a highly automated warehouse management system (WMS) to run day-to-day operations and keep track of inventories. WMS facilitates cross docking that allows a distribution center to direct incoming shipments straight to a shipping dock so as to fill outgoing orders, thereby dramatically eliminating costly warehouse inventory operations including putaway and order picking. More specifically, the Internet has altered how companies distribute goods by adding more frequent orders in smaller amounts and higher customer service expectations. To fill such Internet orders, distribution centers are set up as flow-through facilities, using automated material-handling equipments to speed up the processing and delivery of orders.

Increased supply-chain collaboration has also changed the way orders are placed. Traditionally, distributors place orders with manufacturers when they need products. But, in the new vendor-managed inventory (VMI) manufacturers, instead of distributors, generate orders. Through advanced information systems, manufacturers can monitor the distributor's sales and stock levels, and use this information to create and maintain a forecast as well as an inventory plan. Therefore, the vendor has more control over the supply chain, and the buyer is relieved of administrative tasks, thereby increasing supply-chain efficiency. Collaborative planning, forecasting, and replenishment (CFPR) is the next evolutionary phase of VMI. Unlike VMI, CFPR is totally collaborative. It incorporates joint forecasting thereby eliminating any potential discrepancies in forecasts. Moreover, sharing forecasts within such a collaborative system ultimately results in a significant decrease in inventory levels for both the manufacturer and distributor.

Another recent trend in logistics is the outsourcing of distribution activities to third-party logistics (3PL) companies.[19] The underlying reason is that outsourcing allows firms to focus on core competencies and at the same time take advantage of the expertise that distribution companies have developed. 3PL companies have their own warehouse facilities, fleet, and other logistics assets. The degree of outsourcing varies, and the outsourced activities differ greatly in complexity. The 3PL arrangements cover straightforward arm's length relationships involving simple logistics activities to advance logistics solutions including value-added activities such as secondary assembly of products. More recently, a new concept of 4PL focusing mainly on administrative services has been introduced. Most 4PL companies have no assets like warehouse facilities, fleet, etc., and they provide services to the customers in the form of responsibility and knowledge of how to fulfill the customer requirements. The physical movement of goods is then outsourced to other 3PL providers. In general, providers of administrative services including 4PL, Web marketplaces, etc. are termed as *logistics service intermediaries* (LSI).

QUALITY MANAGEMENT

Quality is considered as one of the key competitive priorities of many organizations. Quality has been defined differently, depending on the role of the people defining it. Some people view quality as conformance to specifications, although others view it as meeting the customer's needs, or satisfying the customer.[20] From the manufacturer's standpoint, deviation from specifications cannot be tolerated. The quality attributes of the product or service must be carefully specified, and the underlying specifications need to be met to ensure its quality. Whether the resulting product or service meets the customer's requirements, or not, will subsequently be judged by the customer. The management of quality, termed *quality management*, has stood for different philosophical meanings over the years. In the early 1900s, it meant inspection, which was the primary method of ensuring the quality of products after the production process. Currently, the meaning of quality management has been expanded to include the entire organization as all functions can help in designing and producing quality. In this section, some of the key concepts within quality management are briefly discussed.

Total Quality Management

To ensure that products and services have the quality they have been designed for, the commitment to quality must be expanded to include the entire organization. This new perception of quality is termed as *total quality management* (TQM) and is designed to build quality into the product and process. A successful TQM program must be planned, established, and initiated by top management and implemented by various functions and employees in the organization. It requires a total commitment from management and employees to monitor and maintain quality throughout the organization. Although different companies use different terminology to refer to this approach to quality, they mean essentially the same and cover similar concepts, including strategic stature of quality, total commitment, continuous improvement, comprehensive focus, employee involvement, job training, etc.

Traditional systems operated on the assumption that once a company achieved a certain level of quality, it was successful, and no further improvements are required. But companies adopting the TQM program believe that it is better to take frequent gradual quality-improvement steps. Continuous improvement, called *kaizen* by the Japanese, requires that the company continually strives to become better through learning and problem solving. Because perfection is unachievable, we must always evaluate our performance and take measures to improve it. TQM also empowers all employees to seek out problems in the processes and correct them. In traditional systems, poor quality was often passed on to the next process so that it becomes someone else's problem. But, on the contrary, TQM rewards employees for uncovering quality problems. Employees are also empowered to make decisions during the production process and correct any problems. To achieve superior employee involvement and empowerment, they are given continual and extensive training in quality-measurement tools.

During the early adoption of TQM programs, companies focused more on internal operations. However, as companies' quality programs matured, they have realized that customer satisfaction not only requires their own commitment to quality, but also the support and commitment from their suppliers. Therefore, for TQM to succeed, a partnership should exist between the supplier and its customer wherein the supplier must manage its own quality effectively so that the company it supplies can count on the quality of the materials, parts, and services it receives. Many TQM companies have reduced their numbers of suppliers to have more direct influence over their suppliers' quality and delivery performance. They enter into a collaborative partnering in which the supplier agrees to meet the company's quality standards and, in return, the company enters into a long-term agreement with the supplier that includes a stable order and delivery schedule. Many manufacturers include their suppliers in the design and planning stages of product or service development, although some of them employ quality teams to help identify supplier problems and improve their suppliers' quality performance.

Service Quality

Service organizations and manufacturing companies both convert inputs into outputs though a process. Both organizations use similar inputs, resources such as physical facilities, capital, materials, equipment, and people. However, in pure service industries, such as law, hotels, entertainment, education, real estate, banks, retail, health care, and airlines, the processes are less similar, and the output is not tangible. A service cannot be held, felt, stored, or used again. The consumer of a service often interacts directly with the production process as it is being produced. Despite these differences, the definition of quality can be applied equally well to services. Service quality has three dimensions, including the facilitating good, tangible (explicit) service, and psychological (implicit) service. Although the facilitating good quality can be measured using dimensions similar to that of manufacturing, the tangible and psychological dimensions of service quality require different subjective measurements.

The most popular measure of service quality is called SERVQUAL and is measured using five perceptual measures of service: tangibles, reliability, responsiveness, assurance, and empathy. Tangibles relate to the appearance of the company's physical facilities, equipment, and personnel. Reliability refers to the ability of the company to perform the promised service dependably and accurately without errors. Reliability for service can be defined more accurately as conformance and is significantly different than reliability for manufacturing. Responsiveness measures the willingness of the company to provide service that is prompt and helpful to the customer. Assurance measures the knowledge and courtesy of the company's employees and their ability to convey trust and confidence. Finally, empathy relates to the caring, individualized attention the company provides to its customers. SERVQUAL uses a questionnaire consisting of 22 items that, in aggregate, measure the five underlying dimensions. It is actually based on the gap between what the customer expects on each dimension and what is provided. Though the dimensions and measurement of SERVQUAL have been extensively debated in literature, it is widely used in practice to measure the quality of retail services such as banking, telephone services, and repair services.

Quality Standards and Awards

Increases in globalization and international trade have created a need for standardization of quality. This requirement has created an impetus for the universal standards, which could be used to objectively document the quality practices around the world. The International Organization for Standardization (ISO) has established international standards for quality management called ISO 9000 and 14000. The ISO 9000 standards specify that a company must have a quality system in place, including procedures, policies, and training, to provide quality that consistently meets customer requirements. ISO 14000 has had a major impact on worldwide environmental quality practices and many companies are requiring this certification as a condition for doing business with their counterparts. Though ISO 9000 addresses the fundamental processes needed to ensure a quality product and high levels of customer satisfaction, it does not provide a complete quality system due to the omission of competitive strategy, information systems, and business results from its standards. The Malcolm Baldrige system has similar requirements as the ISO, but also includes competitive strategy, information systems, and business results within its evaluation criteria.

The Malcolm Baldrige National Quality Award is given by the President of the United States to large and small manufacturing firms, service businesses, and education and health care organizations when earned. There is not necessarily a winner in each division every year. Recipients of this award are judged outstanding in seven areas including leadership, strategic planning, customer and market focus, information and analysis, human resource focus, process management, and business results. This award seeks to enhance management's awareness of quality and recognize superior accomplishments in improving product quality among American businesses. Also, because the winners of this award are required by law to share their experiences publicly, another major objective of this award is to provide ideas and strategies to other firms that are seeking ways to improve their product quality. Subsequently, the Baldrige Award winners have become models or benchmarks for other companies to emulate in establishing their own TQM and other quality programs.

The increasing trend towards economic globalization and the success of the Baldrige Award have spawned a proliferation of national, international, government, industry, state, and individual quality awards. National quality awards emphasize the economic fact that survival in global competition requires improvement to world-class status. The evaluation criteria are publicized to provide guidelines to organizations to measure their progress. National awards include the Rochester Institute of Technology/USA Today Quality Cup, which recognizes exemplary customer service or valuable improvements in a system or process designed to achieve customer satisfaction. The American Society for Quality (ASQ) sponsors a number of national individual awards, including the Deming Medal, the E. Jack Lancaster Medal, the Edwards Medal, the Shewhart Medal, the Feigenbaum Medal, and the Ishikawa Medal. Prominent international awards include the European Quality Award, the Canadian Quality Award, the Australian Business Excellence Award, and the Deming Prize from Japan.

REFERENCES

1. Russel, R.S. and Taylor, B.W., III, *Operations Management*, 4th ed., Prentice Hall, Englewood Cliffs, NJ, 2003.
2. Blackburn, J., *Time-Based Competition: The Next Battleground in American Manufacturing*, Business One Irwin, Homewood, IL, 1991.
3. Reid, R.D. and Sanders, M.R., *Operations Management: An Integrated Approach*, 2nd ed., John Wiley & Sons, Hoboken, NJ, 2004; Russel, R.S. and Taylor, B.W., III, *Operations Management*, 4th ed., Prentice Hall, Englewood Cliffs, NJ, 2003; Schroeder, R.G., *Operations Management: Contemporary Concepts and Cases*, 3rd ed., McGraw-Hill/Irwin, New York, 2005.
4. Russel, R.S. and Taylor, B.W., III, *Operations Management*, 4th ed., Prentice Hall, Englewood Cliffs, NJ, 2003.
5. Reid, R.D. and Sanders, M.R., *Operations Management: An Integrated Approach*, 2nd ed., John Wiley & Sons, Hoboken, NJ, 2004.
6. Russel, R.S. and Taylor, B.W., III, *Operations Management*, 4th ed., Prentice Hall, Englewood Cliffs, NJ, 2003.
7. Sasser, W.E., Olsen, R.P., and Wyckoff, D., *Management of Service Operations*, Allyn and Bacon, Boston, MA, 1978.
8. Russel, R.S. and Taylor, B.W., III, *Operations Management*, 4th ed., Prentice Hall, Englewood Cliffs, NJ, 2003.
9. Russel, R.S. and Taylor, B.W., III, *Operations Management*, 4th ed., Prentice Hall, Englewood Cliffs, NJ, 2003; Schroeder, R.G., *Operations Management: Contemporary Concepts and Cases*, 3rd ed., McGraw-Hill/Irwin, New York, 2005.
10. Schroeder, R.G., *Operations Management: Contemporary Concepts and Cases*, 3rd ed., McGraw-Hill/Irwin, New York, 2005.
11. Russel, R.S. and Taylor, B.W., III, *Operations Management*, 4th ed., Prentice Hall, Englewood Cliffs, NJ, 2003.
12. Hammer, M. and Champy, J., *Reengineering the Corporation: A Manifesto for Business Revolution* (revised and updated), HarperCollins Publishers, New York, 2003.
13. Rehg, J.A., *Introduction to Robotics and CIM*, 5th ed., Prentice Hall, Englewood Cliffs, NJ, 2002.
14. Reid, R.D. and Sanders, M.R., *Operations Management: An Integrated Approach*, 2nd ed., John Wiley & Sons, Hoboken, NJ, 2004; Russel, R.S. and Taylor, B.W., III, *Operations Management*, 4th ed., Prentice Hall, Englewood Cliffs, NJ, 2003.
15. Shingo, S., *Modern Approaches to Manufacturing Improvement*, Productivity Press, Cambridge, MA, 1990.
16. Reid, R.D. and Sanders, M.R., *Operations Management: An Integrated Approach*, 2nd ed., John Wiley & Sons, Hoboken, NJ, 2004; Russel, R.S. and Taylor, B.W., III, *Operations Management*, 4th ed., Prentice Hall, Englewood Cliffs, NJ, 2003; Schroeder, R.G., *Operations Management: Contemporary Concepts and Cases*, 3rd ed., McGraw-Hill/Irwin, New York, 2005.
17. Chen, I.J. and Paulraj, A., Towards a theory of supply chain management: the constructs and measurement, *Journal of Operations Management*, 22(2), 119–150, 2004.

18. Chen, I.J., Paulraj, A., and Lado, A., Strategic purchasing, supply management, and firm performance, *Journal of Operations Management*, 22(5), 505–523, 2004.
19. Russel, R.S. and Taylor, B.W., III, *Operations Management*, 4th ed., Prentice Hall, Englewood Cliffs, NJ, 2003.
20. Reid, R.D. and Sanders, M.R., *Operations Management: An Integrated Approach*, 2nd ed., John Wiley & Sons, Hoboken, NJ, 2004; Russel, R.S. and Taylor, B.W., III, *Operations Management*, 4th ed., Prentice Hall, Englewood Cliffs, NJ, 2003; Schroeder, R.G., *Operations Management: Contemporary Concepts and Cases*, 3rd ed., McGraw-Hill/Irwin, New York, 2005.

11

HUMAN RESOURCES

In the systems approach, we have discussed how inputs are taken and transformed into outputs through the use of raw materials, equipment, and people. Managing people is the key to successfully creating an efficient and effective organization. Within a firm, there are line and staff personnel. Line personnel are those who are directly involved with producing the product or service, whereas staff personnel provide support for the line managers and employees. Examples of staff departments include human resources (HR), accounting, finance, and legal. The responsibility for effectively managing human resources belongs primarily to line managers. In most firms, line managers have more power than staff.

In today's complex environment, however, any CEO or other line manager who does not work in conjunction with a competent human resources (HR) manager is courting financial disaster. The competitive environment and the legal environment are such that a single misstep in managing people may cost a company millions of dollars. The old "personnel manager" as a record keeper is extinct. Indeed, today's HR manager sits as a close advisor to the CEO and other senior managers, participates in formulation of corporate strategy, and proposes policies that will keep any individualistic line managers from making gaffes that are costly to undo.

Despite flowery phrases, solid human resource management is concerned with maximizing long-run productivity. Failing to reward employees on the basis of performance and external rates, failing to develop and train employees, failing to respect the dignity of employees, and not providing a good physical workplace can yield only short-term productivity gains. With this concept in mind, let us look at the changing environment that has created such complexities for a company managing its human resources.

CHANGING ENVIRONMENT

About 80 percent of the workforce is employed in services, and this number continues to increase. Very little manufacturing actually occurs in the United States today. We do assemble products from components, but the majority of components are shipped into the country. In fact, many of our imports are components that are shipped intracompany among divisions of multinational firms. These products are assembled and sold, some domestically, whereas others are exported as entire products.

Women at work represent more than fifty percent of the workforce but hold less than four percent of senior managerial positions. The workforce has become more educated and, in the future, many people will be overqualified for their jobs. They may become bored with routine, repetitive jobs. It is an ongoing challenge to motivate the workforce to assure that employees arrive for work each day (low, or no absenteeism), are productive, and maintain quality output.

Immigration is currently a hot topic for the government and our citizens as illegal immigrants continue to arrive, primarily from Mexico. These people are willing to take jobs that many Americans consider not suitable for themselves. Since September 11, 2001, the government grapples with the issue of illegal immigrants who have resided in the United States for decades as productive citizens. It will take years for public policy to be decided in this area as illegal immigrants have not contributed to the social security system and yet would be allowed to withdraw support after meeting requirements.

Our culture is also changing. Through TV and other mass communication media, values are changed more easily through repeated exposure to other cultural norms and mores. Past affluence and increased material expectations appear to have changed the work-hard ethic of the past. The youngest generation of workers and teenagers are now known as generation plastic in that the majority of their purchases are made on credit (or debit) cards. Savings in the United States are at an all-time low.

Drug abuse, alcoholism, gambling, spousal abuse, AIDS, more ex-convicts, an aging workforce, and problems with sexual harassment and homosexuality have produced important areas of concern for human resource management (HRM). Nontraditional workers such as retirees often enter the workforce in pursuit of medical coverage. The work ethic is strong in the older workers but health issues are more frequent.

Health and safety now have large dollar values attached to their maintenance. Workers' compensation must be provided although this is generally a state-based system, which is a combination of public and private insurers. It is one of the mandatory benefits that must be provided to workers. Other required benefits are discussed later in the chapter.

Now that we have covered some of the environmental changes that HR managers face, let's review the overall range of their responsibilities.

HUMAN RESOURCE MANAGEMENT

HRM is essentially concerned with the following processes:

1. Planning for HR needs — It includes addressing questions such as: Is there any planning of HR staffing requirements and forecasting of supply? What types of people (skills) will the firm need over the next five years? What policies should govern subcontracting, outsourcing, and the hiring of foreign workers? What is the competence of top-level managers and key professionals? Is there a possibility of retirement of a number of top managers all at the same time? Do we have a succession plan in place for managers? A management analysis report as shown in Table 11.1 can identify the key managers, along with the education levels, experience, and qualification. This type of information helps in succession planning for future promotions.

2. Work design and job analysis — In the current legal environment, a company must clearly define jobs and job-related qualifications to defend itself against claims of discrimination of all kinds. "Comparable worth" is an ongoing issue that requires documentation of job design and analysis. Does the company have a position guide and job specifications based on work analysis, such as functional job analysis, position-analysis questionnaire, or time and motion studies? Are performance appraisals and compensation tied directly to the job description?

3. Recruitment issues — Does the firm have a continuing recruitment program or is it intermittent? Should we recruit managers from outside or promote from within? There are benefits to promotion from within in terms of morale, understanding of the corporate culture and the company's policies, and familiarity with employees and customers. However, fresh ideas come from hiring people outside the organization who have different work experiences and qualifications. Are equal employment opportunity (EEO) and affirmative action policies clearly stated and implemented? Affirmative action plans are only required where there has been past discrimination by a firm, or if a company accepts federal contracts, which are paid by the government (tax dollars). EEO must be used by all firms except where there is a *bona fide* occupational qualification that allows discrimination to achieve company goals. Have sources of candidates been identified? Have managers supplied adequate job specifications so that HR may review the candidates

Table 11.1 Management Analysis Report

Name and Title	Actual Responsibilities	Age	Experience Years and Kind	Educational Qualifications	Summary of How Well-Qualified	Philosophy and Views of the Business
Walter White Executive VP	Sales and order processing, merchandising	62	25 years with Vogue	Not known	Appears to be well-qualified by experience	Cut out reports, cut prices, cast out merchandising and advertising people and contract out advertising; believes quotas, industry potentials are worthless; increase finished goods inventory; get out the goods and stop worrying about control; wants to broaden line further
B. H. Winslow VP–Production	Production except for production control	61	25 years with Vogue	At least high school but not a college degree	Appears to understand his work and be doing a good job	Feels need for strong president to get a unified sense of direction for the company

Name/Title	Responsibilities	Age	Experience	Education	Assessment	Comments
Robert Kelley VP–Operations	Accounting, real estate, secretary–treasurer, purchasing, production control	59	25 years with public accounting firms, VP in charge of loans for a bank; about 5–10 years with Vogue	College degree in accounting, CPA	Extremely well-qualified	Recognizes limitations in merchandising and production
Paul Trout Advertising manager	Advertising and sales promotion	54	J & J Apparel: salesman for 4 years, advertising manager for 3 years, asst. sales manager; P. L. Brooks: sales manager for 8 years, VP-marketing for 10 years	MBA, University of Chicago	Very strong qualifications for his job; overqualified	Sees need for management team with unified sense of direction; believes strongly in marketing concept and integration of all activities
Sam Chapman Merchandise manager	Implementing merchandising decisions of Walter White	39	3 years as merchandise manager with Vogue plus unmentioned experience	Not known	Seems OK	Understands market segmentation; desire to reduce styles and price lines; concentrates on medium quality, mass market in 20–45 age group

Table 11.1 (continued)   Management Analysis Report

Name and Title	Actual Responsibilities	Age	Experience Years and Kind	Educational Qualifications	Summary of How Well-Qualified	Philosophy and Views of the Business
Tom Evans VP–Systems	EDP systems	48	Apparently broad business and systems experience	Not known	Appears qualified	Believes EDP could be expanded for management decision making
Toni DeMarco Head designer	Designs the apparel	34	13 years of designing for Vogue	Graduate, School of Design	Well-qualified	Believes design is more important than production modifications to reduce cost
Richard Roberts Chief engineer	Manufacturing equipment design	32	7–10 years with Vogue	Mechanical engineering degree; graduate work in wide range of subjects including management	Very well-qualified	Believes in concentrating on his own job despite his broad academic qualifications
Harry Thomas Human resource manager	Routine personnel activities	41	Not mentioned	Certified SPHR	Well-qualified	Likes prestige of reporting to the president

for required skills? Is the total recruitment program measured and found to be cost-effective?

4. Selection planning — Questions such as the following are addressed: Is the HR department providing adequate background evaluation of candidates to managers, e.g., credit checks, reference checks, etc.? Are reasons for selection/rejection acceptances/nonacceptances identified and analyzed to improve the process? Are valid selection techniques used? What is the average length of employment with the company by job classification?

5. Developing communications — Does the company have a good formal mass communication system (publications, newsletters, public address system, group meetings, intranet, employee handbook)? Does the company facilitate informal communications? Does the company have a good informal system of communication up and down the organization? Are safety rules established and safety procedures maintained in the production shop, in the office, on the floor of the retail store, or on walks and drives leading to buildings? Safety rules and regulations must be developed and communicated to be effective. Safety committees to review overall levels of security and safety are popular at many firms.

6. Training and development — Is the policy to train and develop people or hire trained people from outside? Is there a management-development program? Have training and development needs been identified for the next five years? Are there training programs matched to the needs of all groups of employees? Are courses or programs to be given on company time, after hours, or part of each? Are individual training courses and programs measured in terms of cost/benefits? Does the company have a benefit for education and tuition reimbursement?

7. Appraising performance — Is there a formal appraisal system of each employee's performance at least on an annual basis? Does the system measure performance against predefined objectives for a specified time period? Who is involved in the rating process, and who has responsibility for explaining the rating to the employee? Many firms considered a 360 degree performance-appraisal process whereby ratings are provided by not only the employee's supervisor, but also their peers, their subordinates, their boss's boss, and customers or suppliers that the employee interacts with regularly. However, how does a company distill this to one final rating? They are difficult to implement, so most firms rely on the employee's supervisor or manager. Other questions to consider include: Do appraisals meet stringent criteria for validity under the uniform guidelines on employee selection procedures to meet the court-held

view that appraisals are a form of selection? Are informal measures collected on a monthly basis and then aggregated into the annual formal appraisal?

8. Compensation and benefits — The reward system is a critical element in establishing the individual worker's relationship to the organization because it offers the opportunity for the employee to achieve major personal objectives. The total reward system consists of extrinsic financial and nonfinancial rewards and intrinsic rewards from the work itself. Extrinsic rewards may be tailored to each individual through the "cafeteria" approach. This is a flexible approach that offers the individual options as to the form and timing of the compensation package, that is, the mix of benefits, salary, stock options, pension plan, and so on. More details are discussed later in the chapter. Some policy areas for compensation are:

   a. Should the company pay minimum rates established by federal and state laws or always exceed them?

   b. How should the compensation structure relate to that of other firms in the area? Should the company be below market, meet market rates, or pay above market rates?

   c. Should the compensation structure be the same in every area where plants are located? Consistency is simple, but many cities or states have higher minimum wages. Some cities require almost $10.00 per hour for minimum wage as the cost of living is much higher there.

   d. Is it a better policy to pay low salaries to key managers to keep expenses down or pay high salaries to obtain better individuals? What compensation plan will best motivate key managers to produce profits?

   e. What policies should be established for golden parachutes (large severance to top managers in case of takeovers or acquisitions), golden handshakes (large separation benefits in case of turnovers), or tin handshakes (large separation benefits to middle managers)? Does the company have a downsizing plan? How can it attract people to voluntary separation without overpaying or making it so attractive that there would then be a shortage of workers?

   f. What should the company do about compensation for "comparable worth" jobs in the light of possible future liability?

9. Career management — This area is poorly developed in most firms. The average length of time for employees to stay with a company is between four and five years for most employees. Should the firm do nothing, act if asked, or actively promote career planning for employees? A company may choose to hire good young people and let the cream rise to the top (or hope it does). It may have a policy

of achieving high turnover and low payroll and low average age by developing people, giving small raises, and encouraging them to seek better opportunities outside. Is there a succession plan that is available and up-to-date, to plan for and fill vacancies with qualified staff?

10. Labor management relations — Many policies have been tried in this arena and some have succeeded, according to economic conditions and government regulations. We have a history of adversarial policies because it is difficult to get the two sides to agree on a fair division of the pie. Japanese success has caused some new experimenting in the United States in terms of joint management–labor relations to more cooperative relations. This involves increasing workers' responsibilities, total equality management (TQM) and continuous improvement to increase quality, fewer layers of management, and less autocratic supervision.

11. Governmental impact — Since the 1900s, the federal government and, later, state governments, have increasingly affected the way companies treat employees. Companies have resisted laws and regulations by both illegal and legal means. Sometimes, policies that forestall the impact of a particular law will give a company a tremendous advantage. For example, IBM's treatment of its employees has been so liberal that unions have not been able to gain a foothold in this giant company. Other companies have fought actions to delay the impact and costs of some of the legislation and regulations. Many companies have been trapped in no-win situations due to recent affirmative action and antidiscrimination laws. Corrective policies must be developed quickly to make adjustments and minimize large fines. It is apparent that policy makers must take into account both the main thrust of legislation and the particular points involved in making a variety of decisions on HR problems. Table 11.2 provides a brief guide. Company EEO and affirmative action plans are clearly long-range in nature. Companies must prepare goals and timetables for recruitment, training, and progress up the ranks for men and women: handicapped, military veterans, and minorities classified as black, Asian, and Hispanic. An availability analysis and a utilization plan of the general form shown in Table 11.3 is required.

12. Automation in HRM — Managers may now obtain, upon request, all sorts of analyses and performance indicators relating to organizations and individual. They may track easily the progress of subordinates in their careers from hiring to retirement. In addition, the burden of keeping accurate maintenance records (vacation time, sick leave, insurance, medical contributions, pensions, etc.) and producing required government reports is greatly lightened.

Table 11.2 Impact of Legislation on Human Resource Management[a]

	Year	Main Thrust	Policy Implications
Sherman Anti-Trust Act	1890	Designed to limit business combinations in restraint of trade; it was also applied against union activities interfering with interstate commerce	
Clayton Act	1914	Exemption of union activities from antitrust actions except when in combination with business group to restrain competition by affecting labor outside of the bargaining unit	
Railway Labor Act (amended in 1934, 1936, 1966)	1926	Established unionization rights of employees and collective bargaining procedures for airline and railroad management and unions of employees in appropriate unit as determined by National Mediation Board; outlaws yellow dog contracts	Legal constraints imposed on management and unions in use of power to provide for self-determination by an employer and selected by majority employees, with procedures of collective bargaining for negotiating differences over wages and conditions, to promote peaceful settlement of disputes; management policy as to organizing efforts of unions must be within limits established by the antitrust and the labor relations acts and consistent with leadership philosophy, its personal values, and economics of situations

Act	Year	Description
Federal Anti-Injunction Act (Norris-La Guardia Act)	1932	Restricted federal courts from enjoining or restraining legal labor organizing, picketing or strike activities, or from holding legal yellow dog contracts by which employees agreed not to join unions
National Labor Relations Act (Wagner Act)	1935	Business activities affecting interstate commerce subject to management unfair labor practices; prohibiting interference in employees freedom to organize and to bargain collectively; majority in appropriate unit can select a union, as determined by the National Labor Relations Board, which enforces unfair labor practices
Davis-Bacon Act	1931	Provides minimum wages and conditions of overtime for construction and for other workers
Walsh-Healy Act	1936	Contracts with U.S. Government

Table 11.2 (continued)   Impact of Legislation on Human Resource Management[a]

	Year	Main Thrust	Policy Implications
Fair Labor Standards Act	1938	Provides minimum wages and overtime conditions, with child labor prohibitions, or industries producing goods for interstate commerce; amended to prohibit lower wage for females than males on work requiring similar skill, effort, and responsibility or exclusion of females from highly paid jobs	Management, subject to coverage, must meet statute requirements in employment, compensation, overtime, promotion, and recordkeeping practices or be subject to penalties; expert human resource staff is essential
Labor-Management Relations Act (Taft-Hartley Act) (includes National Labor Relations Act provisions)	1947	Adds to NLRA union unfair labor practices restricting interference with management or affecting public health and welfare; allows suits in federal court against violation of labor agreements; establishes the Federal Mediation and Conciliation Service	Management has to make decisions regarding its attitude toward unionization efforts and type of bargaining with union, to contain its power or for accommodation with cooperation in administration of contract and grievance processing; necessary legal and labor relations advisors for management
Labor-Management Reporting and Disclosure Act (Landrum-Griffith Act)	1959	Covers in detail a Bill of Rights for union members with the responsibility and liability of members, officials, and unions for unlawful conduct; employer and union reports required as to management payments to influence unions, or agents, or employees on collective bargaining matters	Management must maintain financial as well as administrative separation from internal union affairs and employee–union matters

Act	Year	Description	Impact
Executive Order 11246	1963	Applied only to contractors and subcontractors on federal work	Same impact as Civil Rights Act; Title VII
Civil Rights Act, Title VII Amended by Age Discrimination in Employment Act of 1967 and Equal Employment Opportunities Act of 1972	1964	Elimination of employer and union discrimination against applicants and employees on basis of race, color, religion, sex, age, or national origin, with regard to hire, terms of employment, compensation, or union membership, or apprentice programs; administered by Equal Employment Opportunities Commission with individual right to court suit	Burden placed on all employers, including state and local government management with 15 or more employees; all subject to injunction and affirmative action orders including hiring with back pay for prohibiting discrimination unless based on bona fide occupational qualification necessary to normal operation; any job test or qualification may cause reverse discrimination order and cost
Occupational Safety and Health Act	1970	Requires employment free of recognized hazards to employees, subject to severe penalties	Cost of meeting OSHA requirements; consideration of reasonableness of standards and regulations for acceptance or to legally oppose
Vocational Rehabilitation Act	1973	Affirmative action to employ and promote qualified handicapped persons	Revisions of recruitment and hiring and medical programs; effect on productivity, labor cost, work procedures, promotions, and layoff policy
Employment Retirement Insurance Security Act	1974	Required standards for pension programs to protect employee benefits and fringes established by company or by collective bargaining	Name fiduciaries within company; long-range and immediate costs; pension and benefit plan changes; impact on turnover, productivity, recruitment, on acquisitions or mergers

Table 11.2 (continued) Impact of Legislation on Human Resource Management[a]

	Year	Main Thrust	Policy Implications
Civil Service Reform Act	1978	Statutory standards for Federal Service Labor Relations under a federal labor relations authority, similar to private labor-management standards (except no right to strike); established an Office of Personnel Management and a Merit System Protection Board	Expansion of grievance arbitration and compulsory arbitration for disputes over new agreements in public sector may affect policies toward strike substitutes (like basic steel industry Experimental Negotiation Agreement)
Americans with Disabilities Act (ADA)	1990	Prohibits discrimination against qualified individuals with disabilities; expands the Vocational Rehabilitation Act of 1973, extending protection to most forms of disability if perceived or real — including those afflicted with AIDS	Firms are required to make reasonable accommodations to provide a qualified individual access to the job; ADA extends coverage to private companies as well as all public service companies
Family and Medical Leave Act (FMLA)	1993	Provides employees in organization with 50 or more employees the opportunity to take up to 12 weeks of unpaid leave each year for family matters, to include child birth, adoption, or illness	Firms guarantee employees their current job or its equivalent, upon returning to work; employees retain their employee offered health insurance coverage during the unpaid leave period

| Civil Rights Act | 1991 | Prohibits discrimination on the basis of race and racial harassment on the job; permits women and religious minorities to seek punitive damages in intentional discriminatory practices | Employer again must provide burden of proof that discrimination did not occur |

Table 11.3 EEO Work Force Analysis

By Job Title within Department

Department _____

Page _____ of _____

As of _____ 19 _____

(Date)

Job Group Number	Job Title	Eeo-1 Category	Salary Code	All Employees			Minority Employees									Progression Lines
							Male				Female					
				Total	Male	Female	Blk.[a]	Asian	Hisp.[b]	N. Amer.[c]	Blk.	Asian	Hisp.	N. Amer.	Total	
Total - This page																
Grand total - Last page																

[a] Blk. = BLACK.
[b] Hisp. = Hispanic.
[c] N. Amer. = Native American.

Now that we have reviewed the primary responsibilities of the HR manager, let us consider in more detail some of the key issues facing HRM. The president of one of the country's leading management consulting firms says that most business problems stem from having misplaced people in management positions, often in top management. He believes that HRM is probably less understood and more poorly executed than all other management functions combined. The first step, if we are to improve the operation of the business, is to analyze and update the processes by which inputs are transformed into outputs. Then, if there are continuing quality issues, identify the people who are causing the problems.

Once identified, such misplaced people must be shifted to positions where the firm can build on their strengths and work to improve their weaknesses, or they must be terminated. Management training and development in most companies is best conducted by on-the-job coaching and occasional brief in-plant or outside seminars. Larger companies can afford broad management development programs, which pay off.

When we analyze a company or a case, we usually search for functional problems and recommend policies, systems, procedures, and corrective action to prevent repetition of the problems. Too often, we fail to examine the weak links, the broken processes or individuals who originally failed to recognize an operating or a strategy problem. Fix the system, train the employees or managers, and then make changes if performance problems continue (Figure 11.1). However, unions can be problematic in making work assignments, reducing the management's flexibility.

UNIONS

By contracts, specifics of working conditions, wages, benefits, and job assignments are spelled out in great detail. This drastically restricts the management's flexibility and limits moving workers around to areas where shortages exist. Unions are careful to follow the elaborate job descriptions that exist. Unions handle grievances for their members when workers have conflict with managers.

With foreign competition, job security has become an even more important issue. Unemployment is managed by each of the fifty states and varies in amount from about $150 up to $450 per week, depending on how long you have been employed, and how much you earned per week. It is not needs-based, so it usually does not cover all of the unemployed worker's expenses. Typically, unemployment lasts 26 weeks, unless extended by an act of Congress. If your job is lost because of foreign competition (e.g., Boeing layoffs due to Airbus, a European consortium), additional funds are available.

The president of a management-consulting firm said that the following scenario points out the often-met confusion between *functional business problems* and *human resources problems:*

Several years ago we were called in to improve a firm's order processing system. Our mission appeared to be straightforward, to reduce costs and improve inventories. During the orientation phase, it became apparent that high costs and high inventories were symptoms of other problems.

Sure, we could save a modest amount by improved systems, but we could never substantially increase profits unless we faced up to the real problems. These were excessive product proliferation and poor sales forecasting that generated short factory runs, frequent schedule changes, large inventories of slow moving items, and constant back orders on fast moving, wanted merchandise. As a consequence, manufacturing and order handling costs were high. Approximately 70 percent of the orders had to be handled four to eight times before finally completed.

Excessive product proliferation and poor sales forecasts led us directly to the vice-president in charge of marketing — who incidentally was a protégé of the president.

What became readily apparent was the fact that the vice-president of marketing was the *wrong person* for the job. Although he had been a tremendous success in sales and possibly the reason for the firm's position of dominance in the market, he was not familiar with the managerial aspects of marketing. The vice-president had no experience in product development or cost analysis. Because he had been the best salesman the firm had ever had, it was assumed he would be the best choice for vice-president of marketing. Sales forecasts became extremely inaccurate and new products proliferated with the result that inventory cost soared. No amount of sales pitches seemed to reverse the trend.

The president had to make a serious decision — demote his friend back to sales, or continue to suffer poor forecasts and high inventory costs, or find help immediately for his vice-president of marketing. These decisions weighed heavily on his head.

Figure 11.1 People job fit scenario.

Unions are extremely concerned about job security. Of all of the things that unions focus upon, job security is number one, followed by increases in benefits, and increases in base pay. With the decline of smokestack industry in America, only about 15 percent of the workforce is employed in manufacturing. There has been a corresponding decline in union membership because of this, and because service workers are harder to unionize. Further, management has been more sophisticated in appearing to treat its workers openly and fairly. Many new laws also protect workers, which was an original benefit of becoming a union member. In right-to-work states (primarily in the southeast), where companies are unionized, the union must represent all eligible workers, whether they actually join the union and pay dues. Dues vary based on the union and may be anywhere from $30 per month to one percent of base pay with no upper limit. Alternatively, in the northeast, in some states you must be a union member to be hired, although in other states, you must join the union within 30 days of accepting a position.

Do employees have a channel for presenting possible unfair treatment and other work issues? In unionized settings, there is a mechanism for handling grievances at different levels of the company. Should the company be unable to resolve the grievance with the union, often mediation or arbitration are specified in the contract. Mediation is a review of the issues by an independent party who makes recommendations to the union and the company. However, you do not have to follow the recommendations of a mediator. Alternatively, arbitration is binding, which means that whatever decision the neutral arbitrator makes, after reviewing all of the evidence, must be followed and implemented.

FLEXTIME, FLEXIBLE WORK WEEKS, AND PART-TIME WORKERS

Flextime for workers, part-time workers without health and pension benefits, and related employees (e.g., husband and wife combinations) represent policy areas. Flextime is working an eight-hour shift, but on a variable schedule. One worker may work from 6 a.m. to 2 p.m., although another may work from 7 a.m. to 3 p.m., and others may be scheduled from 8 a.m. to 4 p.m. A common core time is scheduled to facilitate communication. These types of flexible arrangements allow flexibility in terms of workers' needs. This is different than a flexible work week where the traditional five-day work week is replaced with four ten hour days, or three twelve-hour days, which are quite popular in the medical profession, nursing in particular. The flexible work schedule makes many firms attractive.

Nepotism is frowned upon in the United States where we tend to not hire related workers (either genetically or by marriage) to avoid appearances of unfairness. Yet, as firms have gotten larger, it becomes more difficult to attract the people you need. Many companies will now allow related workers to work in different departments or divisions. Internationally, hiring related workers is quite common and often seen as a reward to superior employees to hire their family members.

Wal-Mart is one of the companies that first realized that by hiring part-time workers, benefits would be greatly reduced. Part-timers are not required to be offered benefits although many firms today grant part-time benefits after a period of time. In 2006, Wal-Mart makes part-time employees (which is most of their hourly workforce) wait 24 months to be eligible for benefits. This lowers their total payroll costs and makes them more profitable than their competitors. United Parcel Service (UPS) is another firm that heavily utilizes part-time workers. In the last decade, UPS unions have struck twice over the issue of using part-time workers to work more than 40 hours each week on a regular basis. Finally, the workers were hired as full-time employees during the last contract negotiation (strike), and the union agreed to lengthen the period of the new contract.

BENEFITS

The cost of employee benefits continues to skyrocket. On average, they cost a company approximately 40 percent of base pay, although unionized firms have greater benefits. For example, a $10-per-hour employee actually costs the firm about $4 per hour for the cost of benefits, for a total of $14 per hour worked up to 40 hours. Overtime pay at 1.5 times the hourly wage is required for nonexempt (hourly) employees after 40 hours per week. However, benefits do not increase; thus, many companies will use overtime for short-term increases in demand instead of hiring workers where benefit costs increase.

Benefits include mandatory and optional, market-based benefits. The mandatory benefits include unemployment insurance, which is completely paid by the company. Workers' compensation for injuries on the job is also paid by the firm. Lastly, Federal Insurance Contributions Act (FICA) (also known as social security) is paid by both the employee and the employer.

For wage earners above a minimum income, social security as of 2006 is paid at a percentage of the first $90,000 earned by the employee. The company contributes 7.65 percent, which is matched by the employee at 7.65 percent for a total of 15.3 percent of the first $90,000 earned each year. This includes 6.2 percent for social security and 1.45 percent from each party toward Medicare/Medicaid. There is no cap on the earnings, which are subject to Medicare/Medicaid. Medicare is for older Americans whereas Medicaid is for low-income Americans with no assets. Employees must pay in 40 quarters over their work careers to be able to draw full retirement benefits. However, you can draw from social security funds if you are permanently disabled as well.

To reduce payments from social security, full retirement is estimated to be 66 years and 8 months as of 2006. Monthly payments to the retirees increase if you wait until 70 years of age to begin withdrawing social security. In addition, the amount subject to FICA, currently $90,000, has increased each of the last ten years. There is also talk of increasing the 7.65 percent.

These mandatory benefits cost firms anywhere from 9 to 12 percent as a percentage of total payroll. The other benefits are market based. The two largest and most popular benefits are pay for time-not-worked and medical insurance. Pay for time-not-worked includes vacations, holidays, sick pay, jury duty, etc. Medical insurance is heavily subsidized by the company, and most employees pay only 20 to 50 percent (but much less in unionized firms) of the actual cost for themselves although they pay a higher percentage toward family benefits. Other popular benefits include vision care, dental insurance, tuition reimbursement, and others.

Cafeteria compensation will permit the company's pay to be packaged as salary and benefits according to each worker's desires. Most companies will not offer each employee his or her own personal benefits selections, as, administratively, this is a nightmare to accommodate. However, many offer packages designed for young, single workers, married workers with kids, married workers without kids, empty nesters whose children are grown, and older, nontraditional workers. Companies are also offering sheltered income that comes off the top before taxes are taken out. Retirement contributions (up to $14,000 in 2006) can be sheltered as well as medical funds such as Flexible Spending Accounts (FSAs) and Medical Savings Accounts (MSAs). There are positives and negatives to each of these types of accounts.

DISCRIMINATION

In a society where the ratio of lawyers to the general population is by far the highest in the world (more than 2.2 lawyers per 100 people), it is not surprising that companies are being sued for discrimination in hiring and firing, for work-related injuries, for sexual harassment, for age discrimination, and for many other actions. Although such suits are often needed to rectify injustices, and many more could probably be justly filed, they point out the need for companies to develop a comprehensive, fair, and legal set of policies to protect both workers and employees. Lawsuits originate from the onset of applications and selection through on-the-job infractions. HR is responsible for providing the training to supervisors and managers to be able to avoid these types of lawsuits. Laws such as the Civil Rights Act, Pregnancy Act, American Disabilities Act (ADA), and Health Insurance Portability and Accountability Act (HIPAA) all provide specific regulations with which companies must comply.

PRODUCTIVITY AND TECHNOLOGY

The old seat-of-the-pants intuitive approach to increasing productivity no longer works. New systems of management that allow workers more control over their work have led to high-quality products with increased output. Although theorists argue over methods of getting higher performance from workers by needs satisfaction, operant conditioning, or contingency theory, the implementation for all theories is the same: Create the work environment and reward system appropriate for each organization's goals.

Record keeping and documentation have become voluminous but are now primarily computerized, which increases productivity. HR information systems (HRIS) allow for resume scanning for key word searches for job skills along with scheduling, promotions, transfers, and training assessments. Most resumes are never seen by a human reviewer, and it is estimated that of those that rise for review after the key word search done via technology, only seven seconds is spent on a personal review.

In addition, more employees are using computers and technology to perform their jobs. Finally, the speed and sophistication of technology requires that employees be better educated and specially trained so that more poorly educated people are becoming unemployable. Improving productivity is one of the primary HR functions.

PERFORMANCE IMPROVEMENT AND TURNOVER

There are two approaches that may be used to make sure it is people who are performing inadequately, rather than poorly defined system processes and procedures that are being utilized.

1. Conduct in-depth interviews with key people connected with a particular problem area. Determine if it is the system that needs to be modified so that the process works well. If the system is working well, it may be the particular person involved. Sometimes, it will be immediately obvious where the weak link is. At other times, several or all of those concerned may lack competence. In some cases, personal conflicts will surface that have resulted in lack of cooperation, blocking of communication, or just plain sabotage (Figure 11.2).

2. Start with the symptoms of problems as they appear in the operating statements. Work backward until the individual processes ultimately responsible are identified. Fix the processes, and then monitor performance of the individuals to ensure they improve. If not, suspension or ultimately termination may be needed. A progressive discipline system is recommended, which is discussed in greater detail on the following subsection.

Company X, a manufacturing concern, was a fair-sized division of a billion dollar corporation that had fallen on hard times. Despite increased sales in five out of the last eight years, profits had vanished. Each of the six vice-presidents blamed their problems on one or more of the others. From in-depth interviews lasting about two to four hours each, it became evident that the first and most important problem was the president of the firm. When our confidential report was given to the chief executive officer of the parent organization, and verified by two VPs of his own group, replacements were made. Not only the division president but also two of his VPs were moved out. Within one year profits were up substantially.

Figure 11.2   Managerial consulting report of executive performance inquiry.

A goal of zero turnover is not recommended as some deadweight, nonproductive employees need to be let go, to increase performance of the firm (Figure 11.3). However, too much turnover is expensive. The capabilities, experience, and dedication of individuals in business cover a wide range. If all the not-great workers were fired, it is probable that we would only replace them with not-great workers. The cost of continually replacing employees would be great. Each individual should be appraised in terms of his or her potential to the company with proper training and guidance. From a practical standpoint, unions, civil service regulations, company traditions, or legal problems may knock out firing as a means of disposing of problem workers. Terminating employees without cause leads to increased unemployment payouts, which increases the costs of unemployment insurance that the firm pays to the government.

If the company is subject to seasonal layoffs, does it hire people who desire only seasonal work or does it have some policy for taking care of laid-off employees? It will reduce costs if you can hire the same workforce each year, as training costs and company orientation would be much lower. Companies should also budget for the increase in unemployment costs, which must be paid to the state.

Progressive Discipline

For minor infractions, a progressive discipline system is recommended. Verbal warnings are the first step, and those are given. If the behavior continues, written warnings should be issued, signed by the employee and placed in their file. If nothing changes for the positive, suspension without

A large retail store was selling $1.5 million annually in women's shoes, far higher as a percent of total shoe sales than the National Retail Merchants Association figures for stores of similar size. The problems were lower-than-average turnover, higher markups, and such high markdowns and high advertising costs that contribution to store profit was extremely low. Both the store controller and the merchandise manager admitted the buyer was a genius at promotion, had the wanted merchandise at the right time, and inspired the sales force. However, he was unable to control his operations, as profit and loss statements proved. The general merchandise manager decided not to fire the buyer — he merely placed the department under the control of another merchandise manager who was a lavish man with praise for a job well done. While the new man was tough and figure conscious, he was a fine leader, and within a reasonable time, had the buyer eating out of his hand. The important improved turnover and profit added to the buyer's bonus but more importantly, to his self-esteem — "I can master figures that formerly were a deep mystery to me."

The sales figures proved the buyer knew his business. He could promote and sell. At the same time, the slow turnover and large markdowns proved the buyer needed a good controller that led the general merchandise manager to the real culprit, the buyer's boss — the merchandise manager who had failed to manage!

Figure 11.3 Managerial consulting report of managerial performance inquiry.

pay may be used. Lastly, termination should occur after you have been through all of these steps. This documentation in the employee file will reduce unemployment claims on the basis of cause. You may be called to the local unemployment services office to provide this documentation.

For major policy and procedure violations such as alcohol use, drugs, stealing, weapons, etc., a progressive discipline system is not utilized. Companies should go straight to either suspension without pay, or termination, depending on the previous work history of the employee.

SUMMARY

The HR manager should not concentrate on purely technical solutions to general management and functional problems and issues. It is extremely important to pay attention to the people in the organization for it is people who cause problems, correct problems, and prevent future problems. The staffing, training, and motivating activities are of utmost importance to the success of the firm. Great strides have been made toward professionalizing

the HRM field by offering Professional in Human Resources (PHR) certification, and senior PHR (SPHR) certification by the HR Certification
Institute of the Society for Human Resource Management. For managers
going into the HR field, these certifications provide external documentation
of knowledge and achievement.

12

MANAGEMENT INFORMATION SYSTEMS

William A. Sodeman

Organizations rely upon the effective and efficient exchange and use of information to create and maintain their core competencies and competitive advantages. In this chapter, we shall examine the various components of the organization's information systems, and the strategic and tactical roles that these components perform.

INFORMATION SYSTEMS

People have always used some kind of system to store, maintain, and report important data about themselves and their groups. Although there are many definitions for an information system, many of these definitions include four primary components: people, infrastructure, processes and the information itself. This model of an information system is, in some ways, a timeless model, as it does not require specific sets of technologies for the basic stages of implementation.

People

The most important part of an information system includes the people who use the system or rely upon the system's inputs and results. It is significant that in most information systems, people control the fundamental business roles that are used to operate that system. Moreover, people must also identify and use various assumptions to control the scope of the system.

As we shall demonstrate in this chapter, managers must place specific limits on an organization's information system for practical reasons of efficiency and effectiveness. In some situations, society prescribes additional limits through ethical and legal constraints. This tension between what can and what should be done with an information system is central to good managerial practice.

Information

The information that is stored and maintained in the system is another critical element. Managers and users must decide what information should be entered into a system, and how it should be stored. Manual information systems that relied on written information are still widely prevalent in managerial practice. Many employees still keep handwritten to-do lists and notes in a paper notebook, though others use high technology such as Blackberries.

Managers also use information systems to create reports that describe or categorize data in forms that provide additional value. Among these, highly detailed information may have far greater value when it is tabulated and interpreted. Managers may use these reports to analyze past trends and help predict upcoming patterns and events. In some information systems, the system itself uses reports to maintain or change system and business processes, and operations.

In many countries and industries, organizations are required to maintain and archive detailed information about individual transactions. In the United States, comprehensive legislation such as the Sarbanes–Oxley Act of 2002 requires the executives of publicly traded companies to certify the accuracy of the firm's reports, and charges the board of directors with oversight of the company's information systems. Professional organizations may also have their own requirements, which, in some cases, can be far more stringent than the legal requirements.

Since Alvin Toffler and Peter Drucker first began to talk about the "third wave" and the "knowledge economy," economists have begun to write about knowledge itself as a new form of capital in the postindustrial economy. A knowledge economy exists in contrast to the old concept of manufactured "capital goods," which involves production equipment and facilities such as refineries, railroads, and factories to produce and deliver other goods and services. Economist Paul Romer writes, "Instead of just capital and labor and raw materials producing output, it is the ideas themselves and the economic incentives that lead to their creation and diffusion that are the fundamental determinants of economic well-being." For example, FedEx and UPS sell "tracking" to other firms (see Table 12.1).

Table 12.1 Old and New Concepts of Nonfinancial "Capital"

	Old Concept — Capital Goods	New Concept — Intellectual Capital
Examples	Railroads	Collective knowledge of workers
	Refineries	Innovations and ideas
Type of economy	Industrial	Knowledge

Infrastructure

The *infrastructure* of an information system includes the various resources, devices, and storage media that are used to actually operate the system. Most people are familiar with the components of a typical paper-based information system: paper files, cabinets, and the buildings or structures that may provide storage or work areas.

The postal system is an essential element of infrastructure that provides a regular, efficient means of moving or transmitting large amounts of data. For example, despite the many advances in video technology, it is still more efficient and less expensive to send a movie in an optical disk than it is to transmit that same movie across the Internet. Netflix, Amazon, and many other online services and retailers have relied heavily on this cost differential to build and maintain a healthy market share, even as cable and satellite television providers continue to test and deploy various video delivery technologies. The swift ascent of online audio services such as iTunes, Rhapsody, and podcasting show that people are willing to abandon long-held pieces of infrastructure, such as physical stores and catalogs, when these reliable systems provide different or greater forms of value.

Telecommunications has redefined our basic assumptions regarding infrastructure requirements for information systems. The ability to reliably transmit and receive large amounts of information over distances to almost any point on the planet continues to trigger changes in how people use information. The types and amounts of information that are recorded have grown rapidly as digital storage systems have become less expensive and more reliable.

Processes

The actual operations performed by the information system represent the final item in our model. Those who design information systems tend to model real-world activities, especially when developing information systems for a wide audience. Electronic commerce still uses a "shopping cart" model, in which users select specific items during one or more visits to a Web site, and then purchase them with a single financial transaction. Podcasting uses a subscription model that requires users to ask for ongoing delivery of audio and video files to their device.

Professional requirements and codes of conduct may mandate specific types of processes. Accounting provides one relevant example. Companies are required to maintain accurate records of their financial transactions. Accounting students still learn how to manually post transactions to a paper ledger. Computer-based accounting systems resemble the double-entry form of bookkeeping that was developed for paper-based systems, to efficiently record transactions and quickly identify errors.

Electronic mail is modeled on postal mail and paper-based reporting; distribution lists and attachments are standard parts of paper-based correspondence. However, employees and managers still benefit from learning and applying the most elementary principles of business communication that were developed when correspondence relied on paper-based systems.

Digital versions of these systems may provide far greater efficiency than their paper or manual counterparts. This, of course, assumes that the digital version of these systems can be run accurately and efficiently. Successful operations often require people to adjust or change their accustomed ways of performing actions within these processes. Managers, customers, suppliers, and other members of the value chain often assume that employees are always available and ready to act on text messages and electronic mail. Even if these messages are received, people may not act on them because they are already involved in other tasks. Both e-mail and text messaging have been found to be significant distractions for employees. In some companies, management has tried to limit the amount of electronic messaging that is used. Occasionally, users find that it is much faster to have a conversation than it is to participate in a thread of messages.

TYPES OF INFORMATION SYSTEMS

There are many varieties of information systems used within organizations. This discussion will focus on the most essential systems that are in use. These systems include transaction processing, functional systems, enterprise resource planning systems, communications, and file management.

Transaction Processing

The earlier section on accounting presented an information system based on individual financial transactions. Transaction processing is a core function of many information systems, and this model encompasses far more than financial exchanges. Users make requests to remote servers for information, files, and resources.

E-mail and instant messages are text and binary information transactions between users. These systems have become a popular means of corporate communication because they allow organization members to time-shift their conversations as needed. Many employees use the corporate e-mail and messaging accounts for personal communications, even though every individual message transaction can be archived for future reference and analysis. The U.S. Department of Justice performed extensive analysis of Enron's electronic mail messages in its investigation of that company's business operations. In the United States, financial services companies must capture and store every message sent on its information systems, as required by the Sarbanes–Oxley Act. Health care providers face similar requirements from legislation such as HIPAA (Health Insurance Portability and Accountability Act).

Functional Systems

We may also choose to identify, design, and implement information systems that are specific to a business function such as marketing, human resources, or production. These functional information systems may become highly specialized, depending on the amounts and types of data that must be captured, processed, and analyzed by staff and managers in that area. In some cases, a functional system provides additional layers of security, designed to prevent information from being transferred or used in illegal or unethical ways.

For example, human resource managers often deal with sensitive and confidential information about employees. This may include information about an employee's medical records, age, or social security number. In many countries and localities, organizations must comply with laws that govern or control the privacy of information.

Enterprise Resource Planning

Functional information systems must have some level of integration among them, so that the organization's managers can monitor and understand changes in important tactical and strategic issues. Enterprise resource planning (ERP) systems can help provide this integration by supporting a common suite of business applications that share the same corporate data.

This integration requires certain compromises by any organization that adopts an ERP system. Every ERP makes certain assumptions about the business processes that are used within a company. In fact, some ERP implementations assume that the company's managers are willing to replace existing business processes with versions that are compatible with the ERP software.

It is difficult and risky to customize an ERP to a specific organization's requirements. Some customization is necessary, of course, particularly when strategic factors such as organizational knowledge, core competencies, and markets are considered. Many vendors provide industry-specific versions of their ERP suites, so that much of the customization that would be required in a specific line of business is already incorporated in the base or default version of the software.

Even so, ERP vendors and consultants are often asked to tailor the ERP solution so that it can use existing systems and data. These requests can burden the organization over time, by preserving business processes that may not be appropriate to the ERP's design or the changing nature of the company's business. Too much customization may produce an ERP that the vendor cannot support or maintain, leaving the organization with increased costs over the entire life of the system.

Communications

In the earlier section on transaction processing, we discussed how messages can be handled and stored as units of information. A communications system conveys these messages and more basic information that is included in a message.

Communications systems tie the organization's information systems, servers, and infrastructure together so that information can be exchanged within and outside the company's networks. We tend to classify these networks as local or wide area, depending upon the geographic scope of the system. The Internet itself is a redundant collection of wide area networks (WANs) and metropolitan area networks (MANs), which are themselves composed of other WANs that help connect many smaller networks together.

Telephone systems record the time, duration, and telephone numbers involved in a conversation. Electronic mail systems can track the journey of an e-mail message across corporate systems and the Internet, using information stored in mail servers and in the electronic mail message itself. Network appliances such as intrusion detection systems can automatically notify employees when certain kinds of attacks are mounted against corporate systems.

File Management

The final type of system helps manage files, which are bundles of more specific digital information that are stored on a computer or network. File management systems work with communications systems to deliver information within a computer and across a network.

Recall our earlier discussion of mainframe computers. Punch cards provide a ready example, as a single card may hold a few hundred bits of information. Several punch cards may be linked to create a single file, just as a paper file might include several pieces of paper.

Storage media, such as tapes, hard drives, and storage area networks (SANs) provide ever-increasing amounts of storage space for users and their organizations. In the mainframe era, storage was a precious commodity that was expensive to create and maintain. Managers were extremely conservative in selecting the types and amount of digital information that was created and stored in these computer systems. In the twenty-first century, users may find this conservative attitude difficult to understand. Users and organizations have tended to create and save increasing amounts of information, which in turn must be archived, stored, and transmitted by the organization.

DISTRIBUTED INFORMATION SYSTEMS

The wide acceptance of the Internet in corporate computing has led to a resurgence in distributed information systems. In this model of information systems, computing power, data storage, and user input may occur in different parts of a process and in different physical locations.

The distributed model has its origins in the early history of computers, when large mainframe computers used vacuum tubes instead of transistors, and punch cards instead of magnetic storage. These devices were extremely expensive to operate, requiring round-the-clock attention from dedicated teams of engineers and technicians, and large air-conditioned rooms. There were a wide variety of vendors, many of whom were either acquired or went out of business as the industry matured. Corporate customers were forced to consider the long-term viability of their vendors, as well as the technical and economic advantages of the computing products and services that they provided.

The personal computer provided the opportunity to move more of the processing power away from a centralized mainframe or server toward the end user's physical desktop. One major benefit of this transition was the development and acceptance of the graphical user interface (GUI), which provided a user-friendly alternative to command lines.

Personal computers also brought massive storage and memory capabilities to the desktop. This storage is used for a variety of purposes, including the installation of large and complex operating systems and applications, and the caching of data at the user's location. This is one method by which computers provide an illusion of fast access to information, as the computer does not depend upon its telecommunications link for all of the information needed in a session. This design also allows a client-server computing model that provides a rich level of information and interaction between the user and remote computers.

NETWORKS AND THE CONNECTED ORGANIZATION

As organizations develop their information systems, these systems must be interconnected to create additional operational and strategic value. Networks combine aspects of the five types of information systems we discussed earlier, along with distributed computing.

The Internet

At the broadest level of our discussion, the Internet provides organizations and individuals with access to a widely accessible, highly redundant, scalable communications network. The term "Internet" is derived from "internetwork," which is a communications network that combines several smaller networks into a single, interoperable system.

The Internet itself relies upon the best efforts of communications carriers, governments, organizations, and individual users for its ongoing operations. An exchange between a user's computer and a server may require multiple paths or hops across international networks that are operated by competitive partners or rivals. All participants or stakeholders in the Internet must use a common set of communications protocols and file standards to support the distributed exchange of information.

Intranets

Organizations have used internal communications systems as one way of coordinating strategic and tactical activities. An intranet is a secure internal network that allows employees to access and share organizational information that is confidential or sensitive. As companies gained more experience in deigning and deploying intranets, the technology has progressed in two directions. Some intranet features are almost a commodity that are included in operating systems, ERP platforms, and other applications. These features include messaging, e-mail, search, and knowledge bases.

In some companies, executives and employees have come to expect or even demand highly specific designs and features that are commonly found on commercial Web sites. Implementation of these features can help a company maintain its sense of identity in a competitive market, but after an acquisition or a merger, the removal or replacement of these features may present some employees with a sense of defeat or loss. One can also question the overall value of highly customized intranets, as these systems often require the company to maintain or replace experienced staff and vendors over the life of the system.

Extranets

Organizations must communicate with their partners in the value chain. An extranet can facilitate this communication in a secure manner that the organization's managers can limit and control. An extranet can be defined as a portion of the corporate intranet that may be accessed by customers, suppliers, and other partners.

Extranets can complicate relationships in a value chain, especially when participating organizations fail to compromise or cooperate over issues including data format, interface design, and software requirements. In some value chains, a coalition of partners may take control over these issues, by creating or adopting a set of standards, or developing a common portal that incorporates best practices in the industry.

SUMMARY

In this chapter, we examined the various components of the organization's information systems and the strategic and tactical roles that these components perform. Companies may gain a huge source of sustainable competitive advantage through effective development and implementation of information systems. However, the benefits should always outweigh the costs of the information systems to be an effective user of organizational resources.

SELECTED BIBLIOGRAPHY

Bender, D.R., Information overload requires knowledge management, *Houston Business Journal*, 1998.

Davis, M.C., Knowledge management, *Information Strategy: The Executive's Journal*, Fall 1998.

Drucker, P., *Management Challenges for the 21st Century*, Harper Collins, New York, 1999.

Edvinsson, L. and Malone, M.S., *Intellectual Capital*, Harper Collins, New York, 1997.

Egan, M. and Mather, T., *The Executive Guide to Information Security*, Symantec Press, Upper Saddle River, NJ, 2005.

Henderson, J.C. and Venkatraman, N., Strategic alignment: leveraging information technology for transforming organizations, *IBM Systems Journal*, 1999.

Mason, R.O., Mason, F.M., and Culnan, M.J., *Ethics of Information Management*, Sage, Thousand Oaks, CA, 1995.

McNurlin, B.C. and Sprague, R.H., *Information Systems Management in Practice*, 5th ed., Prentice-Hall, Upper Saddle River, NJ, 2002.

Shulman, S., *Owning the Future,* Houghton Mifflin Co., New York, 1999.
Stewart, T.A., *Intellectual Capital*, Doubleday/Currency, New York, 1997.
Umbaugh, R.E., Defining a corporate information policy, *Journal of Information Systems Management,* Spring 1984.

13

ANALYZING GLOBAL BUSINESS

GLOBALIZATION

Global business involves much more than simply applying all that has previously been covered in this text to commercial activities and interactions with the rest of the world. For many years, many American corporations attempted to do that and found themselves at increasing competitive disadvantage to many companies based overseas — in fact, they even began to lose market share in the United States to those companies. For example, both Ford and GM have lost market share to Toyota, which has the vision to become the world's largest automobile company.

The old approach to doing business outside of the United States involved companies viewing their international activities as a "step-child" with lower importance, which was secondary to domestic U.S. activities. Such companies could be compared to the colonial empires of the past in which the so-called "mother country," aka home country, was given highest priority and the "colonies" (host countries) were of importance only to the extent that they strengthened the mother country. Most top managers were from the home country, which is known as an *ethnocentric approach* to human resources.

Such companies were sometimes referred to as "international" as long as they were involved in any aspect of international business such as exporting or importing while primarily producing goods and services in the United States, and sometimes they would be referred to as "multinational" if they had production or operations in more than one country. Multinational enterprises still tended to be primarily American, Japanese, German, etc., and their operations outside their home-based country might play a vital role for their overall world goals, but each country's operation was viewed as distinct, regardless of the amount of autonomy or home-based domination of the subsidiary in that country. Today, when people refer to a "multinational" enterprise they are usually using the term as synonymous with "global business."

A global business may have its headquarters located in a given country but it often could really be in many other countries just as well. Its activities tend to not be restricted by the location of its headquarters. A U.S.-based global company will not simply look for a U.S. national as its CEO; it may pick a person from Europe or Asia. If it needs to fill a position at operations in the Netherlands, it may pick someone from the United States or the Netherlands or a third country national, for example, Brazil or Australia. This is known as a *geocentric approach* in that the best person for the job is selected, regardless of their nationality. When a multinational enterprise uses top managers from the host country, often because of necessity of customization of their product or service (multidomestic strategy) to the local country, this is known as a *polycentric approach* to human resources.

Global firms not only simply raise funds in U.S. financial centers but also in Hong Kong, London, and Frankfurt. The whole world is their marketplace. Unilever and Royal Dutch Shell have their headquarters split between two countries: the Netherlands and the United Kingdom.

Royal Dutch Shell is an example of a global company. Most Americans think of Shell as an American corporation. Part of the worldwide Royal Dutch Shell Group is indeed American. However, it is based in the Netherlands and the United Kingdom. This is one of the few petroleum companies that has not merged or acquired other firms. BP–Amoco (Gulf oil, was also swallowed up by BP), Chevron–Texaco, Exxon Mobil, and others have joined together for economies of scale and reduction in exploration costs. Fina is a French petrochemical company that also competes on a global basis.

Increasingly, people entering the workforce during the twenty-first century who spend the rest of their lives working here in the United States may actually be working for a company based overseas or for a company that is controlled by an overseas-based corporation. Table 13.1 gives examples of overseas companies and their ventures in the United States. Also, those who spend part of their careers overseas may do so as employees of a corporation based in the United States. Table 13.2 shows the top 20 companies of the world that include U.S., European, and Asian firms.

In this chapter, we will begin by looking at some of the benefits of investing in business operations outside of the United States. We will then go on to see some of the approaches to doing business globally, approaches that range from relatively little or no investment overseas to

Table 13.1 The Ten Largest Foreign Investments in the United States

Rank Foreign Investor	Country	U.S. Investment	Percentage Owned	Industry	Revenue ($million)	Net Income ($million)	Assets ($million)
1. Daimler Chrysler AG[a]	Germany	Daimler Chrysler (North American)	100	Automotive, aerospace, credit	**78,845**	NA[b]	NA[b]
2. BP Amoco Plc[a]	United Kingdom	BP Amoco	100	Energy	**33,160**	NA[b]	35,987
3. Deutsche Bank AG[a]	Germany	Bankers Trust	100	Financial services	12,048	73.0	133,115
		Deutsche Bank Americas	100	Financial services	<u>8,484</u> **20,532**	NA[b]	86,839
4. Sony[a]	Japan	Sony Music Entertainment	100	Music entertainment	**18,533**	NA[b]	NA[b]
		Sony Pictures Entertainment	100	Movies			
		Sony Electronics	100	Consumer electronics			
5. Diageo[a]	United Kingdom	Burker King	100	Fast food	10,300	NA[b]	NA[b]
		Pillsbury	100	Food processing	6,010	NA[b]	NA[b]
		Utd Distillers & Vintners (North America)	100	Wines and spirits	<u>2,100E[c]</u> **18,410E[c]**	NA[b]	NA[b]
6. Toyota Motor[a]	Japan	Toyota Motor Manufacturing	100	Automotive	9,400E[c]	NA[b]	NA[b]
		New United Motor Manufacturing	50	Automotive	4,900E[c]	NA[b]	NA[b]
					<u>3,100</u> **17,400E[c]**	NA[b]	1,666
Denso[d]	Japan	Denso[d] International America	100	Automotive systems			

Table 13.1 (continued) The Ten Largest Foreign Investments in the United States

Rank Foreign Investor	Country	U.S. Investment	Percentage Owned	Industry	Revenue ($million)	Net Income ($million)	Assets ($million)
7. Royal Dutch/Shell Group[a]	Netherlands/United Kingdom	Shell Oil	100	Energy, chemicals	17,034	–1,727.0	26,543
8. Royal Ahold[a]	Netherlands	Stop & Shop	100	Supermarkets	6,187	NA[b]	NA[b]
		Giant Food Stores	100	Supermarkets	3,417	NA[b]	NA[b]
		Tops Markets	100	Supermarkets	3,061	NA[b]	NA[b]
		BI-LO	100	Supermarkets	2,887	NA[b]	NA[b]
		Giant-Landover	100	Supermarkets	837	NA[b]	NA[b]
					16,389		
9. ING Group[a]	Netherlands	ING Insurance (United States)	100	Insurance	14,227	NA[b]	NA[b]
		ING Barings (United States)	100	Financial services	615	NA[b]	NA[b]
					14,842		
10. BG Plc[a]	United Kindom	Dynegy[a]	25	Gas and electricity	14,258	108.4	5,264

[a] Publicly traded in the United States in shares or ADRs.
[b] NA = not available.
[c] E = estimate.
[d] Some foreign investors on the list own U.S. companies indirectly through other companies (in italics).

Table 13.2 Global Top 20 Leading Companies

Rank	Company	Industry	Sales ($million)	Profits ($million)	Assets ($million)	Market Value ($million)
1	Citigroup	Banking	108,276	17,046	1,484,101	247,655
2	General Electric	Conglomerate	152,363	16,593	750,330	372,139
3	American Intl Group	Insurance	95,036	10,909	776,420	173,985
4	Bank of America	Banking	65,447	14,143	1,110,457	188,771
5	HSBC Group	Banking	62,966	9,522	1,031,287	186,742
6	ExxonMobil	Oil & Gas Operations	263,989	25,330	195,256	405,247
7	Royal Dutch/Shell Group	Oil & Gas Operations	265,190	18,536	193,825	221,492
8	BP	Oil & Gas Operations	285,059	15,731	191,108	231,877
9	ING Group	Diversified Financials	92,013	8,098	1,175,157	68,038
10	Toyota Motor	Consumer Durables	165,684	11,133	211,145	140,890
11	UBS	Diversified Financials	62,216	7,096	1,115,904	89,165
12	Wal-Mart Stores	Retailing	285,222	10,267	120,624	218,562
13	Royal Bank of Scotland	Banking	46,645	8,660	1,119,901	108,946
14	JPMorgan Chase	Banking	50,119	4,664	1,138,469	129,979
15	Berkshire Hathaway	Insurance	74,207	6,355	181,860	138,736

Table 13.2 (continued)   Global Top 20 Leading Companies

Rank	Company	Industry	Sales ($million)	Profits ($million)	Assets ($million)	Market Value ($million)
16	BNP Paribas	Banking	55,085	5,802	1,228,035	64,389
17	IBM	IT Hardware & Equipment	96,293	8,430	109,183	152,757
18	Total	Oil & Gas Operations	131,638	8,843	98,690	151,128
19	Verizon Commun	Telecom Services	71,283	7,831	165,958	99,637
20	Chevron Texaco	Oil & Gas Operations	142,897	13,328	93,208	131,524

Sources: Exshare; FT Interactive Data; Reuters Fundaments and Worldscope via FactSet Research Systems; Bloomberg Financial Markets.

very substantial investments. Any attempt to develop a strategy for global business must recognize the barriers that governments have erected to limit opportunities, and we will next look not only at those barriers but also at what is now being done to eliminate or minimize some of the barriers. Because global business involves exchange of money and — despite the common use of the dollar worldwide, even when countries are not doing business with the United States — there is no single currency used for all transactions everywhere all of the time, except possibly euro currency, which has emerged as the second most frequently used currency. As a result, we see why it is important to recognize how the global currency market can impact on your opportunities to export, import, and expand your global assets; you will learn how to avoid the risks resulting from constant changes in the rates of exchange between one currency and another. We will then see how the global business leader uses a situation analysis and builds on the marketing concept as a basis for strategy in the global leadership, planning, organizing, and controlling of global marketing, finance, human resources, and production — and the many issues or questions that global business leaders must resolve in developing their strategies.

In our discussion of global business, we will look at things from the perspective of those who are in the United States. Most of our examples will also be from that perspective. However, the concepts apply to global business, regardless of the country or overseas-based company.

GLOBAL BUSINESS OPPORTUNITIES

Benefits of Global or Foreign Direct Investment

Foreign Direct Investment (FDI) refers to investing in the productive capabilities of a nation other than the country in which the global company is based — it does not refer to investing in securities. To illustrate, let us consider German investment in the United States. In addition to producing cars in Germany and exporting them to the United States (engaging in trade), a German company may wish to invest by building a factory in the United States so that it can also produce its cars in this country, such as the BMW in South Carolina or Daimler Benz (now Daimler Chrysler) producing the Mercedes in Alabama. This is an example of investment. A company in one country (for example, an oil company in the United Kingdom) that develops productive capabilities in other nations (such as refineries in Australia and oil fields in South America) is involved in international or FDI. You may accomplish FDI by purchasing an existing company or by building from scratch (Greenfield investment).

The global company doing the investing can benefit through several means. A few of these include the following three: being able to leap over trade barriers, obtaining transportation efficiencies, and achieving global integration. These benefits to the company do not necessarily result in the loss of jobs in the country in which the company is based.

Leaping over Trade Barriers

A global company can benefit by being able to leap over trade barriers. Trade barriers may be such that a U.S. corporation might be selling none of its products in some specific country. For example, a tariff (government tax per unit) on an imported product might cause it to be prohibitively expensive. The trade barriers may not apply if the product is manufactured or assembled within the country. The same concept applies if a product manufactured in the United States would be too expensive to sell within the country due to transportation costs. Quotas (limits on the numbers sold) are also eliminated by manufacturing and assembling products within a country or regional trade area.

Transportation Efficiencies

Let us consider a second benefit for the global company: transportation efficiency. If a U.S. firm minimizes transportation costs by locating itself close to foreign markets, it may thus be making sales that it could not otherwise have made. Again, if no U.S. jobs were previously involved in making such sales, the overseas investment will not cause the loss of jobs. The larger and heavier the product, the more this benefit applies.

Global Integration

Finally, global integration benefits the firm by enabling it to profitably choose from among worldwide alternatives. It can choose the least costly and most productive sources of inputs such as labor and raw materials. It can choose the best locations to convert the inputs into outputs. And it can choose the most desirable places to market the outputs. (For example, the U.S. market for its products may be stagnant and saturated but there may be a far larger potential market overseas that is largely untapped.) Because of its array of global choices, the company can minimize its costs and maximize its revenues. Table 13.3 provides an example.

APPROACHES TO GLOBAL BUSINESS

There are several means of going into international business. They range from very little, or no, investment outside the home country to very significant investments. They include the following possibilities.

Table 13.3 Global Integration and Expansion: Oil Company Examples

Stage	Vertical	Horizontal
(Of production and distribution)	(Expanding into the various stages of production and distribution)	(Expansion at given stages of production and distribution)
	Examples	Examples
Input	Oil company explores for oil in most productive fields on earth, not just in United States; operates oil fields and transports oil through its tankers and pipelines to next stage	Exploration, production, and transportation includes natural gas as well as oil; tankers carry nonenergy cargo as well as oil and natural gas
Process	Oil company converts petroleum into gasoline at multiple locations on earth, not just in the United States	Petroleum is converted into petrochemicals as well as gasoline
Output	Oil company controls stations where its gasoline is sold and sells its gasoline in the best markets on earth, not just the best markets in one country	Sells nonpetroleum products such as food at the gasoline stations

Exporting and Importing

If you export or import, it is possible that you may wish to have some international investment such as sourcing (purchasing) offices. This method of going international involves the lowest level of risk in that the firm has not invested huge sums of capital in terms of plant, equipment, and home office personnel. On the other hand, you may be able to work through international trade intermediaries (trading houses or agents) without any such investment. To link up with such intermediaries, you may obtain exporting help through specific country desks at the Department of Commerce and many state departments of development offices. There is also the National Trade Data Bank. The trade consulates at most country embassies would be delighted to help in facilitating your imports from their countries. See Table 13.4.

Table 13.4 Tariffs and Demand Elasticity: Examples of Impact from a Tariff Increase

Impact	Elastic	Inelastic
Ability to pass tariffs on to consumers	Difficult	Easy
Effect on imports by passing tariffs on to consumers	Significant decrease	Minor decrease or no change

Licensing and Franchising

Licensing enables you to take advantage of global markets without the firm having to put up the capital. You license the rights to manufacture your product or service to a company, which perhaps already has the production and distribution facilities outside their home country that you need to reach global markets. Someone else puts up the money and facilities and does the work while you receive royalties or a share of the profits. Licensing involves low levels of risk from an investment standpoint; however, you may be creating a competitor when the contract expires. Licensing works well if you continue to make improvements and updates to your products or services. This ensures that the licensee needs to renew the license at the end of the agreement.

Franchising works in the same way but it often involves contracts with a greater number of people and firms and it is usually built around a common name. McDonald's is an example; its franchises are found throughout the planet. In addition to the fact that the franchisee puts up the money to build facilities internationally to do business that will help you make money, as a franchiser, you can make money even if the franchisees do not, and you can make even more profits if they also make profits. Usually, the franchisee pays a fee to the franchiser at the outset and, thus, the franchiser can earn money even if the franchisee's business does not truly get off the ground. If the business is successful, the franchiser shares in the profits but if the business is not successful, the franchiser does not share in the losses. In addition, many franchisers make money from the supplies they sell to franchisees. Subway overtook McDonald's as the largest franchiser in the world recently.

International Strategic Alliances

By sharing and exchanging your product lines and production capabilities here in the United States, with the product lines and capabilities of an overseas company, both your firm and the other firm may mutually benefit. In an alliance, two or more companies work together without necessarily having an ownership interest in each other, such as in the airline industry. Airlines form code-sharing relationships where each airline sells seats on the same flight, providing greater frequency and destinations with fewer overall costs.

Sometimes it may mean piggybacking off each other's capabilities by using products that complement each other's line. Suppose a company in the United States produces inexpensive and medium-priced widgets, and a European company produces widgets that are very expensive. Suppose the U.S. products sell especially well when there is a downturn in the economy and people cannot afford anything better, but when economic conditions improve, they then tend to increase their purchases of the European product. By adding the European product to its line, the American company may benefit, and by adding the American product to its line, the European company may benefit.

International Joint Ventures (IJV)

Joint ventures involve two or more companies cooperating in taking advantage of an opportunity. It could involve several companies pooling their human and financial resources. An IJV involves firms from more than one country. Typically, a third separate entity is created, which limits the liability of the two or more parent firms.

When the petroleum industry was first being developed in the Middle East, usually there were several companies joining in each development. When Saudi Arabian oil production was developed, four American oil companies pooled their resources into a joint venture known as Aramco. This allowed the sharing of the exploration expenses. The Kuwait development involved a British company and an American company. Normally, joint ventures involve some overseas investment, but it is possible that one of the joint ventures might simply be contributing intellectual property such as copyrights, trademarks, or patents. IJVs are growing tremendously in the former Soviet Union states.

FDI and Acquisitions

FDI involves actually building a company's own facilities in another country to do business there. This clearly involves significant capital outlays on the part of the company; consequently, this is the riskiest way of going international. Companies have lost their entire plants and production capabilities when governments have changed, or when the government nationalized (took ownership of) their facilities. FDI clearly creates the most purpose-built facilities for a firm, but it is a slower way to expand internationally.

Alternatively, acquisitions involve buying an existing company with an existing market of customers. When the company does not want to be acquired, it is known as a hostile takeover. International acquisitions involve companies from more than one country. There are many benefits in this approach, as opposed to starting from scratch (as in FDI) internationally. Starting from scratch often involves many years to gain market share and acceptance within the desired countries, to develop a trained and effective work force, and to gain skill at the local languages, culture, and laws. During the expansion process, profits may be unimpressive. However, there are some obvious advantages if one takes over a company that already is profitable, has a proven track record, already has the people and facilities needed, and is intimately familiar with the languages, culture, and laws. Depending on the value of the dollar, compared to the currency used for the company being acquired and certain market conditions at the time, it may actually be less expensive to expand through an acquisition.

BARRIERS TO GLOBAL BUSINESS

Some of the common barriers to global business are detailed in the following subsections.

Tariffs

If your global business involves importing or exporting, tariffs are of concern to you. Tariffs are a tax for each unit imported into a country. They tend to make the imported product more expensive and less competitive, thereby normally enabling the producers of a competitive domestic product to both charge more and sell more. Of course, sometimes the producers or sellers of the imported product may absorb part or the entire tariff themselves and simply accept a lower profit per unit to remain competitive with the domestically manufactured products. What determines the extent to which the tariff will result in a higher price to consumers (the tariff being paid by consumers), or the extent to which the tariff will result in a lower profit per unit (the tariff being paid by the producers or sellers)? The answer is "elasticity of demand."

Elasticity, as we are using the term, refers to the sensitivity of the quantities demanded to alternative prices. As a general rule, the higher the price the less the quantity demanded, and the lower the price the greater the quantity demanded. However, just how much more will people buy at a lower price than a high price and just how much less will they buy at a high price than a low price? If demand is inelastic or relatively insensitive to price, buyers may purchase only slightly less at the higher price — or they may even continue to purchase the same amount. In that case, the tariff will be paid by consumers because their demand for the product is such that they will willingly pay a sufficiently higher price to cover the tariff. If demand is elastic or very sensitive to price, there could be a huge loss of sales if consumers had to pay a sufficiently higher price to cover the tariff, so if the producer or seller of the product wants to continue to sell the same quantity of output, as was the case before the tariff was imposed, the producer or seller will have to be sure that the consumer does not have to pay a higher price due to the tariff — that is, the producer or seller will simply have to accept a lower profit per unit. Entertainment such as movies, DVDs, and dining out are all examples of elastic products.

What would cause a product to be such that consumers would be willing to pay the higher price needed to cover the tariff? Some of the things that could cause the demand to be inelastic could include the following: the product is perceived to be absolutely essential to something very important such as staying alive, there is no substitute for the product or competitive brand available, the product has many uses, the product price represents a very tiny portion of one's income, etc. Petroleum, electricity, and food tend to be inelastic in nature. Higher prices do not significantly lower the quantity demanded by consumers.

Quotas

A quota is even more effective than a tariff as a trade barrier because it imposes an absolute ceiling on how much can be imported. A government imposing a tariff on widgets may have intended to limit the amount of widgets imported into the country but if consumers have a very inelastic demand for the product, they may not cut back on their imports but simply pay a higher price to cover the tariffs. The quota assures that the consumers will not be able to buy more than a given amount, regardless of whether the producers or sellers of the imported product raise or lower their prices. However, there may be ways around this. Nissan (formerly Datsun) shipped cars to Canada when the hot new 240 Z model had reached its quota in the United States. They hired drivers to put enough miles on each new car so that it was considered a used car. They were then able to bring those into the United States without violating the new car quotas.

Export, Import, and Investment Laws

Most people recognize that there are some products that cannot be imported or can be imported under only certain conditions — for example, cocaine. They also realize that there are some products that can be imported — such as oil — but it may not be possible to import the products from certain countries such as Iraq.

There are also restrictions on exports. For example, normally a company producing weapons for the U.S. government cannot also sell weapons to any foreign government without obtaining the approval of several government agencies including the State Department, the Defense Department, and the Department of Commerce. To a lesser extent, there are restrictions on intellectual property, especially inventions and processes involving high tech, that cannot be exported without an export license, even to friendly countries and, sometimes, cannot be exported to particular companies within friendly countries.

Before either importing or exporting, it may be a good idea to check with the Department of Commerce to see if there are any trade restrictions that could cause you or your company to wind up in trouble. There is also a U.S. Office of Export Administration.

Investment barriers restrict the extent to which companies and investors from another country can own or control property in a given country. The restrictions can affect real estate and the percentage ownership of companies in that country. Sometimes, the laws may limit land ownership very severely, thus any property used in conducting business in that country may have to be leased or rented. Sometimes the laws may require that foreigners own no more than 50 percent of local companies because of fear of being controlled by other countries and their companies. A company wishing to do business in such a country will have to find local investors or partners. For example, if you wish to run a hotel in Jamaica, you must have a local partner as noncitizens are allowed not to own land, but allowed just to lease land.

Local Content Laws

To encourage industrial development and lessen dependence on other countries for goods, some countries seek to direct their citizens' purchases to products that are at least partly produced domestically. As a result, they may use tariffs or quotas against products that are totally produced in other counties, but not impose those barriers if, at least, part of the final product was produced or, at least, assembled in that country.

Such a case, an American automobile company might find it desirable not to ship automobiles to such a country but, instead, to simply ship the components and then assemble the components into cars in that country. GM was forced to assemble cars in Australia after the Australian government would not allow cars to be imported there. Their government wanted the job creation and the taxes direct investment would create. Also, local content may be low initially for multinational firms that enter a country with FDI, but over time, the host governments require that more local suppliers be used. This increases the skill levels and creates additional jobs for their citizens, who, in turn, pay more taxes.

Dumping and Price Control Laws

Governments also protect local businesses (not consumers) through dumping and price control laws. The laws enable local businesses to be able to charge a higher price than would otherwise have been the case. Sometimes the government simply sets a particular price for all products in a category (usually at a level that assures local businesses of a profit) and no company — domestic or foreign — can charge less. A company seeking to do business in such a country must then engage in non-price competition — for example, provide better quality, better services, better advertising, longer hours of operation, etc. The price controls may take the form of dumping restrictions.

Dumping involves a foreign company selling products in a given country below cost. However, calculating what is below cost and whether there can be any exceptions is a tricky issue that often has resulted in trade disputes between the United States and other countries.

The issue as to the cost of a product is not as easy as might first seem to be the case. As you probably know, producers have fixed costs, such as rent that will not change regardless of how much or how little they produce. If you rent a facility for $100 for some period of time, you pay $100 whether you produce nothing, one unit, two units, a hundred units, etc. As you also probably know, producers have variable costs that go up as they produce more, go down as they produce less, and that do not exist at all when they are producing nothing at all. Suppose a producer has variable costs of $10 a unit for raw materials; if it is producing nothing it will not have any variable costs, but if it produces one unit it will have total variable costs of $10 and if it produced two units it will have total variable costs of $20, etc. Its total costs will include both fixed and variable costs, and its average costs will simply be its total fixed and variable costs divided by the number of units produced.

Suppose you rented a facility for $100, had variable costs of $10 a unit, and you wanted to make a profit of $10 a unit. How much would you have to charge if you could only sell one? Obviously, the price would be $120. However, suppose you have a chance to sell another unit but you cannot sell it for $120, how low of a price could you charge and still make a $10 profit on that second unit?

You calculate your costs (see Table 13.5). You have $100 of fixed costs and a total of $20 of variable costs for two units. In other words, you have a total of $120 costs for two units or an average cost of $60 for each

Table 13.5 Pricing Based on "Cost" Scenario

	Incremental Cost	Average Cost
Calculation	Because the fixed costs are covered by the first sale, only the variable cost of $10 needs to be covered	The total costs consist of $100 fixed plus variable costs of $10 for each unit (a total of $20 for variable costs for two units) thus total costs are $120; total costs of $120 divided over the two units produced results in an average cost of $60 for each unit
Conclusion	A price of $20 is above cost	A price of $20 is below cost

Note: The fixed cost of a product is $100, the variable cost of production is $10 per unit, and a profit of $10 a unit is desired. One unit is sold in the home country for $120 but more could have been produced. It is possible to sell another unit overseas, but only if it could be sold for $20.00. Under which circumstances would such a sale be regarded as being sold below cost — under an incremental approach or an average cost approach?

of those two units. So should you take the average cost of $60 and add in $10 of profit and sell it for $70? Suppose you could not sell that second unit for $70. Again, how low of a price could you charge and still make the $10 profit?

Because the sale of the first unit for $120 has covered the fixed cost for rent and you will not have to pay more rent to produce that second unit, the only cost you have to cover is the variable cost of $10 and then you add your profit of $10. In essence, you can profitably charge $20 for the second unit. However, some might complain that you are dumping because you are selling it for less than its average cost of $60. Because of their huge economies of scale, multinational firms are often accused of dumping their products at low prices. These low prices may drive the domestic producers out of business.

Bribery Laws

In the United States, one could be thrown into prison if one bribed a public official to do business. However, other countries have different ideas as to what is right and wrong, and have traditions that go back many centuries, sometimes long before the United States came into existence. If one wishes to do business, one may have to comply with those traditions.

Bribery is a tradition in some countries although it may not always be openly called bribery. Local officials may put a different spin on the practice and it may be viewed as a means of demonstrating goodwill and sincerity. Doing business with the king may require demonstration of goodwill to the king's friends and relatives — if enough goodwill is demonstrated to them, then one may be able to see the king, where more goodwill may be expected if one truly expects a favorable decision from the king. If an American business person views the whole practice as corruption and refuses to engage in bribery, the king will likely find business people from other countries who are willing to operate according to the king's ethical standards.

Following the Second World War, American companies greatly increased their overseas trade and investment. The war's destruction resulted in a need for U.S. goods and for American companies to help rebuild industries. Furthermore, the fall of colonial empires after the war opened up new opportunities that had previously been denied to Americans. However, when the American public learned that American companies were engaging in the same kind of bribery that had previously been done by comapnies from Europe and elsewhere, there was a public outcry. The public demanded that Congress not permit these companies to do something overseas that they could not do in the United States. The result was the FCPA, the Foreign Corrupt Practices Act.

Although the intent may have been good, there were a couple of problems with the FCPA as it was originally passed. For one thing, it prevented payments to officials even when the payment was not to obtain a special favor but was simply a gratuity intended to get the officials to do what they are supposed to do. Another problem was that it prevented Americans from bribery, but it did not stop their competitors from Europe and elsewhere.

To deal with the first problem, eventually Congress modified the FCPA to permit the so-called "grease payments" — paying someone to do what the person is supposed to do. According to the grease payments amendment, one still could not pay another country's customs officials to allow banned products into that country or to give the American products a lower tariff than what would be proper. However, the grease payments provision would permit paying a customs official to process a shipment instead of idly contemplating the universe.

To deal with the second problem (companies headquartered outside of the United States not subject to the FCPA), a variety of mechanisms were employed, which put a more respectable spin on bribery by U.S.-based companies such as payments to so-called consultants.

Labor Usage Laws

Governments sometimes restrict foreign companies in regard to the makeup of local versus home country nationals from the foreign headquarters employed in the local operation, and the wage scale paid to locals. The governments may make these demands partly to deal with an unemployment problem in a manner that does not create wage competition for local businesses. Even though some companies may have been attracted to a country because the wage rates are low, many companies still pay salaries or wages in those countries which are remarkably high compared to compensation provided by local employers — thus causing those local employers to lose valuable employees or fueling wage demands (by unions), which may exist. Thus the government may take an active role in labor usage decisions by the foreign company.

Often a foreign company investing in a country must use local citizens for most of its workforce, and technical training must be provided if certain skills are lacking in the local workforce. In some cases, a local citizen must head the local operation — even if that citizen is largely a symbolic figurehead who is publicly visible although the real decisions are made by a person from the foreign headquarters. Furthermore, it has become very expensive to send expatriates to other countries, so generally only home office personnel are used for the most senior positions.

Foreign Exchange Restrictions

Governments, especially in many lesser developed or newly industrializing nations, sometimes try to maintain their economic strength and the value of their currency (what it will convert into in terms of other currencies) by developing exchange controls. For example, instead of allowing citizens in such a country to convert their currency into dollar, yen, or euro at whatever the market rate might be, the citizens might have to make such exchanges through the country's central bank or some other agency at whatever rate is set by the government — if any exchange is even permitted. Such restrictions tend to discourage companies from expanding into these countries. After all, why would a company invest hundreds of millions of dollars building facilities if the company could not take its profits out of the country and deploy them elsewhere?

Of course, some more creative business people have found coping mechanisms to handle such restrictions, mechanisms sometimes referred to as "counter trade." Consider Pepsi when it set up operations in the former USSR (now Russia): instead of taking money it took vodka, which was then sold in the United States.

Government Monopolies and Favored Companies

Many socialistic or formerly socialistic governments have privatized those industries that they previously owned (state-owned enterprises [SOE]), but not all governments have done so. To keep either the government-owned or privatized business viable, special favoritism and protection are often provided, which makes it difficult for foreign companies to compete with them. The favoritism may take the form of subsidies, tax favors, loans, etc. Existence of such a favored business may make it difficult for a foreign company to penetrate the market.

Enforcement of Laws

To gain respectability in the world community, some governments may have laws on the books regarding worker safety or the environment. The problem is that such laws may not be enforced except on a selective basis. They may be applied to those who have lost political favor, those who have not paid sufficient bribes, and to foreign companies that are viewed negatively by local activist groups. Such selective enforcement eliminates the level playing field that many companies feel they must have if they are to begin operations in a country.

The problem is even worse if the country wishes to enforce its laws but cannot — for example, if it is unable to prevent kidnapping and terrorism.

Government Purchasing Policies

In many cases, the government is one of the biggest spenders in the country, but it may restrict its purchases to only those companies owned by local business people or SOE even if a foreign company operating within the country can offer a better product at a lower price. Sometimes, this problem can be minimized by operating as a joint venture with a local organization or by permitting local citizens to share in ownership of the operation.

Threat of Nationalization and Expropriation

Few rational business people would invest massive amounts of money in developing an industry in some country only to have their properties seized (nationalization), once they have become profitable. Nevertheless, such has happened in the past and it is an issue that should be considered before investing in countries, especially those that appear to have unstable governments. After all, suppose the current dictator promises a prospective company, considering expansion in the country, that its production facilities will not be nationalized. What happens when a revolutionary group in which nationalization is one of its top priorities overthrows the dictator? That has happened.

However, those facing nationalization have sometimes found ways to fight back. If the local country does not have all of the technical expertise needed to operate the nationalized facilities, or the output from the local facilities has little value without the company's worldwide distribution facilities, the government and the company may have to reach some sort of compromise. One such compromise is the use of management contracts. The government simply declares that it is now the owner of the company's facilities but it employs the former company owner to manage the facilities in exchange for a share of the profits. Under such a contract, the practical result may be that life goes on for the company and its local facilities much as it was before the nationalization, except that now there is a different name out in front for the local citizens to see. When companies' facilities are expropriated, the firms receive some compensation for their assets, although nowhere near market value. When facilities are nationalized, no compensation is provided.

Culture and Language Issues

Some governments fear that trade and investment may result in damage to their culture, including language and religion. There are a multitude of barriers on trade and investment that may be developed because of such concerns.

It may affect what can be imported. It may affect who may be allowed into the country to conduct business, and how foreign nationals will be permitted to dress (especially women executives and engineers stationed in the country) or entertain themselves while in the presence of local nationals. It may require that all communication be conducted in the preferred language of that country or at least that there be copies of such communication in the local language.

If too many Americans, for example, have caused local radio stations and nightspots to play too much rock or country music, such local businesses may be required to play a certain percentage of the more traditional local music. Of course, although such restrictions may seem to be a deterrent to some international executives, others appreciate efforts to prevent total Americanization of the rest of the world and appreciate the opportunity to observe other cultures and customs.

There is another dimension to the issue of culture and language. Awareness of the culture and language can be important to success, even if the government is not restricting trade and investment for the purpose of protecting its culture and language. Such awareness may help establish rapport with customers and others important to a company's goal, and it may help them recognize that many business policies and techniques, which work very well in the United States, could be disastrous if used in a particular country.

Governmental Reduction of Barriers

As has been mentioned previously, in the post-World War II period there has been a recognition of the potential value of trade and investment and the need to either overcome or minimize as many barriers as possible. There are many understandable reasons for barriers to trade and investment, and it is likely that some barriers will continue to exist one hundred years from now. However, the governments that have erected barriers have also been taking steps to deal with those barriers. Those efforts include negotiations among nations, as well as formalized institutional arrangements to work toward barrier reduction and the resolution of trade disputes.

The United States periodically negotiates trade arrangements with its major trading partners. We have worked with countries throughout the world in various rounds of the General Agreement on Tariffs and Trade (GATT) and continue to do so in the implementations of those agreements through the World Trade Organization (WTO). Here in this hemisphere, we have promoted regional free (or relatively free) trade and investment through NAFTA — the North American Free Trade Agreement. Other areas of the world have also worked toward regional economic integration, such as the European Union — the EU. The EU goes far beyond NAFTA in promoting regional trade and investment. In 1999, the EU (in particular, its related EMU — the European Monetary Union) began the process of integrating its monetary system through a new currency, the euro, to ultimately replace several of Europe's major currencies. There are now 25 member countries in the EU, making it the world's largest group of consumers.

In essence, a major effort of the second half of the twentieth century has been to undo what was done during the first half of the century.

GLOBAL BUSINESS AND THE CURRENCY MARKET

Impact of the Currency Market

First, let us look at currency values. To illustrate, we will refer to the dollar and to a euro. By value of the dollar, we are referring to what the dollar will convert into in terms of another currency such as the euro. As of 2006, 12 of the 25 EU countries used the euro as their currency. To use the euro as your currency, each member country must have financial stability. However, if the domestic currency is stronger than the euro, a country may choose not to use the euro as its currency. This is the case of the British pound.

Transaction Effect

As we buy more internationally, we dump more dollars onto international markets causing the value or exchange rate to go down. There are other factors (besides exports and imports) affecting the supply and demand for dollars on international money markets, but the point is that the changes in the value of the dollar affect exports, imports, and international investment.

For example, supposing that the dollar is equal to 4€ in 2005 and, in 2006, its value decreases to the extent that it will now convert into only 2€. Suppose there is a product selling for $1000 in 2005 and it is still selling for $1000 in 2006. The price has not changed for the U.S. citizen, but it has changed for the German citizen who will exchange euros into dollars to buy the product. In 2005, a German citizen would have paid 4000€ for the product but in 2006 it will cost only 2000€. As a result, we are likely to export more of the product to Germany. If there was a product selling in Germany for 4000€ in 2005 and it is still selling for 4000€ in 2006, the product in 2005 would sell for $1000 in the United States and in 2006 — after the dollar has lost value and will no longer convert into as many marks — it would sell for $2000. As a result, we are likely to import somewhat less of the German product. (See Table 13.6.)

At the same time, property in the United States selling for 100 million dollars in both 2005 and 2006 would become less expensive for the German to buy as the value of the dollar goes down — going from an investment of 400 million euros to 200 million euros.

Table 13.6   Transaction Effect

Period A		Period B	
U.S. product	$1000	U.S. product	$1000
German product	€4000	German product	€4000
Exchange rate: $1 = €4		Exchange rate: $1 = €2	
German buyer of U.S. product pays €4000.		German buyer of U.S. product pays €2000.	
U.S. buyer of German product pays $1000.		U.S. buyer of German product pays $2000.	

Note: Example of the impact on U.S. exports and imports caused by a change in the exchange rate of the dollar and the euro between two periods of time: period A and period B. Note that the price of the U.S. product has not changed in the United States and the German product has not changed in Germany. Period B compared to period A likely effect: Export of U.S. product up, import of German product down.

Generally, as the value of the dollar goes down, it is good news for exporters, bad news for importers, and good news for international companies seeking to buy control of U.S. companies. On the other hand, if the value of the dollar increases, the opposite is true: including the fact that it then becomes less expensive for American companies to acquire foreign companies.

Translation Effect

Using the example above — concerning a change in dollars versus euros — suppose there is a bank in Germany with 400 billion euros in assets in 2005, and it is still the same size bank in 2006. Nevertheless, in a list comparing the world's leading financial institutions in which the comparison is made in dollars, the bank would be valued at 100 billion in 2005 and 200 billion in 2006. It would falsely appear that the German bank has doubled in size whereas the apparent growth is simply because of translating its euro value into dollars. International financial managers and investors need to be aware of the translation effect in evaluating the performance of various companies around the world.

Coping with Changes in Currency Values

How do companies involved in exports, imports, and international investment protect themselves against unpredictable and undesirable changes in currency values? After all, suppose that you have sold products to a customer in Germany for delivery in 60 days and, to make the sale, you agreed to be paid in euros instead of dollars. The buyer will pay you 10,000€ when you make delivery but you do not know how many dollars you will be able to obtain from those euros at that time. Depending on the exchange rate 60 days from now, you might make a significant profit or loss from that transaction. You know what the current exchange rate is, and it may be acceptable to you, but exchange rates are changing continually — you do not know what it will be at that time. Again, how can you protect yourself against such changes, assuming that your German accounts payable and accounts receivable do not perfectly balance?

Coping through International Bank Loans

One common technique involves international bank loans. Suppose you borrow 10,000€ for 60 days at 6 percent interest on a discounted note. You will actually receive about 9900€ that you can immediately convert into dollars at the current acceptable exchange rate and, 60 days from now, you can pay off the loan with the money you receive from your

German customer. The exchange rate at that point will be irrelevant to you because you already have your money and an acceptable profit.

Coping through the Forward Market

Another common technique is the use of the forward/futures market. Currencies, commodities, and securities are traded, involving contracts for their delivery at some point in the future. Such contracts may include the deliveries of assets that do not even exist at the present time. Such contracts could be a simple and unsophisticated arrangement between an exporter who will be receiving a certain amount of a currency at some point in the future and an importer who needs that same amount of the same currency at exactly the same time. Use our previous example of the dollar being equal to 4€ in period A and equal to 2€ in period B, and suppose Smith will be receiving 4000€ in period B from exports, and Jones will need 4000€ in period B to pay for imports. Further suppose that it is now period A, and neither knows what is going to happen in period B. At the current rate in period A, the exporter would receive $1000, but if the dollar were to increase in value to $1 = 8€, the exporter Smith would receive only $500 for the 4000€. On the other hand, the importer Jones would now need $1000 to obtain the 4000€ required to pay for imports in period B, but if the exchange rate goes to $1 = 2€, the importer will need $2000 to obtain the euros required to pay for the imports. Rather than worry about what the future exchange rate will be, the two could enter into a contract for the future delivery of that currency, also referred to as a forward contract, and set whatever exchange rate that they wish to apply to that delivery. Once they have agreed to the rate, they can cease worrying about further changes in the value of the dollar and euros.

In the real world, it is highly unlikely that an exporter and importer with such complimentary needs would happen to know each other. Therefore, financial institutions around the world are linked by computers to engage in currency transactions involving not only exchanges of one currency into another at the rate applying as of the moment, but these institutions can also help international business people by providing forward contracts, which assure them that their future currency needs will cost them no more than a given amount or that the currencies they will receive in the future will convert into at least a known amount of dollars.

One reason that those importers will be able to execute such forward contracts is that they do not have to depend only on exporters who will be receiving currencies in the future — there are speculators willing to provide the currencies because they are hoping to obtain the promised currencies at a bargain price. The importer who needs 200,000€ agrees to pay the speculator $100,000 for the euros to avoid the risk of having to pay more than $100,000 when the currency is needed, whereas the speculator may be hoping that the exchange rate will change to 1€ = $1 by the time the importer needs the currency so that the speculator will pay $100,000 for 200,000€, which will yield $200,000. The exporter in like manner enters into a forward contract to be assured that he or she gets at least a given amount and the speculator assures the exporter that he or she will pay that amount in hopes that the contract will be worth more later. In essence, importers and exporters are able to hedge ("insure," in a sense) and avoid risk by transferring the risk to speculators who assume the risk in hopes of making a profit.

Global Financial Issues

There are many questions you should ask regarding global financial management. What is your forecast of future cash inflows and outflows, both on a short-term and long-term perspective based on strategies for the company's overall global growth? How do those inflows and outflows coordinate with the overall firm's needs and resources? If there is a period of entry and expansion into a country, in which the initial outflows exceed inflows, how will those inflows be met while the operation continues to grow and move toward an ultimate net inflow?

Can the needs be met from within the country through sale of debt or equity interests? Can some aspect of the venture be franchised so that the franchisee finances the activity? Can some aspects of the business be outsourced to others rather than developing one's own capabilities? Can an existing firm be acquired using the stock of the company based in the United States so that no cash is required? Can financing be obtained from other areas of the world besides the United States or that country?

In financing, can the company lock in stand-by commitments at given interest rates or at given rates of exchange between the dollar and the local currency?

How do local government policies affect input/output pricing? If a company produces inputs in Country A and converts those into outputs in Country B and then moves the outputs on to Country C for sale, are there any restrictions among those governments that can affect the price of the inputs from A or the outputs to C, so as to minimize tariffs or corporate profit taxes in any of those nations?

If any part of the involvement in a country involves a minority investment in a local company, how do accounting procedures involving profit calculations and asset valuation differ from the United States?

How liquid is the investment in that country? If changes in markets, technology, or international politics required the company to relocate, could it do so quickly without a substantial loss?

Human Resource Issues

There are many questions you should ask concerning the human resources you will need to achieve your international objectives. Do the skills needed in the country already exist? If not, is it possible or better to bring in employees from the home country or can local people be trained quickly enough to the level of skill desired? If local people are obtained, how much flexibility does the government permit regarding their use or termination if downsizing is desired? Would it be possible to contract with a local company to obtain the needed skills and be able to obtain the flexibility needed that would not be possible if the workers were your direct employees?

Is it possible to integrate your human resources on a global basis so that not only do people move from the home office to international assignments but those in a given international area may move to the home office or to a different international area in accordance with the overall global needs of the company and the career objectives of individuals? Can diversity be achieved not only within the operations in specific countries but also among all operations throughout the world?

Does the government or society have much different values and standards concerning the employment and use of genders, minorities, and child labor? If you were to apply the human resource policies used in the United States, would the operation be in trouble in that country? If you followed the practices and policies of that country, would you suffer adverse publicity in the United States? Even if your company does not have any facilities or employees in the country but contracts with a local company to produce its product but the local company practices discrimination or uses child labor, will that result in damaging publicity in the United States?

Will it work to use a team approach in which the team is empowered and people are encouraged to participate in decisions? Recognition of individual performance is often effective as a motivational tool in the United States: will it also be effective in that nation? Will hands-on managers who successfully work side-by-side in the United States be viewed as lowering themselves and thus not respected if that approach is used in the country? As companies increase the percentage of international sales, the organization structure will need to be changed. (See Figure 13.1.)

Production and Operations Issues

There are many questions you should ask concerning the operations involved in producing your goods or services overseas. Is the infrastructure

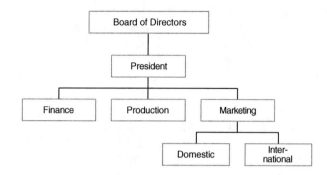

Later International Production:
Establishing Subsidiary Companies in Host Countries

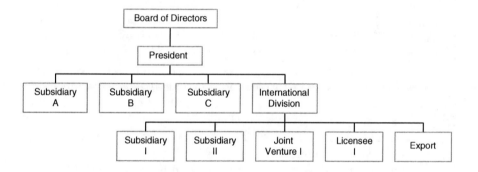

Trans-National Company: Establishing Global Philosophy and Operation

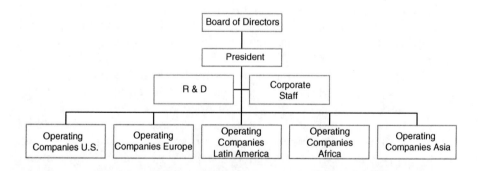

Figure 13.1   Organizational structures as firms increase international sales.

(transportation, utilities, etc.) sufficiently dependable to achieve production objectives? If the company tries to use a just-in-time approach to inventory control, is the infrastructure such that the company can be sure that the needed inputs will arrive just in time?

How reliable are the inputs (supplies, services, etc.) that may need to be purchased locally? To what extent can the company unite both those within the company and those serving the company from without into a team that will work together in pursuing objectives? Or will the presence of a company based in another country be viewed with hostility?

Will the concept of improving not just total production but also improving productivity be accepted by the work force?

Management: Leadership Issues

There are many questions a company should ask concerning leadership of international or global activities. Do all those connected with the management of the operation in the host country, both those in the United States and those in the host country, share a common vision and are all working together toward the same goals? To what extent does inspirational leadership exist which will inspire all involved in the operation to do what is needed and to do so, not just because they have to do it, but to do so because that is what they want. Is the culture sufficiently understood so that anyone acting in a leadership capacity will know how to motivate and obtain such a commitment?

To what extent does the culture permit local managers to be creative, be entrepreneurial, and take risks? To what extent does the company culture permit the same? Is there a pecking order within the global firm in which local managers have less status than those in the home country and are less trusted? For managers who may be temporarily in the country from the home office in the United States, is the international assignment viewed by the home office as an important career move or is it viewed as time-out? (See Figure 13.2.)

Are managers (and their families) from the home office adequately trained in the local culture and language prior to going to the foreign assignment and assisted in readjustment upon return? The inability of the manager's family to adjust to the foreign assignment is a major cause of failure in overseas assignments. The return home is also problematic. One study reported that over 25 percent of managers left their firm within one year after being repatriated from their international assignment.

There are many questions you should ask regarding both the long- and short-term plans you have to achieve your international goals. To what extent do not only day-to-day plans exist (budget, schedules, etc.)

A major American soft drink bottler opened a bottling plant in the Middle East. The plant manager, who had opened many similar plants in the U.S., hired the best available technicians to operate the plant. Because of the political and legal constraints, most of the employees were local nationals. Within a week the main conveyor broke down. The cause was that the main bearings had not been greased upon installation. Luckily the machine came with an extra set of bearings. These were installed and the plant manager instructed the machine custodian to pack them with grease. A week later, the bearings burned out again – the custodian had used the wrong kind of grease. The machine custodian said that he was not at fault because "if Allah wanted the machine to break, it would break, grease or no grease."

Incidents such as this were common at this plant in the Middle East. During the first year over 100 working days were lost because of accidents and down time.

Figure 13.2   Cultural differences impact operations.

but also long-term strategies, and to what extent are the strategies understood and endorsed by those who must carry them out? Do the strategies call for actions that will violate the beliefs and convictions of the implementers? To what extent are those strategies based on careful strengths, weaknesses, opportunities, and treats (SWOT) analysis: the operations' internal strengths and weaknesses plus the external opportunities and threats?

There are many questions you should ask to assure that your international operation is organized in the most effective manner. Is it organized according to the approach used by many companies years ago in which the operation in that country is treated as a stepchild of the home operation and operated as if it were independent of the rest of the global company, or is the company organized according to processes or production stages, customers, etc. without regard to national boundaries?

To assure that your plans are carried out effectively through the organizational structure that is established, there are many questions you should ask. What kind of controls exist over finances, inventory, quality, and human resources, and are they proactive or reactive — do they achieve continuous improvement by avoiding problems or tend to respond as problems arise?

Controls involve comparison of how things are to the way they should be — a standard. Should the same standards apply in the host country as in the United States? Is it possible that an even higher standard may be attained?

SUMMARY

Global business applies to all that you have learned thus far in the text but recognizes that the application may be different as you expand into various countries around the world. There is a need to simultaneously have both a global vision and a local awareness and responsiveness.

You should now be aware of the potential benefits of investing in business operations outside of the United States, the range of approaches from relatively little or no investment overseas to very substantial investments, what you may encounter regarding governmental barriers to global business, as well as what is being done to reduce those barriers, the impact of changes in currency values and how to cope with those changes, how a "situation analysis" and the use of the marketing concept can help you build a global strategy, and the many questions involving global leadership, global management, marketing, finance, human resources, and production.

INDEX

Note: Italicized page numbers refer to tables and illustrations.